Diamond Hitch

The diamond hitch, or rather series of hitches the shape of a diamond, is the combination of rope twists by which a load is kept in position on the back of a pack animal. I am not aware who invented it — he should have been knighted.

A. O Wheeler, *The Selkirk Range*

Diamond

The early outfitters and

by E. J. Hart

Hitch

guides of Banff and Jasper

SUMMERTHOUGHT
BANFF, CANADA

For my daughter Melissa,
who sat on my knee for much of it

ISBN 0-919934-08-0

Published by
Summerthought Ltd.
P.O. Box 1420
Banff, Alberta T0L 0C0
Canada

First printing, 1979
Second Printing, 1989

Designed by Brian Patton
Printed and bound in Canada

Contents

Preface

As one examines the history of the Canadian Rockies it immediately becomes apparent that there were distinct groups of individuals associated with the area's periods of exploration. The earliest recorded work was, of course, that done by the fur traders attempting to cross the Cordillera to the Pacific Slope. They were followed by other early travellers, running the gamut from missionaries such as Father Pierre J. De Smet to scientists like Dr. James Hector of the Palliser Expedition, all of whom added much to the limited knowledge of the rugged landscape. A third group were the men involved in the surveys for the Canadian Pacific Railway as well as those employed by the Geological Survey of Canada and the Dominion Topographical Survey. Finally there were the early tourist-explorers, mountaineers and sportsmen who succeeded in discovering and examining most of the country not reported on by their predecessors.

My fascination with the present topic began as a result of studying the activities of the latter group. It immediately became obvious from reading the fairly large bulk of literature which these people had produced that they had indeed been extremely active and had climbed peaks, examined valleys and rafted across lakes where no white man had preceeded them. However, it was also evident that they were often being given all the credit when a good deal of it belonged to others, namely the outfitters and guides who provided the wherewithal and the knowledge necessary for their clients to achieve their goals. In fact, it seemed to me that the story of this interesting period of exploration would not be complete until these men were given their just due.

Though it was only with the intention of rectifying some misconceptions that the work began, it soon became much more involved. From my initial research it quickly became clear that, in addition to their work in the exploration of the Rockies, the outfitters and guides had played major roles in both the history of transportation in the mountains and the economic history of the Banff and Jasper National Park areas. These factors aroused my interest further.

Similarly, as I found out more about the men involved it became apparent that I was dealing with a group of rather unique individuals. Instead of being drawn exclusively from backwoods environments, as I had supposed, I found that many were from fine English, American and Canadian backgrounds; some were well-educated and most seemed to be of higher than average intelligence. Yet here they were travelling in the mountains with pack trains, living the roughest kind of life imaginable and enjoying it immensely. This seeming contradiction intrigued me and added fuel to the fire.

Hoping to shed some light on my questions, I spent many enjoyable hours talking with those of the old trailmen who are still among us and listened to the tape-recorded interviews or read the accounts left behind by those who are not. The result of these pleasurable experiences was this book and it is dedicated to the spirit and zest for life that was so manifest in these men.

I would like to thank all of those who took the time and effort to help me in my research. The staffs of the Archives of the Canadian Rockies, the Glenbow-Alberta Institute, and Mrs. Constance Peterson of the Jasper-Yellowhead Historical Society constantly provided me with new sources of material. Numerous people took the time to respond to my queries either by letter or by agreeing to meet with me. Though they are too numerous to mention here, I owe them a tremendous debt of gratitude. I would be remiss if I did not extend particular thanks to three men who were always ready to answer my persistent questions. — F. O. "Pat" Brewster of Banff, the late Joe Woodworth of Calgary and George Camp of Salmon Arm. I would also like to thank Mrs. Maryalice Stewart for her kindness in reading the manuscript for historical accuracy, and Mrs. Lillian Wonders for her fine work on the maps.

Thomas Edmonds Wilson.

1 Tom Wilson ~The Oracle at Banff

When William Cornelius Van Horne, the General Manager of the Canadian Pacific Railway, looked at the rather shocking figures which represented the costs of construction for the Mountain Section of the line, it was apparent something had to be done. The numerous steep grades, the expensive blasting and tunnel work and the many wide chasms to be bridged had made the price of the section almost unbelievably high. Not only was it dear to build but also looked to Van Horne's knowing eye as likely to be uneconomical to operate. The Mountain Section promised little sustained traffic, unlike the Prairie Section which had agricultural colonists to bring west and the fruits of their labor to ship back east.

Van Horne's carefully considered solution was to "capitalize the scenery," or, in other words, to invite the travelling public to partake of the area's myriad splendors by utilizing the company's transportation system. One of the first manifestations of the plan was the creation of a system of luxurious hotels to accommodate the expected tourists. These included Glacier House and Mount Stephen House, opened at Glacier and Field respectively in 1886, and the Banff Springs Hotel, opened at Banff in the spring of 1888.

Within a few years Van Horne's concept began to pay excellent dividends as an increasing flow of excursionists, attracted by a well-orchestrated international advertising campaign, travelled to and became enamored with the Canadian Rockies and Selkirks. However, it became apparent after the establishment of these hotels that the transportation system could not end at their doors. The attractions of the mountains — unexplored valleys, unclimbed peaks and plentiful fish and game — lured the more hardy visitors to venture beyond the confines of 'civilization,' requiring the provision of horses, equipment and guides. It was appropriate that one of the first individuals to become involved in the outfitting and

guiding business that resulted had played an important part in the building of the Mountain Section and had discovered some of the area's foremost beauty spots. This was Tom Wilson.

Thomas Edmonds Wilson was born at Bondhead, a small town north of Toronto, on August 21, 1859, but at an early age moved with his Irish-Canadian parents to a farm near Barrie, Ontario. Here he lived the normal life of a farm boy and attended the local public school before completing his formal education at Barrie Grammar School in 1875. His father wished him to attend Guelph Agricultural College while his mother hoped that he would become a minister, but young Tom would hear of neither. Always interested in history and nurtured on romantic tales of the North West, he easily fell victim to the spirit of wanderlust so common to youth. A rangy lad of sixteen already beginning to approach his full height of five feet nine inches, he set out in search of adventure. For three years his travels took him to Detroit, Chicago and as far west as Sioux City, Iowa before he became homesick and returned to Barrie.

Lacking a trade and uninspired by farming, he helped to pass the time by enrolling in the Ontario Field Battery of the Volunteer Militia of Canada in October, 1878. Here he served until March, 1879 when at his own request he received his discharge. He once more began to look for something new and exciting but which would also ensure a reasonable livelihood. With his rural background and experience in the militia, he was an ideal candidate for the six-year-old North West Mounted Police force which was recruiting to supplement its undermanned western posts. From Tom's point of view the force would not only provide an interesting and possibly exciting job but would also allow him to come to grips with the country he yearned to see.

The forces's appetite for manpower was considerable

and upon applying for service at Barrie on July 19, 1880, Tom was immediately engaged at the rank of constable. He was assigned to Fort Walsh in the Cypress Hills country of south-western Saskatchewan, one of fifty-two recruits sent to that post in 1880. After an arduous journey including a voyage across Lake Superior, a train trip from Duluth to Bismarck, then by river boat up the Missouri to Coalbanks and finally by horse to Fort Walsh, he began his service on September 22, 1880.

Life at Fort Walsh revolved around surveillance of a large concentration of Indians. Because of their destitute condition they had gathered in the vicinity with the hope of receiving relief from the police. They were causing few problems with the exception of the self-exiled Sioux chief Sitting Bull and his followers who were still vacillating about returning to the United States, despite several years of efforts by the NWMP to convince them to do so. As Tom remembered it, the high point of his career with the police was the occasion on which he accompanied a detachment to meet with the Sioux's stubborn leader. He claimed to have spent some time in conversation with "the wily chief" during the visit to the Indian encampment.[1]

Apart from this brief interlude, the life of a police constable was routine and did not fulfill Tom's hopes. Boredom quickly set in and, as the job was far from lucrative, soon led to dissatisfaction. When word reached Fort Walsh in early 1881 that the Canadian Pacific Railway was hiring men at Fort Benton, Montana to assist in surveying a route through the mountains, he decided to leave the police force. On May 16, 1881 he purchased his discharge and immediately journeyed to Fort Benton. Here, after a short wait spent working with a cattle outfit, he was hired on as a packer by P. K. Hyndman, Chief Engineer for Major A. B. Rogers, Engineer-in-Charge of the Mountain Section of the CPR line.

When the survey outfit departed for Old Bow Fort, the former Hudson's Bay Company post near the confluence of the Bow and Kananaskis Rivers and the proposed headquarters for the survey at the base of the Rockies, most of the equipment and supplies were freighted by the ox teams of the I. G. Baker and Company of Fort Benton. The packers rode their own saddle horses and were responsible for herding the eighty pack horses that would be used in the mountains after the freight wagons could go no further. Most of these horses were Indian-bred stock, commonly known as 'cayuses,' and were chosen in preference to the American-favored mule because of their larger hoofs, which would aid them in negotiating the treacherous muskegs of the mountain valleys. Although Tom had considerable experience with horses, he soon had to learn to deal with the unpredictability of this unfamiliar breed. At the same time he had to quickly acquaint himself with the tools of the packer's trade.

Primary among his equipment was the pack saddle,

constructed of two pieces of strong wood about fifteen inches long, five to seven inches wide and about an inch deep. These pieces of wood, which were rounded and slightly contoured to fit the horse's back, were connected by means of a wooden "X" at each end, the upper arms of which were considerably smaller than the lower. From these arms hung the sling ropes which were adjusted to support the packs. The packs themselves were of several varieties, but the two most popular were sturdy wooden boxes used for more fragile items and large cowhide bags, or 'alforjas', which could carry articles of almost any size and shape. Each loaded pack weighed approximately 100 pounds as 200 pounds, with one pack balanced on either side of the saddle, was the maximum burden for most horses. Over the top went the pack mantle or cover, a large piece of heavy canvas measuring about six by eight feet. When everything was in its proper place the cinch and the lash rope, which was a half inch thick and about fifteen feet long with an eye spliced into one end, were brought into play. With an intricate series of loops and twists the lash rope was tied into either the diamond, double diamond, three-quarter diamond or squaw hitch by which the entire load was securely fastened to the saddle and the horse. These knots had to be practised endlessly for they were the key to the whole packing operation and their secrets were jealously guarded by the initiated.

A typical cayuse with pack saddle and sling ropes ready for packing.

The trek to the foot of the mountains proved to be an adventure in itself for Tom. Because the outfit left towards the middle of June it had to contend with high water on the numerous mountain-born rivers and streams that crossed its path. Added to the excitement of many hair-raising fordings was a stampede of the stock when some Montana packers became a little too boisterous celebrating the Fourth of July at Fort Calgary.

Despite the delays, time passed quickly and the party soon found itself at the end of the regular wagon road at the Stoney Indian mission settlement of Morley. Here they were greeted by the pioneer missionary Reverend John McDougall who agreed to guide them to Old Bow Fort on a rough trail. At Old Bow Fort it was decided to establish the headquarters further west, and the reverend's brother, Dave McDougall, hauled the equipment by Red River cart on to the Bow River Gap.

With the gear stockpiled at the Gap, Tom's first real work as a packer began; he proceeded to sort the various items, then readied them for the horses whose strength and temperament were thought to be best suited to the load.

Before they could proceed further, though, the party had to await the arrival of Major Rogers who had been doggedly attempting to discover a pass through the Selkirks which would serve as the key to the railway's penetration of that range. He was unsuccessful on this attempt but finally appeared at the Gap on July 15th after an exhausting ride from Spokane by way of Pend d'Oreille Pass, the Kootenay and Columbia Rivers, the Brisco Range, the Cross River and eventually down from Whiteman's Pass via the Spray River and Lakes.

Shortly after the Major's arrival the survey party was split into separate gangs, each charged with the investigation of a different pass which could possibly accomodate the construction of a rail line over the backbone of the Great Divide. Wilson was assigned to the group accompanying the irascible, tobacco-spitting Major and he was soon herding the pack train up the Bow Valley into the mountains on an old Indian trail. As he rode, Tom began to get acquainted with the magnificent, rugged mountain scenery — the towering peaks, the broad U-shaped glacial valleys and their smaller tributary valleys, the verdant forests and flower-strewn meadows, the rushing snow-fed rivulets and streams, and the gem-like lakes and tarns. He was much impressed, but could little realize he was being introduced to the country which would become the scene of his activities for the greater part of his life.

Major Rogers' first objective was to reach the Divide and then await the arrival of his nephew, Al Rogers. This young man had been given the herculean task of taking a pack train from the mouth of the Kicking Horse River up its treacherous valley to the Divide, a feat never before accomplished.

Rogers' perennial bad temper became acutely obvious to his men on their way up the Bow and when he asked for a volunteer to accompany him as a special attendant on his visits to the various survey camps no one felt obliged to accept. Finally, when it became apparent that the request was to go unanswered, Tom agreed to take it on. In the months ahead their relationship was often stormy but both soon learned a grudging respect for the other's abilities and they eventually became fast friends. Tom's decision was ultimately to prove a beneficial one since it allowed him to explore the region more fully.

Upon attaining Kicking Horse (Wapta) Lake at the summit of the Divide and finding that Al Rogers had not yet arrived, the Major immediately became concerned for his nephew's welfare. Feeling that he may have reached the summit before them and continued eastward along the opposite side of the river, Rogers took Tom and began heading back in search of traces of the youth. Reaching a particularly fast flowing creek swollen with meltwater, Tom suggested they postpone their crossing until the morning when such streams usually subsided considerably. Hurling oaths upon his companion's head, the Major insisted on plunging ahead and immediately was swept from his horse into the swirling, bone-chilling water. Fortunately Tom found a branch near at hand and was able to fish him out. The incident provided evidence to Rogers of the value of Tom's services and also gave the creek its name. Whenever it ran high and dirty the men on the survey would jest, "Hello, the old man's taking another bath," and before long it was known as Bath Creek.[2] Two days later Tom and another packer discovered Al Rogers almost starved near the confluence of the Kicking Horse and Yoho Rivers.

While celebrating around the campfire the men of the party discussed the future of the railroad and their own individual plans. Moved by the day's events and their surroundings, someone suggested that they make a pact to keep in touch with each other at least once a year no matter where their travels took them. The "oath of the twenty" was solemnly sworn by all and, surprisingly enough, was fulfilled by most. Forty-five years later Wilson and Al Rogers were still corresponding, but after Rogers' death in 1929 Tom was the sole living member of that historic group.

For the balance of the 1881 season Tom accompanied Major Rogers to various survey camps and packed in provisions and equipment from the supply headquarters at Padmore (Kananaskis). This work provided further valuable experience but was not without its hardships as the packers existed on a rather lacklustre diet of sowbelly and beans and slept covered only by a tarpaulin slung between pack saddles, no matter what the weather.

On one of these overnight stops Wilson made camp close to the site of what would later become the town of Banff, the headquarters for his outfitting and guiding activities for many years. The campsite was on the banks of a small creek and the area was named Aylmer Park after Fred Aylmer, chief of one of the CPR survey crews. The creek subsequently became known as Whiskey Creek because near the springs at its head a certain individual named Gosling manufactured a 'snake bite cure' from potato peelings. In later years Wilson recalled that "two drinks and the snake died if he bit you."[3]

Deciding to leave the survey early, Tom made his way to the Little Snowy Mountains of Montana and spent the winter trapping. Although he had scoffed at Major Rogers' suggestion that he would return to the survey the next year, the spring of 1882 found him unable to resist the lure of the far away precipices and valleys. In May he reappeared at Fort Benton and signed on for the seemingly monotonous chore of hauling in supplies from Padmore to the survey camps with a fourteen to sixteen horse pack train. However, the summer was to prove anything but uneventful.

On the return trip from packing in the second load of the season to the Divide, the outfit camped, as was their custom, at the mouth of the Pipestone River near the present town of Lake Louise. During the evening, while sitting around the campfire with a small group of Stoney Indians encamped at the same site, Wilson heard the thunder of several large avalanches. Tom asked an Indian known as Gold Seeker (Edwin Hunter) about the noise and was told it originated on a mountain above the 'Lake of Little Fishes.' As the following day began wet and unsuitable for travel he asked Gold Seeker to guide him to the spot and after a short horseback ride through the forest they emerged on the shore of the lake. Of the sight Wilson said:

As God is my judge I never in all my explorations saw such a matchless scene. On the right and the left forests that had never known the axe came down to the shores apparently growing out of the blue and green waters. The background, a mile and a half away, was divided into three tones of white, opal and brown where the glacier ceased and merged with the shining water. The sun, high in the noon-hour, poured into the pool, which reflected the whole landscape that formed the horseshoe.[4]

Surmising that he was probably the first white man to lay eyes on this extraordinarily beautiful sheet of water, he named it Emerald Lake. As such it appeared on the reconnaissance map of Dr. George M. Dawson of the Geological Survey of Canada published in 1886. Later the name was changed to Lake Louise in honor of Princess Louise, wife of the Marquis of Lorne, by Dawson and Sir Richard Temple on the occasion of their visit to the spot in 1884. Even though he did not dispute the change of name, Tom in later years, depending on his mood and the circumstances, variously agreed or disagreed with the interpretation of the name. At certain times he agreed that it had indeed been the Princess

A CPR packtrain.

Tom Wilson at Lake Louise almost half a century after his initial discovery.

Louise who inspired the nomenclature but at others insisted that it was a daughter of Sir Richard Temple who deserved the credit.

A second and equally important discovery followed soon after the historic visit to Lake Louise. During one of his frequent trips to the Divide, Tom left some of his extra horses at the bottom of the hill leading to the summit of Kicking Horse Pass and on returning found that they had wandered off. After assuring himself that they were not at another favored feeding spot he picked up their trail leading over the Natural Bridge on the Kicking Horse and through the thick forest to the north. Eventually the trail led to a small stream (Emerald River) which when traced to its source was found to flow from a lake whose charms rivalled those of the recently visited 'Lake of the Little Fishes.' This body of water eventually became known by the name he had originally applied to his previous discovery, Emerald Lake.

Despite the interest of these two side trips they in no way compared with what was to be Tom's most strenuous undertaking in the 1882 season. Staking his faith almost exclusively in the Kicking Horse Pass route for the line, Major Rogers had all but ignored the apparent alternative of the Howse Pass. The Howse had been the traditional fur trade passage to and from the

Columbia River until 1811 when David Thompson, his way barred by hostile Peigan Indians, turned north and discovered the henceforth more popular Athabasca Pass. Because of its historical significance and reports of its viability as a rail route by Walter Moberly, an early CPR surveyor who had examined it, Rogers began to have second thoughts about his decision to gamble everything on the Kicking Horse. Finally, to ease his mind of nagging doubts he concluded that he would have to reconnoitre the Howse himself and asked Wilson to accompany him.

Tom accepted the challenge and for two days the pair toiled on horseback through the interminable muskegs and burnt timber of the upper Bow Valley, making little progress. At this point the Major handily excused himself from continuing further on the pretext of being needed in the Selkirks, but convinced his companion to continue on foot with the offer of a fifty dollar bonus. Estimating the amount of food needed to complete the remainder of the journey, Tom agreed on a rendezvous at the confluence of the Blaeberry and Columbia Rivers ten days hence, and set off with a light pack.

It was not long before Tom realized he had seriously underestimated the difficulty of traversing the pass. He had to crawl over downed timber, swim across swollen streams, and often retrace his steps after following the wrong trail. Upon reaching the summit of the pass he again lost valuable time searching for a westward flowing stream. The descent of the west slope proved harder than anticipated with heavy timber and undergrowth and two narrow canyons whose passage required some rather precarious rock climbing. Due to these unforseen setbacks his supply of food ran dangerously low and it was not until thirteen days after leaving Rogers that he was able to keep his appointment, stumbling into the Major's camp on the Columbia half-starved and totally exhausted.

At the time Tom probably thought that no advantage would accrue to him from his labors other than the proffered fifty dollar bonus, but if such were the case he was mistaken. The trek had enabled him to come in contact with some of the country that the explorers, mountaineers, hunters and tourists of future days would find among the most interesting in the Rockies — the northern Bow Valley, the Waputik Range, the Bear Creek (Mistaya) Valley, the forks of the Saskatchewan River and the Forbes and Lyell Groups. His forte was a keen eye for detail and once over a piece of country he never forgot its every feature, possessing almost a photographic memory in this regard. The value of this gift was to become obvious in the not too distant future.

After the completion of the 1882 season Tom headed for Calgary, intending to continue southward and winter in Montana. But his plans quickly changed. Likely because of his police experience in handling Indians, when he reached Calgary the railway offered him the job of dealing with some stubborn Blackfeet who were holding up the survey work of Charles Shaw near Medicine Hat. He accepted, and after helping to cool the Indians' tempers returned to Calgary, where he was hired by a crew surveying near Padmore on a timber lease belonging to Colonel James Walker, the former NWMP officer and manager of the famous Cochrane Ranch. When the survey was completed in mid-winter he decided to remain in the area and await the arrival of the CPR survey party in June, boarding with the Dave McDougall family at Morley in the interim.

With the coming of June, 1883, Tom began his last summer of work with the CPR survey crews. His unfavorable report to Rogers on the Howse Pass route the previous year obviously had its effect as the Major again focused his attention exclusively on the Kicking Horse Pass. The advancement of the survey work to near the mouth of the Kicking Horse River required lengthy pack trips early in the season but soon a new distribution centre was set up close to Tom's campsite of 1881 at Aylmer Park. The high point of the season was his first recorded guiding activity when he was assigned to accompany Sandford Fleming, the one time Engineer-in-Chief of the railway, and the Reverend George Grant, Principal of Queen's University, along a part of the surveyed route. Fleming later published the story of their journey through the mountains as part of his book *England and*

Canada, A Summer Tour Between Old and New Westminster and it provided a rare description of the daily problems faced by the CPR packers.[5]

After travelling by wagon from Calgary to Hillsdale, a commissary centre about fifteen miles west of present day Banff, the Fleming party met with Wilson on August 26th and discussed his instructions, which were to escort them to Major Rogers' camp at the mouth of the Kicking Horse. The following day the party took a short, toughening up excursion to the vicinity of Vermilion Pass, but the next morning they were underway in earnest with Tom in charge of the six packers assigned to the convoy. Freight wagons were taken part of the way over a rough tote road and then the load was shifted to the ten most trustworthy pack animals for the journey down the treacherous Kicking Horse.

During the course of the descent Fleming noted the rapport between the packers and the horses, stating that "there is always a wonderful link between the man and the horse, and the kinder the man the more gentle the quadruped." His observation included a classic understatement of the manner in which the packers, cultured gentlemen by no stretch of the imagination, addressed these "gentle quadrupeds." "The names of our horses are Black, Coffee, Blue, Calgary, Coaly, Buck, Pig, Bones, Strawberry and Steamboat, and each creature knows perfectly the reproof or the cheering cry addressed to him."[6] Although rather genteel in his descriptions, Fleming was nevertheless accurate, especially in his observation of the link between the packer and the horse which was born of shared trials and tribulations.

Notorious for its danger to both man and beast, the trail down the Kicking Horse consisted for most of its length of a ledge high up on the canyon wall that required a good deal of nerve to travel. Fleming found it almost intolerable:

To look down gives one an uncontrollable dizziness, to make the head swim and the view unsteady, even with men of tried nerve . . . We are from 500 to 800 feet high on a path from ten to fifteen inches wide and at some points almost obliterated, with slopes above and below us so steep that a stone would roll into the torrent in the abyss below. There are no trees or branches or twigs which we can grip to aid us in our advance on that narrow precarious footing . . .[7]

While these conditions made it difficult for him, the situation was far worse for the men who had to see to the horses' welfare as well as their own. The packers' first trouble occurred when in the course of ascending one particularly steep spot one of the horses slipped and went somersaulting over the side of the hill. Fortunately his pack caught, halting the fall after a short distance, but the accident necessitated some rather back-breaking work for Tom and one of his assistants. Together they scrambled down to the prostrate animal and after laboriously unfastening the tightly cinched lash rope and removing his burden were able to get him to his feet and shoulder him back uphill. Further difficulties were encountered when Calgary's footing gave way and he plunged over a fifty foot embankment, requiring a similar rescue operation, and again when the pack train ran into a hornet's nest in a wooded section. These winged devils, the bane of many a packer's existence, sent the horses into paroxysms of agony causing untold confusion and the abandonment of the regular trail.

Eventually, persistence paid off and the 'tourists' were delivered safely to Major Rogers' camp on August 31st. Reflecting on the route, one that the packers were forced to travel almost daily, Fleming concluded that "for my part I have no desire to retrace my steps by the path I have followed in the descent of the Kicking Horse Valley."[8]

In later years when reminiscing about the trip Tom was forced to admit that "I never knew how hard a time we had until I read the book." However, he recalled another occasion when one of his fellow packers had a much worse time on the same trail. As Tom told it, the packer was taking a string of eleven horses along the path 700 feet above the river after a few inches of soft snow had fallen. The horses' hoofs quickly balled up with the sticky substance and the lead horse, or bell-mare, lost her footing, plunging to her death in the canyon below. Immediately the other horses panicked and within a few seconds seven more followed her over the precipice, leaving three shaking animals and a pale packer "standing on the edge of nothing."[9]

Although there wasn't anything extraordinary about the Fleming-Grant trip it did provide Tom with one of the most embarrassing moments of his life. Often when forced to cross a heavily swollen stream it was the packers' practice to cut some trees and construct a makeshift bridge to prevent the wetting of the packs. At one bad crossing, after building such a bridge, Tom found that one of his animals had decided to ford the stream. The animal soon found himself sunk to his knees in soft mud and to prevent himself from sinking further simply lay down on his side. Tom then had to wade into the mire and attempt to heave the recalcitrant to his feet. As the day was hot and the flies and mosquitoes were taking advantage of the fine weather, his temper soon got the better of him. He addressed his charge "in the language he was accustomed to hear" and armed himself with a stout club. To his amazement, the horse suddenly leapt to its feet and scrambled free of the muddy prison. Still fuming he turned to extract himself and looking up was surprised to see the Reverent Grant standing on the bridge above him:

. . . I guess I turned seven or eight shades redder than I had been before. I hadn't the sand even to apologize for my talk. But I felt kind of glad when he looked at me with a laugh and said: 'It seems to help sometimes, Tom.'[10]

So much for Fleming's "reproofs" and "cheering cries."

This historic and eventful journey was one of Tom's last duties as a packer for the CPR survey. Early in November he accompanied Major Rogers by sleigh from the Kicking Horse summit to the end of steel near Castle Mountain (Mount Eisenhower), and then joined him on the caboose of a work train as far as Calgary. There he officially ended his employment. The job had provided him with the opportunity to gain valuable experience at packing and to become knowledgeable of a great deal of the country along the railway's right-of-way through the Rockies and Selkirks. But it was time to look elsewhere for a livelihood.

In the course of his work for the railway he had on numerous occasions found traces of mineral deposits at several locations and a bit of prospecting seemed like the most obvious, and possibly lucrative, course of action. With this in mind, he located at the base of Castle Mountain where the boom town of Silver City, fed by rumors of fabulous silver and copper deposits in the nearby mountains, was beginning its short-lived existence. Either because he found this area too crowded or felt there were better prospects further west he moved on to Holt City (later Laggan and eventually Lake Louise). After spending the remainder of the winter there in a cabin built for him by a friend, he went into partnership with fellow prospector Jim Wright in 1884.

Apparently their first site of exploration was around the base of Mount Stephen, but they soon shifted their attention to an area that had attracted Tom while packing for the railway, the North Fork of the Wapta (Yoho River). In company with Wright and another prospector he blazed a foot trail up this unknown valley and prospected extensively, unfortunately without much success. However, the enterprise was by no means a complete loss as Tom gained his first glimpses of the strikingly beautiful Takakkaw, Laughing and Twin Falls, and knowledge of yet another area for future reference. Following this he pushed on west and spent the month of August on a mineral claim at Quartz Creek, a tributary of the Columbia River near Donald, but found the weather too inclement to make any real headway on a mine.

At the end of this rather fruitless season of prospecting Tom returned to Silver City and focused his attention on more romantic pursuits. During the course of the winter he made the acquaintance of Minnie McDougall, a native of Owen Sound, Ontario, who with her brother Mose ran a boarding house known as 'The Miner's Home.' Given the overwhelming majority of males in the town, apparently 237 men to 5 unmarried women, he must have been rather persistent in his advances as before the snow left the ground he had become engaged to the pretty young relative of the missionary McDougall family of Morley. Part of the winter was also spent near Padmore working at the saw mill on Colonel Walker's timber lease which he had helped to survey in 1882.

The spring of 1885 found Tom beginning one of the most eventful and memorable years of his life. In April he received a wire from Major Sam Steele requesting that he join Steele's Scouts which were being organized to take part in subduing the recent outbreak of Metis and Indian violence known as the second Riel Rebellion. The previous year Steele had been in charge of the Mounted Police at the CPR construction camps which followed the railhead through the mountains. He spent a considerable time headquartered at Laggan and probably became acquainted with Tom there. With his knowledge of horses and experience in packing, Tom was an ideal candidate to help with the transport of Steele's mounted corps and he made for Calgary to answer the call.

Most of his service with Steele's Scouts was spent in the unsuccessful pursuit of the renegade Cree chief Big Bear north of Fort Pitt in Saskatchewan. With the cessation of hostilities early in July Tom returned to the mountains for a short time, but by mid-October was once more headed north, this time for Edmonton. This trip was required because of some unfinished business from the winter before, as that city had become the temporary home of the girl who had so attracted him at Silver City. On October 19, 1885, Tom Wilson and Minnie McDougall were married by the Reverend John Howard with the bride's two cousins, D. M. McDougall and Clara Hardisty, acting as witnesses.

To this point the year would seem sufficiently exciting to make it memorable but there was one more noteworthy event in which he was to participate before it ended. After their wedding the Wilsons returned to Morley to visit the McDougalls and while there Tom heard of the special excursion trains going to Craigellachie for the driving of the railway's last spike. He boarded one of the trains at Morley and with several former fellow workers made his first complete trip over the section on which he had labored for three years. Probably his thoughts were much like those of Sandford Fleming, also a passenger, who recalled that "for myself I could not help contrasting the luxurious travelling which the railway afforded with the experience of my little party journeying westward through the mountains in 1883."[11]

When Craigellachie was reached on the cold, raw morning of November 7th, Tom disembarked with the others and watched Donald Smith officially complete the line. In one of the most famous of all Canadian photographs his stetsoned head is just barely visible peer-

Donald Smith driving the last spike, November 7, 1885. Tom Wilson is just visible in a light stetson to the right of center at the rear.

The Wilson homestead near Morley, ca. 1889.

ing over the crowd of onlookers as Smith drives home the historic spike.

The driving of the last spike marked the end of an era in Tom's life. Only five years had elapsed since he had first come west with the NWMP but they had been very exciting and, as the future was to prove, very profitable for the experience and knowledge gained. Being a bachelor had allowed him to move freely without the worry of responsibility during this period. However, from the end of 1885 onward the need to support a wife and soon a growing family demanded a more permanent and dependable mode of existence.

Tom and his wife returned to run the boarding house at Silver City for the winter of 1885-86. But even though blacksmithing supplemented Tom's income they could not make a go of it when the population of the town diminished to just twenty souls as rumors of mineral strikes proved false and new finds were reported near Golden. Consequently he began searching for a suitable homestead and early in the spring found one northeast of

Morley. Here they built a house, stable and corrals, registered the famous powder horn brand, and settled down, planning to thereafter devote themselves entirely to the raising of horses and cattle. But when he found that he needed to supplement the living made on the homestead, the memory of the mountain trails soon lured Tom back to the scene of his former exploits.

On first returning to the mountains early in the summer of 1887, Tom must have been amazed at the changes that had transpired near his old camping ground of 1881 on Whiskey Creek. When he left for Morley in the spring of 1886 the small community around the station at Siding 29, near the foot of Cascade Mountain, had seemed to be making good progress. But when he returned it was being rivalled, if not outstripped, by another settlement further to the south around the base of Tunnel Mountain. The reason for this development was the presence of hot springs on the lower slopes of Sulphur Mountain.

Tom had first become aware of the hot springs while

with the CPR survey in 1882. During the intervening period several squatters had located at the springs and each had attempted to develop them for commercial purposes, resulting in conflicting claims of ownership. In September, 1885, William Pearce, Superintendent of Mines for the Dominion Government, visited the area and after talking to the claimants returned to Ottawa and recommended that a crown reservation be established in order that the "sanitary advantages" of the springs be made available to the public. With visions of spas on the order of those at Hot Springs, Arkansas and Baden, Germany, the government complied, setting aside a ten square mile reservation by an Order-in-Council on November 25, 1885. During the same year a preliminary survey of the springs was conducted by P. R. A. Belanger of the Dominion Topographic Survey and in 1886, George Stewart, another surveyor, was instructed to lay out a townsite and roads on the north side of the river.

By the time Tom arrived a flurry of building had commenced in the new townsite, which had been named Banff after the birthplace in Scotland of George Stephen, the President of the CPR. This construction had been spurred on by the beginning of work on the large CPR hostelry, to be known as the Banff Springs, at the confluence of the Spray and Bow Rivers. Meanwhile another interesting development had just taken place with the passing of an Act of Parliament which extended the crown reservation to encompass a full 260 square miles. This enlarged area, which the government had decided should become Canada's first national park, was named Rocky Mountains Park and George Stewart was appointed Superintendent.

Obviously Banff was the place for Tom to search for employment and the most logical employer was his old friend the CPR. He found its officials receptive to his request for special assignments because of his knowledge of the area and his successful completion of similar tasks previously. The year after he had left the survey he had undertaken several jobs for them when not out prospecting. Among these were the blazing of a foot trail to Lake Louise and escorting the first two ladies to pay a visit to the spot, the Madames Ross and Brothers, wives of the Chief Engineer and Assistant Superintendent of Construction of the Mountain Section. Later the same year Tom had received notice of the impending railway-organized excursion of the British Association under the presidency of Sir Richard Temple and had blazed another trail to Lake Louise for their benefit.

The railway had decided that the attractions provided by Lake Louise warranted development and as a preliminary measure decided to send in a construction gang during the summer of 1887. Tom was instructed to blaze a new and larger trail to enable a boat to be taken along. The boat was the first one used on the lake and the construction gang erected a rough log shelter, a forerunner of the Chateau Lake Louise. This was, of course, a milestone for the CPR, but for Tom there was a

far more important event later in the year. At the railway's request he agreed to accompany a party interested in hunting big game during the month of September. This was the first hunting party taken out from Banff and launched Tom's career in the outfitting and guiding business.

While working as a packer for the survey he had been struck by the lack of game in such seemingly ideal surroundings. Its absence had been attributed to overhunting by Indians in the Bow Valley, to numerous forest fires and not least of all to the presence of the large body of men associated with the building of the railroad. However, there was one area which he felt sure to be the haunt of substantial numbers of bighorn sheep and perhaps some bear, goat and deer as well. The region was the upper reaches of the North Saskatchewan River which he had viewed while making his crossing of the Howse Pass in 1882, and he decided to escort his clients there.

Departing his homestead early in September with three saddle horses and two pack horses, Tom proceeded to Laggan and joined his party of two English sportsmen, H. W. Calverley and Arthur Brearley. They wished to spend approximately a month in pursuit of big game of all varieties. Little is known about the details of the trip but it is probable that the North Saskatchewan was descended as far as the Kootenay Plains, a favorite Indian hunting ground. Either for variety or because of its historic significance, when the time came to return the hunters insisted on going out to the railroad by way of Howse Pass. Undoubtedly Tom attempted to dissuade them by reciting the litany of his former trip but in the end their desires held sway. The experience proved to be no more enjoyable than previously as the downed timber and steep canyons that had caused him so much grief in 1882 again brought progress to a virtual standstill. Finally the horses had to be abandoned and the three hiked the remainder of the distance down the Blaeberry to Moberly. As a rather inauspicious ending to his first private guiding venture, he had to hire some axemen to return with him and free his animals from their timbered trap.

Despite its problems, this initial endeavor at outfitting and guiding opened up a whole new vista for Tom. With the success of the CPR's international advertising campaign and the opening of the Banff Springs Hotel, numerous hunters, fishermen and sightseers began to arrive. Soon the CPR and the government began cooperating in the construction of roads and bridle paths in the vicinity of Banff to accommodate the less hardy visitors. The Canadian Pacific Railway Transfer Company built and began operating a livery barn which provided rigs and saddle horses to be used for short trips on these roads and paths. The principals of this company were Colonel James Walker and Major John Stewart. However, they were not interested in providing horses and equipment to the few wishing to probe the mountain wilderness away from the rail line. Thus when W. L.

Packing up in Wilson's corral. Tom Wilson is on the right.

Mathews, the hotel's manager, was approached by guests seeking information on longer trips he put them in touch with Tom. Before long he was granted the privilege of advertising his services as 'Guide to the CPR.'

To properly outfit these parties a local headquarters was needed for the summer season. Tom was able to secure the lease on a piece of property at the corner of Banff Avenue and Buffalo Street on which there was a substantial corral. Some of the horses raised on the homestead were brought to this location during the summer to use as saddle horses and he also began to buy horses from the Stoneys for use as pack animals. Henceforth his corral, because of its central locale, would be a favored rendezvous for residents and tourists alike as they frequently gathered to watch the activities which accompanied the preparation of a pack train.

During the summer season 'Wilson's' is frequently the scene of no little excitement when some party is getting ready to leave. Then you may see ten or fifteen wicked-eyed ponies, some in a corral and the rest tied to trees ready for packing. If the horses are making their first trip of the season there will be considerable bucking and kicking before all is ready. Several men are seen bustling about, sorting and weighing the packs, and making order out of the pile of blankets, tents, and bags of flour or bacon. The cayuses are saddled and cinched up one by one with many a protesting bite and kick. The celebrated 'diamond hitch' is used in fastening the packs, and the struggling men look picturesque in their old clothes and sombreros as they tighten the ropes, bravely on the gentle horses, but rather gingerly when it comes to a bucking bronco.

A crowd of the businessmen of Banff, who usually take about 365 holidays every year, stands around to offer advice and watch the sport. Then the picturesque train of horses with their wild looking drivers files out through the village streets under a fusillade of snap-shot cameras and the wondering gaze of new arrivals from the east.[12]

In addition to his guiding and outfitting for the CPR, Tom also worked for the Dominion Topographic Survey between 1889 and 1893. Government survey work in the mountains had begun in 1884 when Thomas Fawcett completed the extension of the township system from the

Gap to Kicking Horse Pass, laying out corner monuments along the Bow Valley and other smaller tributary valleys. The following two years Otto Klotz had been employed determining meridians of longitude from the Divide to the Columbia River along the rail line, thereby completing the first non-CPR survey through the Rockies. But these were, in effect, only preliminary surveys and Surveyor-General Edouard Deville was anxious to have more extensive work done which would show the course of all rivers and creeks, the location of passes and valleys, and the altitudes of various peaks. Some valuable information had already been gathered by Dr. George M. Dawson of the Geological Survey of Canada, in the course of his work through the mountains in 1883 and 1884, but much remained to be done.

In 1886, J. J. McArthur was appointed to begin a topographic survey, and he would continue on the project, with the aid of other surveyors, until work in the vicinity of the CPR line through the Rocky Mountain, Selkirk and Gold Ranges was completed in 1893. The surveyors had to travel through rough mountain country where few trails existed, as they were required to visit a large number of mountain peaks to carry out their triangulation and photo-topographic work. In 1891 McArthur ascended 43 peaks between 8,000 and 10,000 feet in altitude and travelled 400 miles over rugged terrain. Of course, this type of travel necessitated hiring a packer who, in addition to caring for surveyor, horses and supplies, was often called upon to assist in carrying the bulky twenty pound camera and plates and the fifteen pound transit to the summit of the chosen photographic station. Tom's familiarity with the Rockies and Selkirks made him well qualified for such a job. Although he may have accompanied McArthur sometime between 1886 and 1888, it was not until 1889 that it is certain he was hired on by the survey. During that year he accompanied W. S. Drewry, who had joined McArthur in 1887, on his summer's surveys.

The results of the season included the first ascents of Wind Mountain (Lougheed) and Storm Mountain by Drewry and Wilson and a visit to Marble Canyon on the Vermilion River, the first recorded by white men. After these initial successes, Tom accompanied both McArthur and Drewry at various times until the survey's comple-

George Fear and Tom Wilson in the doorway of the Wilson and Fear store, ca. 1895.

Tom Wilson and his family, 1896. Left to right — Tom Jr. (Eddie), Tom, Ada, Rene, John, Bessie, and Minnie.

tion four years later, taking part in the ascent of many more unclimbed peaks and discovering several other noteworthy points of interest.

Beginning in 1891, Tom also performed another important function for the Department of the Interior under whose auspices the survey was carried out. Previously it had been the practice of the surveyors to return the pack horses and other equipment to Calgary upon completion of each year's work. This often caused delays in resuming operations the following spring as it demanded a minimum of a three-day trip to get the pack train to the scene of the survey's activities. Tom minimized these problems by agreeing to keep the equipment and winter the horses at his Morley homestead for the sum of ten dollars each. This service made it possible for the surveyors to wire ahead both their expected time of arrival and proposed scene of operations, and be assured that everything would be awaiting them when they appeared. Under this arrangement he was keeping more than twen-

ty head of the Department's stock on his range by the winter of 1892-93.

There was a further activity that occupied Tom at this time, one which resulted directly from his participation in the guiding business. A side benefit of his trips, particularly the big game hunting variety, was the large number of animal hides and heads procured in the course of hunting food and trophies. At an early date, probably shortly after 1890, a Banff acquaintance suggested that they go into business, selling these articles along with furs that could be gathered in the course of winter's trapping. The acquaintance was William Fear who, with his brother George, had been one of the original residents of Siding 29. Tom liked the idea and formed a partnership with the brothers in a store known as Wilson and Fear. But in a few years, with his outfitting and guiding activities demanding more attention, he found he did not have time to properly hold up his end of the bargain. The partnership was dissolved and the Fear brothers turned part of the store into a curio shop which, with the later addition of a photographic department, became a well-known fixture in Banff.

By 1893 the growth of Banff into a thriving tourist resort had convinced Tom to make the town his permanent residence. Accordingly, he brought his wife and four children from the Morley homestead, first to a small log house on Banff Avenue near the town's school and then later to another, more spacious abode adjoining his corral. The latter eventually became the gathering place of travellers from around the world anxious to learn about the mountains, and the hospitality they received earned it a reputation as a home "where the latch string hung on the outside."

The soundness of the decision to stake his future on Banff and the trail business immediately became apparent as the 1893 season proved to be his busiest to date. Of particular interest was a one month trip taken in the fall with Robert L. Barrett, a Chicago paper manufacturer and businessman. Returning in late August from a three week outing with L. A. Hamilton, CPR Land Com-

missioner, Tom received word from Mathews that Barrett was enquiring about making a trip whose objective was similar to that of two other young men he had met earlier in the summer — the climbing of a difficult mountain strictly for sport. His curiosity aroused, Tom met the would-be alpinist at the hotel and after discussing the matter suggested that he attempt Mount Assiniboine, the highest known peak south of the railroad. Tom had originally learned about the mountain from Dr. Dawson, who had provided its name, and had himself glimpsed its wedge-like 11,870 foot summit in 1889 while with Drewry in the Simpson Pass region. Barrett eagerly concurred and arrangements were immediately made to leave by the first of September.

Acting in the capacity of guide, with George Fear assisting as cook, Tom led the pack train out of Banff on that date, proceeding up Healy Creek as far as Simpson Pass on old Indian trails. Once over the pass they descended into the valley of the Simpson River which was then followed to a point where a south branch flowed in. Here no trails existed and the best route to follow was not

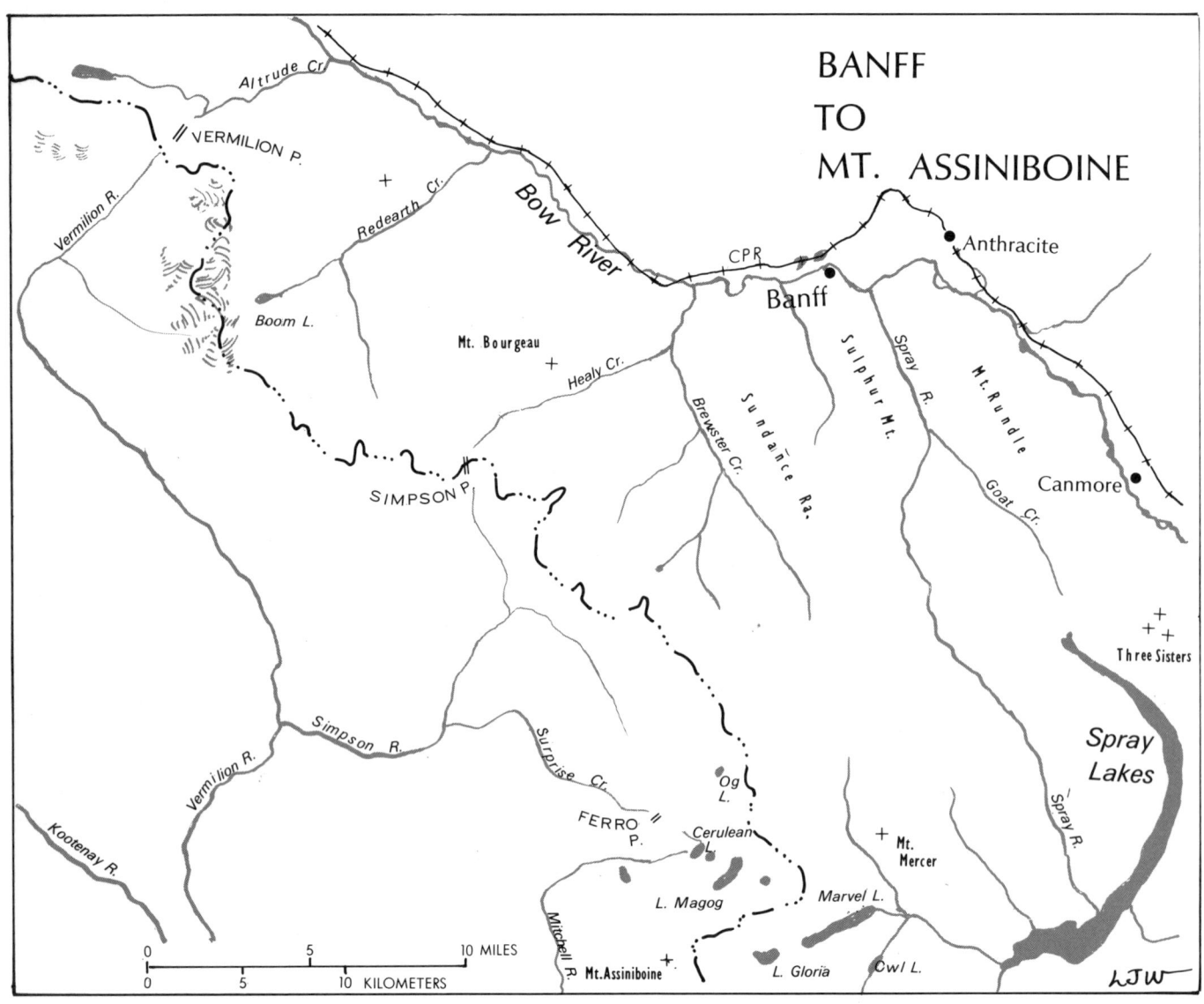

An early party at Mount Assiniboine — the 'Matterhorn of the Rockies.'

immediately evident. After finding a good camping spot and resting for the better part of a day, he and Barrett struggled up a heavily timbered ridge to obtain their bearings. They were rewarded for their labors with the first close-up view of the 'Matterhorn of the Rockies,' a sight which would remain indelibly impressed on their memories. Even as late as 1924, Barrett would remark in a letter written to Tom from his camp at the foot of the second highest peak in the Himalayas that "I don't think even old K2, the 28,000, looked to me as high and imposing, and as terrible as old Assiniboine when you and I finally won through to where we could have a good look at him."[13]

The next day Barrett again mounted the ridge and upon traversing it spotted what appeared to be a suitable pass into the adjacent valley. As there was no trail Tom had to do some back-breaking axe work to the top of the pass (Ferro Pass) and then down again into the valley of the Mitchell River. From there it proved a fairly simple matter to ascend this river to its headwaters in the picturesque lakes at the base of Assiniboine. Unfortunately, though, Barrett was to be denied his attempt on the giant because of the lateness of the season. After a short stay at its foot they returned by way of the Simpson River and Vermilion Pass, visiting Marble Canyon en route.

Earlier in the summer of 1893, Tom had made the acquaintances of two other young travellers with interests similar to Barrett's. The two were Samuel E. S. Allen and his classmate at Yale University, Walter D. Wilcox, who was destined to play a major role in Tom's future.

Wilcox, a native of Chicago, had attended Andover Academy before enrolling in the class of 1893 at Yale. Later he attended Columbia University as well. As a young man he had taken a world tour which had included a stop in Cuba, where he would eventually establish a large mahogany plantation, and in several countries with mountainous terrain. The trip had included some minor climbing and his interest in the sport had been awakened to the extent that he made an ascent of Oregon's Mount Hood in 1890. During 1891, in the course of returning from a summer trip to Alaska, he visited Banff and Lake Louise and resolved to return at a later time and test his mettle on some of the area's interesting peaks.

Allen had been born in Philadelphia and after an early education there became a member of the class of 1894 at Yale. He would go on to receive his M.A. at the same university in 1897, but shortly afterward would become a victim of "dementia praecox" and spend the rest of his life confined to a mental institution. His first visit to the Rockies and Selkirks was also in 1891 when he attempted some minor climbs, including the Devil's Thumb near Lake Louise. Equally impressed, he too decided to return but first turned his attention to the Alps and ascended the Matterhorn in 1892.

Obviously at some point after their 1891 trips, Wilcox and Allen met at Yale, discussed their ideas about climb-

ing in Canada and agreed to combine forces. Allen was the first to disembark at Banff early in the summer of 1893 and while waiting for his companion climbed Mount Rundle and obtained a view of Mount Assiniboine. Upon Wilcox's arrival they found they needed some camping equipment as the original shelter at Lake Louise had recently burned down. After acquiring "outfit from Mr. T. E. Wilson of Banff" they went on to Lake Louise where Willoughby Astley, the manager of the new chalet being built, provided them with a horse and a Stoney guide, Enoch Wildman. Wildman quickly found the temperatures of the high altitudes too uncomfortable for his liking and returned to Lake Louise, but Wilcox and Allen remained in the field in order to attempt the first ascents of Mounts Temple and Victoria. Even though they were unsuccessful the two immediately decided to try again at a later date when they were better prepared and equipped.

Although it was not immediately evident, the appearance of Barrett, Wilcox and Allen at Banff marked the inauguration of the last great era of Rocky Mountain exploration and discovery — the age of the mountaineer, sportsman and tourist-explorer. Following on the heels of the fur trader, railroad builder and surveyor, this group was to make known over the next three decades most of the remaining secrets of the Canadian Cordillera's geography. The Alps of Europe, the hills of Skye and the Appalachians and Rockies of the continental United States were growing stale for the European, British and American climbing fraternities. They thrived on first ascents and new explorations, making the relatively untouched 'Canadian Alps' seem like an obvious area on which to focus attention. The impetus was provided by the CPR's advertising campaign and by published reports of pioneer mountaineers such as William Spotswood Green who had begun climbing in the Selkirks in 1888. Anticipation of future mountaineering and exploration was attested to by Wilcox's report that upon stopping at Glacier House in 1891 he found a group of enthusiasts "who were accustomed to gather every evening around a blazing fire and read selections from Green's *Among the Selkirk Glaciers* just as our forefathers were wont to read a daily chapter from the Bible."[14]

It was impossible for Tom to know at this early date just how closely linked his future would become with the lives of these people. But it was becoming increasingly apparent as the mountaineers began to gather for their assault on the unknown peaks that they could not set forth on their adventures without the aid of experienced guides and packers. Thus in 1893, with his well-established outfitting and guiding operation at Banff and his familiarity with the country, Tom stood on the verge of a potentially bright future in which both his services and knowledge were to be in great demand.

Walter D. Wilcox, ca. 1896.

Bill Peyto.

2 New Faces and New Places

Wilson's decision to concentrate on the outfitting and guiding business and an increasing number of customers required some immediate changes in his operation. Fundamental among these was the need to recruit additional help to deal with the requests being made for his services. Certainly on previous occasions he had periodically employed assistants, as for example when his business partner George Fear served as cook during the trip to Assiniboine with Barrett. But due to the shortness of the season, full-time, trustworthy and competent men who could take out parties on their own were needed if the venture was to become a paying proposition. Tom's success in recruiting such men demanded a further change, namely his own partial retirement from trail work in order to devote his time to the running of the business. Despite this, he was able to retain his reputation as the most reliable source of information available on the mountains by religiously gathering and memorizing details of any new ground covered in the course of his employees' trips.

Finding men suitable for the trail proved to be, by virtue of this particular time in history, no great problem. In the early eighteen-nineties the forerunners of what by the end of the decade would become a flood of immigrants were already beginning to trickle into Western Canada from the British Isles. Augmenting these was a steady stream of eastern Canadians and a few Americans heading west in search of better prospects or a fresh start. Many of these early arrivals were of an adventurous mien and it is not surprising that some eventually gravitated to the rough-and-ready atmosphere of pioneer Banff. Mainly from rural backgrounds, these individuals possessed exactly the right mixture of toughness, independence and humor necessary for survival during long periods on the trail. They also quickly picked up the skills required to handle their specific jobs in the efficient team that composed the crew of a pack outfit.

The key position in this team was that of guide. While on the trail he was charged with the well-being of the clients, or "dudes," and the other crew members, as well as the care of the animals and equipment. In addition, he was responsible for guiding this entourage to the proposed destination and back again. Required attributes were, therefore, a well-developed sense of direction, leadership, good judgement and, above all, an excellent knowledge of horses. A sense of direction was essential because parties often wished to go where no trails existed. In such circumstances the guide had to make the right decision since the margin for error was often very slim, and the complete success or failure of an expedition depended on such choices.

Leadership and good judgement were needed for a variety of reasons. The guide attempted to avoid the many serious situations which could befall an outfit while travelling in the wilderness, but he needed the ability to extract the pack train from any ticklish predicaments, or "jackpots," it did get into. Death by drowning, starvation or any number of other mishaps was an ever present possibility and it took a strong personality to inspire the necessary confidence in other members of the crew.

Finally, the knowledge of horses was indispensable since the welfare of the party could usually be correlated with the state of the horses on which it depended. The guide had to know the particular quirks of each animal to enable him to handle it properly in a given situation; he had to know each one's capabilities and how to rate it to achieve maximum performance during a typical day's march of five or six hours (approximately twelve miles); he had to know how to pack each one to prevent the dreaded saddle sores which could make a valuable horse

Top: the guide and packer saddle a packhorse and firmly tighten the cinches.

Middle: packs in place, the diamond is tied and securely tightened.

Bottom: with everything ready to go the packtrain sets off with the guide in the lead.

useless when most needed; and lastly he had to know what was suitable pasturage when picking a camping spot for the night. In short, he had to know each horse as an individual personality and respond to its needs.

Assisting the guide and acting under his instructions was the packer, sometimes referred to as the horse wrangler, whose desired skills were, to a lesser degree, the same as those required of his boss. The packer's job was the performance of the thousand and one chores which were essential to the success of a pack trip. Beginning at the crack of dawn he was out to round up the horses and bring them to the campsite. There they were saddled and packed, usually with the guide's help, as the camp was dismantled. When it came time to pull out he took up a position in the middle or at the rear of the string, herding along stragglers, gathering up strays and "eating dust" all day. Usually the only respite came when the guide called him forward to aid in chopping out deadfall or clearing a new trail. After the day's march was completed and the guide had selected an appropriate camping spot, the packer assisted in unpacking the horses, cutting teepee poles if none were available, setting up the teepee and/or tents, chopping a sufficient supply of firewood for the night and preparing mattresses from freshly trimmed spruce boughs. After supper the horses had to be taken to the night grazing area where they were often picketed or hobbled, and often a smudge had to be lit to keep off the flies. It was his final responsibility to see to it that all the packs and other pieces of equipment were properly covered to prevent wetting in any overnight storms.

Last, but by no stretch of the imagination least, in the ranks of the crew was the cook. His abilities were, of course, slightly different from those of the rest of the men. Anyone could cook if he had to but the mark of the true trail cook was his success in producing a light and toothsome bannock — a bread substitute made from flour, salt, baking powder and water and baked to a golden brown in the campfire, often with the aid of a metal reflector. In addition to whipping up a batch of this delight every two or three days, the cook also had a busy daily routine. Up with the guide and packer at dawn to start the fire, he had to have breakfast ready by the time the dudes rose and the horses were brought in. Lunch also had to be prepared in advance before quickly washing up and packing the cook boxes. With the exception of the brief lunch break when a pot of tea or coffee had to be brewed, he could ride along in comparative peacefulness until camp was made. Then his real work for the day began. The late afternoon or evening meal was the heartiest and most important of the day and it had to be ready to serve by the time the rest of the men had finished their chores. Even after cleaning up from this meal his job was not completed as he had to prepare the rudiments of the next morning's breakfast before joining the evening parley around the fire.

These were the usual positions which an outfitter had

A packer making a smudge for hobbled horses.

to fill in organizing a trip for a party of two or three. But there were many permutations and combinations possible depending on the size of the party, the number of horses taken along, the men available and the client's wishes. If the party was composed of a single individual, as sometimes happened, only one capable man had to perform the duties of all three positions If there were a particularly large number of dudes it often required the assignment of two or three packers and on rare occasions two cooks. However, to prevent any divisions and facilitate decision-making there was always only one guide.

The man who rates the distinction as being the first guide to be hired by Wilson was a young Irish immigrant named James Tabuteau. His first recorded expedition was in 1895 when he was given the unenviable chore of guiding Colonel Robert O'Hara, one of the earliest tourist-explorers in the Canadian Rockies, to the lake which bears his name.

Colonel O'Hara was a retired British army officer who paid his first visit to the Rockies in 1887, at the age of fifty-two. During a conversation with J. J. McArthur he learned of an interesting lake which the surveyor had seen from a peak while working in the region of the Ottertail Valley. O'Hara visited the lake in that year and

again in both 1889 and 1894, using a trail which he had discovered leading up Cataract Brook. At the conclusion of the 1894 outing he appeared at the recently completed chalet at Lake Louise where he evidently proved to be a somewhat irascible guest. Wilcox, who was there at the time, later reported with rather unconcealed glee that the other patrons were able to have the last laugh at the expense of the reclusive and often ill-tempered Colonel. On one of his jaunts in the neighbourhood of the chalet O'Hara was forced to cross Louise Creek on two slender poles which had been placed there as a makeshift bridge. The unfortunate hiker had armed himself with a stick in each hand so as to be sure not to lose his balance on the treacherous footing. Lose his balance he did, however, and after a plunge in the ice cold water of the creek came into the chalet "all dripping and swearing mad." [1]

Upon returning to the mountains in 1895, O'Hara had two objectives in mind — to reach Simpson Pass from Vermilion Pass via Twin Lakes, and to make another visit to Lake O'Hara. Because of a rough time the previous year when he had been led astray by an inexperienced guide, he approached Wilson to provide men for the present explorations. Two were hired and with them he accomplished his first objective of reaching Simpson Pass. However, when he attempted to engage

Colonel O'Hara and Tom Wilson during a later trip, 1925.

the same men for the second trip they refused to accompany him because he had run his camps on such a strict military basis. Although he had ·been planning to use Tabuteau with another party, Tom turned to him to guide the tempestuous Colonel into the lake. He, like the other guides, at first refused to go but relented when Tom promised him extra pay if he undertook the task.

It quickly became apparent as Jim led the Colonel up Cataract Brook that their personalities were not going to mesh too well. The deadfall on the trail demanded some heavy chopping and after much cussing on his guide's part, O'Hara was soon moved to comment, "Tabuteau, you swear entirely too much." Jim wryly enquired what he suggested be done about it. The Colonel retorted, "When you feel the urge coming on you stop and think once, then think twice, then think a third time and by then the urge will have passed." Apparently taking the suggestion to heart, Jim did much better until the two reached the lake and made camp. After setting up the tent and lighting a campfire in front of it, a strong breeze came up, fanning the flames and sending sparks flying. Suddenly Jim leaped to his feet with a perplexed look on his face and was about to let loose an exclamation when the Colonel, sitting with his back to the tent, stopped him with, "Tabuteau, remember what I told you." Jim stared at him a moment, pulled himself together and carefully repeated, "Tabuteau, think once . . . Tabuteau, think twice . . . Tabuteau, think thrice." Then, while making a

wild dash for the water supply, he blurted out, "Colonel, your goddam tent's on fire!"

The fire was easily extinguished but not so the Colonel's temper and most of the rest of their stay in the lake's vicinity passed in uneasy silence. On returning to Banff, O'Hara sought out Wilson and delivered what sounded like an ultimatum; "I want that man Tabuteau dismissed — he swears too much and isn't a very good guide." Tom was only too aware of the Colonel's bluster by this time and paid no attention. But he was somewhat surprised eight months later when he received a letter from O'Hara composed of only one crisp sentence, "Wilson, I've thought the matter over — don't dismiss Tabuteau." [2]

While the O'Hara trip was one of the thornier expeditions Tabuteau guided, his Irish temperament and thick skin made him invaluable for difficult parties and he was awarded several more tough assignments. Unfortunately, though, he soon decided to leave Tom's employ in order to join the North West Mounted Police. He was stationed in Canmore for a number of years and eventually went on to New Westminster where he became chief of the city police force. However, his brother Fred Tabuteau obtained a position with Tom a short time later, more than adequately filling Jim's shoes. "Tabby," as he was known to his friends, would in time become one of the legendary trailmen of the area. Described by a close companion as "wild as a hawk but the kind of man who would stick with you through any kind of trouble" he was to be noted not only for his trail sense but also for diverse other abilities. Among these was an unfailing talent for being able to sing 'Show Me The Way To Go Home' backwards when "well-lubricated." [3]

During the O'Hara expedition in 1895, two of Tom's other top trailhands were involved in a major excursion to Mount Assiniboine. The pair, Bill Peyto and Ralph Edwards, were to achieve reputations in the guiding business second only to Wilson himself, especially Peyto who was undoubtedly one of the most colorful characters ever to inhabit the Canadian Rockies.

Ebenezer William Peyto was born in the village of Welling, Kent in 1868, the third son in a family of nine children. His father Augustus was a farm bailiff and as a result Bill spent most of his youth in the country before going on to attend Foster's Endowed Church of England School. Possessed of a wandering spirit he left England in 1886 at the age of eighteen and after arriving in Canada travelled it end to end. In 1887 he appeared at Moberly, B.C., working for the railway, and soon afterward moved on to the Cochrane district, taking out a homestead in the Montreal Valley west of the town in 1890. He also did some prospecting and trapping in the mountains and eventually, in 1893 or 1894, hired on as an apprentice guide with Wilson, whom he had probably met as early as 1887. Before long he was favorably impressing the dudes he was engaged to take out, as he did Wilcox who accompanied him on several occasions.

I soon grew to admire Peyto . . . He was efficient, daring, highly imaginative, an excellent man with the horses and a good friend. He spoke in the low, quiet voice of the true westerner, but even so he spoke rarely. His forte was doing things, not talking about them. [4]

It was not only Bill's ability which impressed Wilcox, however, as his appearance on the trail was also something worthy of note.

Peyto assumes a wild and picturesque though somewhat tattered attire. A sombrero, with a rakish tilt to one side, a blue shirt set off by a white kerchief (which may have served civilisation for a napkin), and a buckskin coat with fringed border, add to his cowboy appearance. A heavy belt containing a row of cartridges, hunting knife and six-shooter, as well as the restless activity of his wicked blue eyes, give him an air of bravado. He usually wears two pairs of trousers, one over the other, the outer pair about six months older. This was shown by their dilapidated and faded state, hanging, after a week of rough work in burnt timber, in a tattered fringe knee-high. Every once in a while Peyto would give one or two nervous yanks at the fringe and tear off the longer pieces, so that his outer trousers disappeared day by day from below upwards. Part of this was affectation, to impress the tenderfoot, or the "dude" as he calls everyone who wears a collar. [5]

Peyto's wild appearance was often matched by his behavior and he soon became famous for many of his escapades. On one occasion he live-trapped a lynx, tied it up securely and carried it on his back to a bar in Banff where some miners he was known to dislike were wont to drink. Nonchalantly walking in, he released the cat and stood back to enjoy the scene as it proceeded to wreak havoc among the terrified victims. It is not known how they fared in the match-up but the lynx came through unscathed and soon became one of the prime attractions in the Banff Zoo.

Another incident, which illustrated his rather bizarre sense of justice, occurred when an acquaintance accompanied him to one of his mining cabins in the Simpson Pass region. On arriving at the cabin the acquaintance was about to enter when Bill restrained him and began throwing stones in the door. The loud snap of a bear trap issued from within and when questioned about it by the amazed guest Bill told him that he suspected a certain trapper from Banff was stealing his grub. Pointing out that the intruder could have died if caught in the trap the guest was further amazed to hear him reply, "you're damned right he would have, then I would have known for sure it was him."[6]

Ralph Edwards, although not quite so colorful as Peyto, played an equally important role in the early days of Wilson's business. In fact, although only in his early twenties, he was regarded as Tom's most reliable guide

Bill Peyto with the lynx tied on his back.

during the years around 1895 and was thus given the responsibility for guiding many of the major parties. Born in 1869 at Ramsgate, Kent, Ralph later went to London where he received his formal education at City of London School. Coming to Canada in 1888 he spent four years in the east before arriving in Canmore to work in the mines. He remained two years before giving it up in 1894 to accept a job with Wilson. He later related in his interesting and highly entertaining book of reminiscences, *The Trail to the Charmed Land*, the motivation which led him, and undoubtedly many others, to adopt the trail as a way of life:

Dowered at birth with the itching foot, it was but natural that I should grasp the earliest opportunity of entering the packing business, for, like the Athenians of old, I was ever desirous of seeing and hearing some new thing. Some of my detractors basely asserted that the real reason for my adoption of the life of a trail guide was a rooted objection to real work of any description and that riding around the hills on a horse was about all that I was

Ralph Edwards.

ever likely to do. In refutation I rise to remark that any one who imagines that following a pack train, in all kinds of weather, over all kinds of country, with the attendant thousand and one jobs that seem to appear from nowhere in particular, does not provide some of the steadiest and most continuous work conceivable is making just about the biggest mistake of his life. But we who followed the lure of the mountain trail loved the life and would not willingly exchange it for any other.[7]

The party taken into Mount Assiniboine in 1895, with Edwards as guide and Peyto as packer, was the largest Wilson had outfitted to date. It obliged him to provide nine horses, extensive equipment and supplies, and two extra men to act as cook and second packer. Filling the latter position was Harry Lang, an Englishman who had been sent to Canada by his father, a hotel owner at Brighton. Like most of his confrères he was quiet, competent and a good outdoorsman, and was particularly fond of children, the young boys and girls of Banff affectionately calling him "Uncle Dudley." The dudes included Robert Barrett, making his second journey in three years to Assiniboine, his friend J. Porter, and Walter Wilcox, who joined in at the last moment.

Wilcox had spent the summer of 1894 with Sam Allen and three other Yale men in the vicinity of Lake Louise doing some of the pioneer exploratory work of that region. Astley had provided two Indian guides and two horses, but the guides promptly deserted, leaving the alpinists with the difficult chore of managing the animals themselves. Despite major problems with loose packs, bogged down horses and lost trails, they had performed amazingly well and their season was crowned with many notable achievements. Among these were the first ascent of Mount Temple, the discoveries of Paradise and Prospector's Valleys and the Valley of the Ten Peaks as well as the first recorded visits to Sentinel, Wastach, Wenkchemna and Opabin Passes. Unfortunately, though, Wilcox and Allen came to a parting of the ways at the end of that season due to a misunderstanding over the data gathered for a map of the Lake Louise area. This led Wilcox to write Wilson to see if the outfitter could arrange for him to join Barrett and Porter on their trip to Assiniboine, before his rival Allen could do likewise.

Tom was successful in convincing Barrett and arrangements were made to leave on the sixth of July. Meanwhile, as they were preparing to depart, the trio of adventurers frequently visited at his home where he related "every detail of swinging stream and ford, of rockslide and lake and mountain pass" on the route into the great mountain.

A review of the trip illustrates some of the problems and situations which Wilson's men had to deal with on the trail. Peyto began by having to ferry the three patrons one by one across the cold, swift-flowing Healy Creek on the back of his horse Chiniquay since they had chosen to walk rather than ride, a common occurrence in the early days of tourist exploration. Immediately afterwards he had to take over responsibility for guiding the party when Edwards realized his axe was missing and had to return along the trail to try to locate it. The following day one of the horses became slightly lame and subsequently fell at a soft spot breaking its leg, forcing Bill to shoot the crippled beast and repack its load on the back of his own saddle horse. Next, six to eight feet of snow was found to be covering Simpson Pass and the men had to go ahead and pack down a trail to enable the horses to get through.

After encountering many similar problems the party arrived at the base of Mount Assiniboine and a permanent camp was set up. Then, after resting briefly, Peyto began to retrace the way back to Banff to find out what had become of Edwards who was now long overdue. Bill reappeared a week later with a replacement horse and the missing guide, who had lost the trail and returned to Banff.

This accomplished, Peyto set out on foot with the now well-rested Wilcox and Barrett to attempt to find a way around Assiniboine to obtain a view of its hitherto unseen south side. The venture, which according to Wilcox was "attended by considerable hardship," turned out to be a forty-six hour circuit of the mountain covering some fifty-one miles of the toughest country imaginable. They had to make their way spider-like over miles of downed timber sometimes ten feet off the ground and find a way over areas where contact with burnt trees turned them "black as coal heavers." At one particularly bad spot where a sheer wall of rock five hundred feet high appeared to block their advance Peyto went ahead over an old goat trail and forged a path across "a slope that appeared nearly vertical."[8]

Before the weary and footsore hikers finally regained their headquarters they stumbled upon a camp on the Mitchell River. Their hosts were Sam Allen and Dr. Howard Smith who had left Banff on July 3rd with a guide, a packer and six horses. Allen had penetrated to the same locale the previous fall with Yule Carryer, an Indian who had been working on the railroad, but because of low cloud and snow their views of the mountain had been limited. On that occasion they had started from Castle Mountain and had proceeded by way of Vermilion Pass and the Simpson River but had taken an unexpectedly long time to reach their destination. They had used only one pack horse to carry their equipment and provisions and with the consequent privations Allen had quickly realized he would be wise to prepare better for future trips. Accordingly, Wilson was approached in the summer of 1895 and he was able to provide men and horses. The guide was probably Joe Barker who had come to Banff from England around 1890 and had been in charge of Walker and Stewart's livery stable for several years before going to work for Tom.

After a short day's rest Bill and the other hands dismantled their camp and, once again under Edwards' guidance, headed back towards Banff via Vermilion Pass. Another strenuous journey ensued as the Vermilion River had to be constantly crossed and recrossed and the men were frequently forced to rescue endangered horses from the swirling waters. Finally on August 5th they reached Banff after twenty-nine days of absence, a period which had seen Peyto constantly in action. The exact rate of pay Wilson's men received at this time is not known, but since he charged two dollars for a man and his outfit per day, it was undoubtedly somewhat less than a dollar a day. Bill had earned every penny coming to him on this occasion.

Immediately after returning from Mount Assiniboine Wilcox again approached Wilson, deciding that enough of the season remained to explore another region. Tom suggested the area around the Waputik Range and the sources of the Bow and Mistaya Rivers. He related details of his trips through the rugged terrain for Major Rogers in 1882, with Calverley and Brearley in 1887, and later again for the Topographic Survey. Because Peyto had been found to be "most efficient" on the Assiniboine trip, his services were requested and the outfit, which included a cook and five horses, set out from Banff on August 14th. As it pulled out of town ahead of him, Wilcox was moved to remark on the sight that a Peyto-led pack string presented:

Peyto, as packer, always rode in the saddle, for the digni-ty of this office never allows a packer to walk, and besides, from their physical elevation on a horse's back they can better discern the trail. A venerable Indian steed, long-legged and lean, but most useful in fording streams, was Peyto's saddle horse. The bell-mare followed next, led by a head-rope. The other horses followed in single file, and never allowed the sound of the bell to get out of hearing.[9]

During the course of the trip Bill was able to show his prowess as a fisherman and hunter, keeping the grubpile well-stocked with fish, one a twenty-three inch lake trout taken from Bow Lake, and small game. The game included the ever-plentiful grouse, or "fool hen," which were easy pickings for the sharp-shooting marksman. Wilcox related that "many a time, when on the trail, I have seen him suddenly take his six-shooter and fire into a tall tree, whereupon a grouse would come tumbling down, with his neck severed, or his head knocked off by the bullet."[10]

Wilcox's growing friendship with his guide allowed him to induce Bill to partake of a "sport" until then studiously avoided — mountain climbing. While notoriously fearless in the face of any danger on the trail, be it enraged grizzly or swollen mountain torrent, guides and packers were usually sceptical about risking their necks in what they felt was sheer foolishness. Bill was no exception and spent the time his "gentlemen" were engaged in their alpine pursuits either hunting or prospecting for minerals. However, on this occasion he allowed himself to be convinced, probably because Wilcox would have had to climb alone, and the two conquered a 10,000 foot peak to the north of the lake which would later bear Peyto's name. Reaching the summit and viewing the panorama that lay at his feet he grudgingly allowed that he could now understand "the mania which impels men to climb mountains."

The trip required twenty-three days on the trail and covered 175 miles. In the course of it Peyto and Wilcox examined the areas around Hector, Bow and Peyto Lakes and, because of an elaborate plan for the return journey laid out in advance by Wilson, the Sawback Range, Edith Pass and Forty Mile Creek.

With the unprecedented demand for outfits being made by Wilcox, O'Hara, Allen and several others in the summer of 1895, Wilson soon found himself unable to supply enough men and horses for prospective parties. This could have produced serious economic repercussions as an outfitter's reputation was usually established on the basis of the service provided during the first trip taken by a party. Fortunately for him, though, he held a virtual monopoly on outfitting in Banff at the time and the eagerness of mountaineers to bag their quarries was such that they would venture out under almost any conditions. Such was the case with a group of alpinists from the Appalachian Mountain Club who were to play an important part in the future of his business.

The Appalachian Mountain Club had been formed in Boston in 1876 for "the advancement of the interests of those who visit the mountains of New England and adjacent regions, whether for the purpose of scientific research or summer recreation."[11] The moving force behind the organization was Charles E. Fay, a Professor of Modern Languages and Dean of the Graduate School at Tuft's College in Massachusetts. As a lover of the hills he had joined with other enthusiasts to create the club and served as its vice-president in 1877, president in 1878 and 1881 and editor of its publication *Appalachia* for forty years beginning in 1876.

By the mid-eighteen-nineties the Appalachian Club had become a rather moribund organization and there were those within it who wished to see included in its framework an alpine section for members who wanted to ascend major peaks outside the Appalachians. The leading voice among them was Philip Stanley Abbot, recognized as one of the foremost mountaineers in America at the time. A native of Brookline, Massachusetts, Abbot entered Harvard in 1885 and, after time taken out for travel in the West Indies, California and Alaska, graduated in law in 1893. He then became General Solicitor for the Milwaukee and Lake Winnebago Railroad Company. Previous to and during his college career he had done considerable climbing in the British Isles, California, Alaska and Mexico and then had gone on to conquer some of the most formidable summits in the Swiss Alps.

When Abbot was giving consideration to areas which might merit the attention of an alpine section, Fay was able to offer a suggestion. In 1890, while returning from a trip to California, he had paid a visit to Canada. Stopping in the Selkirks for a day at Glacier House, he had made a partial ascent of Mount Sir Donald and was so impressed that he had returned for a closer inspection in 1894. On that occasion his curiosity had taken him to Lake Louise where he met Wilcox and Allen returning from their successful ascent of Mount Temple. The region was a natural for Abbot's designs and when the club's annual excursion was being planned for 1895 it was decided that Fay's suggestion of Lake Louise would be an appropriate choice. This was the first time that a club outing had gone beyond the Appalachian mountain system.

The 1895 excursion numbered twenty and surprisingly the majority were women. Quite understandably, given their previous mountaineering experience, most of the group were content to busy themselves with some of the easier climbs in the vicinity of the chalet. But not Fay and Abbot. With Charles Sproule Thompson, also a Harvard graduate and at this time the Chicago freight contracting agent for the Illinois Central Railroad, they looked forward to indulging in more challenging mountaineering. They quickly found out the best way to accomplish this was by making arrangements with Wilson.

Our first step was to get hold of Wilson, the best guide and outfitter for that region, and to hold a council of war. Many plans were proposed but none hit our fancy. Finally, for about the tenth time since he joined us, Thompson brought forth his fixed idea. Mt. Hector . . . had never been climbed; better still it had been attempted without success; and it was high, because the Canadian surveyors, when they turned back, had already reached 10,400 feet. It further appeared that Wilson himself had been with that party; and he said he believed the peak could be climbed. He also told us of an enormous snowfield lying to the west of Hector on the main watershed, and stretching away to the north for fifty miles, which was absolutely unexplored.[12]

The only problem in the way of successfully completing preparations for the trip was Tom's lack of men and horses. However, the eagerness of Fay, Abbot and Thompson to have their mountain was such that they agreed to commence the journey to the base of Hector from Laggan on foot and without pack animals. Because there was no on else available, Tom had to guide the party himself and engaged as porter "an admirably patient individual named Hiland who . . . carried an enormous and shapeless pack composed of the tin things and all the other articles which the rest refused to touch."[13]

Evidently the trio were somewhat dissatisfied with the guide service, probably due to the lack of time that Tom was able to devote to it. The problems began when he insisted they attempt to reach the shores of Lower Bow (Hector) Lake to camp, a point well past Abbot's estimation of the proper place to turn off for the ascent of the peak. The error was compounded when it became obvious that the hikers, fresh from their office desks, could not reach the shores of the lake before dark and were thereby forced to camp on a swampy hummock alive with mosquitoes. After camp was made Tom chose the opportunity to tell the party what he had neglected to mention before setting out — because of the pressure of business his return to Laggan the next day was imperative. A further irritation resulted from the directions given them to reach the large snowfield lying to the west of Hector. When they reached the point where they had been told the river could be crossed it was found to be unfordable and Abbot remarked that "we could have hung somebody with pleasure."

Fortunately for Tom the trip did prove to be at least partially successful. The mountaineers accomplished the first ascent of Mount Hector, the only time to that date an alpine peak had been conquered by an Appalachian party without the assistance of climbing guides. Given the benefit of some time to reflect on the accomplishment, Abbot was moved to admit that "It certainly was a glorious trip. I think in my present state of mind I should say that the mosquitoes at the foot of Hector soothed us by their melody. . . ."[14]

Taken as a whole, the 1895 season must have proved

surprising to the seemingly well-prepared Wilson. Although he had taken measures to ensure that he could handle all the business coming his way, the sheer volume of it had proved his preparations inadequate. Part of his problem stemmed from the fact that he had no way of knowing what parties were coming or when they would arrive. This tended to make advance planning difficult, if not impossible. Undoubtedly he informed his customers of his quandry and in the years ahead correspondence between client and outfitter to make appropriate arrangements in advance became much more common. But the fact remained that despite his increase in personnel and his ever-growing string of pack horses, the demand was outstripping the supply. To remedy the situation he purchased additional stock during the winter of 1895-96, mainly from the Stoney Indians, and hired more men. As in the past, most of these were newly landed Englishmen, but the two most noteworthy, Fred Stephens and Tom Lusk, were recent arrivals from the United States.

Fred Stephens was born on a farm in Michigan around 1868 and early in his youth went to work in the lumber camps of that state. Later he headed west to Montana where he was employed at various times as a hunter, trapper and logger. Finding the north-western United States becoming too populated for his liking he gradually drifted north until he landed in Banff during 1896 and went to work for Wilson. Stanley Washburn, at the time a Minneapolis student but later a noted war correspondent, described him when he was introduced by Wilson in 1897:

Fred Stevens [sic] stood six feet and one inch in his stockinged feet. Twenty-nine years old then, he was, with the shoulders and muscles of an athlete, and soft blue eyes that drifted back and forth from the gentleness of a woman's to the glint and fire of a savage's. Big hands, big feet, and a big soul. He was then, and is to-day, a big man, as big a one as I have met in travels in many far corners of this world; big not only in bulk, but big in the qualities of heart and soul that go to make the best type; ... To be Fred Stevens' friend is all the introduction that a man needs, to get the best that the trail offers in western Alberta and eastern British Columbia.[15]

Soon after becoming a packer Stephens gained a reputation on two counts which made him an invaluable addition to Tom's staff. He was undoubtedly the best axe-man ever to work for the outfitter and in addition spared no effort in the care of his horses. Given his early background in the Michigan woods it came as no surprise that he was skilled with an axe but at times his exploits with the tool almost defied belief. When the deadfall was particularly heavy he was known to spend ten to twelve hours a day for three or four days chopping the trail ahead of the outfit. On a lighter note, a fellow guide recalled that "as soon as he got to camp he would take off his boots and socks, grab his axe, which he would later take to bed with him, and go out cutting wood in his bare feet."[16]

Although physically hard on himself Fred felt that the guide who was hard on his horses deserved nothing but contempt and he would often spend several days letting his pack train recuperate when he felt they were becoming run down. Washburn, while on a trip up the Athabasca, was witness to the manner in which he justified such delays to the members of his party.

"Now old Sorrel," remarked Fred, as we sat around the pack-cover at dinner, "He's sure gotten skinnier'n h - - - these last few days, and I don't think the old devil's got the ginger under his hide to cut the mustard, when it comes to swimmin' this young flood which you fellers see abilin' past. The little Bay now, he's some peaked too since he fell down the mountain and skinned his knees. He ain't a bad horse, the Bay ain't, and I don't want to see him get his'n in this rampagin' river. And then there's the old White — he's just barely been draggin' his hinders over the trail this week, and besides, Nick's saddle horse has been gettin' down in the dumps worse and worse every day for a month. Now, fellers, if we was to tackle the job this minute, a lot o' them critturs would just naturally turn up their toes to the surface and drift off down the river to the Arctic Ocean.[17]

Needless to say, such logic was irrefutable and Fred usually won his point.

While Fred Stephens quickly established a reputation for excellence on the trail, his new co-worker, Tom Lusk, gained quite another kind of reputation. Lusk's background, what little is known of it, may best be described as shady. He had apparently spent the greater part of his life travelling the Chisholm Trail with various cattle outfits before heading across the Canadian border with someone else's steers and with a Texas sheriff in hot pursuit. The stock formed the nucleus for a small ranch he established to the south-east of Morley. In 1896, although probably already in his sixties, he went to work on the trail to supplement the living made from the ranch. Before long he had distinguished himself as the hardest drinking member of Wilson's crew and his feats in this regard soon became legendary. When introduced to Martin Nordegg, whom he later guided on the trip resulting in the discovery of the famous Nordegg coal field, the young German immigrant was quite amazed at his prowess.

In strutted an old cowboy dressed in buckskins. He was properly introduced to me as the famous Tom Lusk, our head packer. He squatted on the floor. The factor offered him a glass of beer with a knowing grin and a winking eye. Tom declined emphatically with a shudder and pulled from his chaps a large squash bottle of whisky and took a long drink interrupted by gurgling, then smacked

Tom Lusk.

his lips . . . As long as we were at Morley, his eyes appeared to me glassy and I began to believe that this was their natural appearance. But when I noticed the copious drinks which he took frequently, I had my doubts and asked Dowling. He told me Tom never took a drink while on the trail for good reason. Bottles are too fragile and the weight [of] many cases of supply during many months had to be taken into consideration, as they would require a few more pack horses. But at the return to civilization after the season's work, this reason did not exist anymore and then Tom invested his earnings in liquor, retiring with several cases to his cabin near Morley. I never saw his cabin but heard that his outhouse had been constructed from such empty cases. The Indian Agent and Tom's neighbors watch out for the smoke from Tom's chimney. When they could not see any smoke, they pay him a courtesy call to convince themselves if they have to prepare for a funeral or just relight the fire for Tom after his usual carousel. Tom was methodical in his habits: he divided his cases and bottles carefully into the weeks and months of the long winter allowing to himself double quantities for Christmas and New Year, thus constituting a whisky budget.[18]

In all fairness to Lusk it must be said that he was not the only guide or packer to be overly fond of the bottle. Almost to a man their feats could rival those of the most notorious imbibers. The King Edward Hotel in Banff quickly became known as the "packer's bar" and many a trailman's idle time between trips was spent within its confines. To Lusk's credit, the knowlege of horses he had gained in Texas was second to none. Wilson realized this and gave him the position of a head guide.

Tom was fortunate in finding two individuals of the calibre of Stephens and Lusk as they were able to take out a party on their own the first year they were employed. Spurred by the success of their 1895 expedition to Assiniboine, in 1896 Barrett and Wilcox decided to explore the country north of Bow Pass. The lure of the area was provided by the continuing mystery surrounding the two legendary sentinels of the old fur trade route over Athabasca Pass, Mounts Hooker and Brown. Described by the famous Scottish botanist David Douglas, who travelled through the pass in 1827, as being not less than 16,000 or 17,000 feet above seas level, the two giants had long ranked as the highest known peaks in Canada.

The noted geologist Professor Arthur P. Coleman of the University of Toronto had undertaken a trip in 1893 with his brother L. Q. Coleman of Morley and Professor L. B. Stewart of Toronto to check the accuracy of Douglas' observation. They succeeded in reaching the supposed location of the twin monarchs and ascended one of them but found to their amazement that it was only about 9,000 feet in altitude. Nevertheless, there were still some sceptics, Wilcox among them, who believed that the party had perhaps climbed the wrong mountain and that the question was worthy of further examination.

Coleman had begun his journey from his brother's ranch at Morley travelling by way of the Front Ranges and then entering the mountains at the lower end of the Red Deer River Valley. Wilcox believed that this was the most suitable route to follow but not so Wilson. He insisted that an easier and more scenic route could be found by way of the Bow River, Mistaya River, North Fork of the Saskatchewan and then over a pass which should connect with a tributary of the Athabasca River and ultimately with the Whirlpool River flowing from Athabasca Pass. Realizing that this as yet unknown country would need some difficult trail blazing and would be hard on the pack animals, he decided that Stephens and Lusk would be the most suitable candidates for the job.

The outfit for the trip, in addition to guide Lusk, packer Stephens and cook Arthur Arnold, consisted of five saddle horses, ten pack horses and provisions sufficient for sixty days on the trail. Following the valley of the Bow they were plagued by two of the pack train's worst enemies, muskeg and forest fires, but eventually succeeded in crossing the Saskatchewan and gaining the old Indian trails on the North Fork. Making headway up this stream proved to be exceedingly trying but fortunately Barrett proved to be everything a guide could desire in a dude and aided progress considerably. According to Wilcox, "he would join up with Fred Stephens after seven or eight hours on the trail and explore the new region ahead for half a dozen miles and return to camp with full knowledge of every ford and burnt timber patch in that distance."[19]

Fred Stephens and Tom Lusk packing, ca. 1896.

The pass to the Athabasca (Wilcox Pass), the whole key to the trip, was eventually discovered by Wilcox but it was found to be long, tedious and extremely wet in some spots. Finding a suitable route leading off the pass to the Sunwapta River, a tributary of the Athabasca, was not a simple matter. Stephens finally found a safe path, but in the meantime Barrett had for once proved overzealous as he had gone off on his own and become lost in the burnt timber of the Brazeau River country. Three days later he casually walked into camp around eleven o'clock in the evening without so much as a word of explanation. Meanwhile, Wilcox, whose photographic work was later to be acknowledged as the finest done in the early days of exploration, contented himself with taking exposures of the exciting new country which lay stretched out ahead of them.

Unfortunately for the intrepid explorers, after discovering the correct route they were unable to reach their destination. Advancing down the Sunwapta and then up the west fork of the Athabasca for eight days they reached Fortress Lake where, as a result of earlier delays, their time and provisions allowed them to go no further. Barrett and Wilcox did, however, climb a peak north of the lake from whence they thought they could spy Mount Hooker and satisfied themselves that it was not over 10,-500 feet high. After exploring Fortress Lake on a raft built by the skillful Stephens, the pack train was turned back in the direction of Lake Louise.

The return trip proved to be more of a forced march as two-thirds of the provisions had already been used, but Barrett and one of the men did make one side excursion to explore the Molar Pass region. Forging on ahead the rest of the party quickly reached Lake Louise where some very disquieting news of a recent incident on Mount Lefroy awaited them.

Early in 1896 Wilson had been contacted by Abbot, Fay and Thompson. Along with a fourth Appalachian Club member, George T. Little, they expressed interest in making an attempt on Mount Lefroy, which had defeated them after their return from the climb of Mount Hector in 1895. Following the expected first ascent of Lefroy they wanted to outfit with Tom for a trip up the Bow River in order that they might tackle Mount Balfour, a snowy peak to the west they had caught sight of from the summit of Hector. Tom agreed and arranged to rendezvous with the foursome at the Lake Louise Chalet on the morning of August 4th.

When he reached the chalet with Willoughby Astley who had accompanied him from Laggan, Tom was greeted by three distraught, rain-soaked climbers. Fay, Thompson and Little hurriedly related how, at Abbot's insistence, they had begun their ascent the previous day through "The Death Trap," a narrow snow couloir between Mounts Victoria and Lefroy. Once it was surmounted Abbot had proclaimed there was a clear route to the summit, but they had experienced some difficulty with an immense, seventy-five foot bastion guarding the final snowslope. Abbot, who was leading, had unroped and while making his way up a gully had apparently slipped. His horrified companions had watched helplessly as he fell backwards and tumbled down several hundred feet before coming to rest. After making their way to his limp form the three had attempted to lower him gently down but it had soon become apparent that he was dead. Realizing that any attempt to bring the body further without aid was fruitless, they had decided to try make it to the chalet for help. Darkness intervened and after a cheerless night spent on the pass that would forthwith bear Abbot's name they reached the chalet in the midst of a driving rainstorm.

Wilson and Astley immediately volunteered their services for an attempt to recover Abbot's remains and by 10 a.m. were on their way with Fay, Thompson and Little. The pass was reached by 2:30 p.m. but snow squalls soon enveloped them and made progress difficult. It was not until four o'clock that the work of bringing down the body was begun. They were only able to reach the Victoria Glacier before nightfall and the recovery attempt had to be abandoned. The following day a party of six laborers sent by the CPR completed the task, and the body was conveyed to Banff for an official inquest.

The inquest jury ruled the death accidental and thus ended the events surrounding the first climbing fatality in the Canadian Rockies. It also marked a premature end to Tom's business for the 1896 season as, quite understandably, the proposed trip to Balfour was immediately cancelled. For the remainder of 1896, with the exception of a brief visit with Wilcox to Lake O'Hara, he had to rely on hunters to pay his bills. This type of customer had been an important consideration since 1893 with popularity being divided between spring bear hunts and fall outings in quest of trophy sheep and goat heads. As hunting expeditions were not nearly as well publicized as mountaineering and exploring trips it is difficult to determine who Tom's customers were at this time. However, General Fred Pearson and a Mr. Dickerson, two names that constantly reappear, were probably quite typical of the wealthy sportsmen out in search of fish and game in the years prior to the turn of the century.

Pearson was a retired officer of the United States Army while Dickerson was a millionaire New York stockbroker. When they first arrived to participate in a hunting trip they assumed they would relax in camp until the guide had spotted a suitable trophy. They were soon informed that despite their wealth and social position Tom's men were not their lackeys and they would be expected to take part in the hunting as well as the shooting. Once the air was cleared they greatly enjoyed the sport offered by big game hunting in the Rockies and found the fishing the best they had encountered anywhere. In one notable evening of angling in the Bow River below Bow Lake they succeeded in landing eleven "brook trout" weighing a total of eighty-two pounds, falling short of a world's record for the weight of that number caught at one time by a mere half pound.

News of such accomplishments in the sporting world spread as quickly as did that of the ascent of an 11,000 foot peak in climbing circles. Thus within a short time steadily increasing numbers of hunters and anglers from the eastern United States and Great Britain were being attracted to the area, substantially adding to Tom's business. But despite this popularity, his main concern during the winter of 1896-97 was whether the accident to Abbot would dampen the enthusiasm of other mountaineers.

The party on the way to recover Philip Abbot's body. Left to right — Tom Wilson, George T. Little, Willoughby Astley and Charles E. Fay.

A guide clearing trail through burnt timber.

3 Muskeg, Burnt Timber and Bad Language

In writing of the accident on Mount Lefroy for *Applalachia* Professor Fay concluded that "it occurs at the very dawn of a new era of genuine alpine climbing, for the extension of which among our young countrymen Abbot was so earnest an advocate."[1] His observation was soon to be proved correct for rather than discouraging new expeditions Abbot's death seemed to have the opposite effect. The publicity and interest it generated became a factor in attracting both new and old visitors alike, particularly the mountaineering variety, to the Canadian Rockies. Wilson's fears were, therefore, quickly allayed and, in fact, it soon became obvious that he would have to expand his services further in the period ahead.

In 1888 many of Tom's customers were Banff Springs Hotel guests taking hunting, fishing and sightseeing trips lasting only a week or ten days, but by 1896 he was outfitting major mountaineering, exploring and hunting expeditions up to two months in duration. This change demanded increases in manpower, the number of horses and the amount of outfitting equipment, but there were also several other interesting developments.

One consideration was the additional supplies which longer trips required. In the late eighties and early nineties foodstuffs had been of the most basic variety, mainly consisting of flour, salt pork, tea, coffee and "the omnipresent bean." But as the time away from the sumptuous menus of the CPR hotels increased, the clientele became more particular in their diet. Witness, for example, the requests the Fay party had made for their proposed trip to Mount Balfour:

As to food: — we want plenty of jam and marmalade (but very little strawberry jam, as Mr. Thompson can't eat it). No butter; no sweet crackers; **plenty of lemons;** *lit-tle potted meat, and that either chicken or lamb's tongues, preferably the former, and certainly not ham or corned beef or beef tongues; more coffee than tea; and a number of cans of soup — canned ox-tail or tomato being the best. We will provide our own chocolate and raisins, as we can do it more cheaply and get somewhat better quality, and will charge up to you whatever proportion of the price seems fair. We will also bring our own protection against mosquitoes.*[2]

All of this was to be provided along with the men, horses and the rest of the outfit for $3.50 per day apiece. Tom acquired most of the requested items from one of the general supply stores of Banff, usually that of pioneer merchant Dave White. In fact the large quantities of these supplies and other equipment bought over the course of a season helped support the fledgling economy of Banff.

A second change brought about by the increased length of the trips was an expansion of Tom's bases of operation. At the outset all outings had originated in Banff, usually at the Banff Springs Hotel or his corral, but as the distance covered and the time on the trail increased, most parties preferred to meet the pack train somewhere en route. Many mountaineers gained the railway's permission to ride on the freights running between Banff, Laggan and Field. This enabled them to start out several days later and still catch the outfit before it left the railroad right-of-way for its particular destination. As time went on some parties chose to stay in the Lake Louise Chalet or Mount Stephen House and begin their journeys from these points. To tailor his operations to meet these changing preferences, Wilson stationed guides, packers, cooks and horses at these locales for the summer season in order to simplify the

A party preparing to depart from Lake Louise Chalet.

preparations and to cut down on wear and tear on both man and beast.

The greater duration of many of these pack trips also put more pressure on the relationship between the guide and the party. Short tempers and personality conflicts were bound to arise. Often the party's members decided that they knew better than the guide what route should be followed or where a camp should be placed, but it was the unwritten rule of the trail that the guide's word was law. Instances of confrontation between guide and dude were legion, but a particularly interesting one occurred when Fred Stephens had a visiting German army officer out with him. After breakfast the first morning on the trail the officer, map and ice-axe in hand, took up a position on a nearby rock and began to inform the men of the day's route as if delivering orders for one of his campaigns. The packers were somewhat taken aback and stood dumbfounded while the harangue continued. Finally Fred interrupted, asking the "god damned silly fool" if he was finished and advising that if he wasn't he would personally knock him off the rock on which he was preaching. He then proceeded to inform the amazed officer that the men weren't soldiers, that he himself was

perfectly capable of guiding the party to its destination and that he didn't want to hear any more of his "sauerkraut." [3] Presumably this settled the issue once and for all.

One final development, a consequence of expeditions into largely untrodden regions, was the difficulty Wilson's men experienced with the trails. While the earlier, shorter trips had usually followed well-defined trails in the neighborhood of the railroad, the longer trips often followed faint Indian and game trails which crossed numerous high passes and wild rivers. But the greatest obstacles proved to be the many forest fires, burnt over areas (brûlés) and muskegs encountered.

Prior to the establishment of an adequate warden service there were many forest fires which were left to burn unchecked, resulting in large tracts of timber being completely razed. For instance, Wilcox reported in 1891 that "a very large percentage of the forests, from Bow Pass to Banff were desolated by fire" and that when he later visited them "the borders of Moraine Lake and Consolation Valley were a waste of bare poles and fireweed."[4] These fires were ignited by lightning, the sparks thrown off by coal and wood burning locomotives and through carelessness by man. A forest fire usually meant that the regular trail had to be forsaken and a tedious, out-of-the-way detour made with the consequent loss of precious time and energy. Equally frustrating was the occasional forced passage of a recently burned area, which called for the chopping of the charred and fallen trees blocking the trail.

The muskeg problem was largely related to the fact that most old Indian and game trails followed river bottoms where the oozing muck was most likely to occur. A horse caught in muskeg meant time-consuming and back-breaking labor for a packer since in many cases it had to be unpacked and then pushed, pulled, lifted or otherwise cajoled back onto solid ground. Perhaps the most extensive muskegs were to be found on the trail up the Bow River from the point where it turned north to its source at Bow Pass. All the way along there were major and minor patches, some of the worst beneath the slopes of Mount Hector, where it was common to lay corduroy, and around the shores of Bow Lake, where pack trains often took to the shallow water to avoid becoming hopelessly mired.

Even considering these hindrances the old trails were often found preferable to constructing new ones. Not only would this have meant more work than most outfits were prepared to expend, but new trails would have bypassed the traditional camping spots with their good pasturage, wood, water and neatly stacked teepee poles, each a normal day's journey from the previous camp. Still, the desire of an increasing number of parties to penetrate into country cursed with forest fires, brûlés and bogs makes one observer's description of being constantly surrounded by "muskeg, burnt timber and bad language" quite believable.

The first order of Wilson's business for the 1897 season was providing the means for the Appalachian Club members to complete their interrupted quest of 1896. Abbot's father was anxious to have the feasibility of his son's route up Lefroy proved and in the course of the winter had appealed to Fay to organize a new attempt. Fay agreed to resurrect the plan of 1896, which would call for a move up the Bow to attempt Balfour after their revenge on Lefroy. He decided to make it an international affair by inviting the Alpine Club (London) to send representatives. Accepting the offer were Professor Harold B. Dixon, who had climbed with Abbot in the Alps, and Dr. J. Norman Collie, recognized as one of Britain's leading mountaineers and soon to establish an equally celebrated reputation in Canada.

Collie was a professor of organic chemistry who taught at various English colleges and later held the prestigious post of director of the chemical laboratories at University College, University of London. He had grown up near Aberdeen, where he spent much of his free time in solitary rambles through the hills, and at Bristol, where he often practiced climbing on the sheer cliffs. His appetite whetted, he had continued to participate in mountaineering ventures in the British Isles and the Alps during the years of his education and early career. Drawn further afield as time went on, in 1896 he had accompanied two other well-known British alpinists, A. F. Mummery and Geoffrey Hastings, on an ill-fated trip to the Himalayas. The party succeeded in reaching the 20,-000 foot level on the giant Nanga Parbat, but the expedition ended in tragedy when Mummery perished in an attempt to cross Diama Pass. The heartfelt loss led Collie to forsake the Himalayas and turn his attention towards some other area which would offer new and unconquered peaks. Professor Fay's invitation could not have come at a better time.

The party assembled at Lake Louise and undertook the climb of Lefroy on August 3rd. In addition to Dixon and Collie it included Fay, A. Michael, Reverend Charles L. Noyes, Herschel C. Parker, J. R. Vanderlip and Charles S. Thompson, all from the Appalachian Club, and the Swiss climbing guide Peter Sarbach. Sarbach, brought from his native Saint Niklaus by Collie, had accompanied Abbot in the Alps and was the first Swiss guide to appear in the Rockies.

After an early morning row across the lake and the ascent through "The Death Trap," the large group reached the 9800 foot level and split into three separately roped parties. They proceeded carefully but with no real difficulty to the summit, which was reached at 11:00 a.m. Two days later the first ascent of Mount Victoria was completed by Fay, Michael, Collie and Sarbach. They then waited for a third Alpine Club member, G. P. Baker, before setting out for the attempt on Mount Balfour.

After Baker's arrival at Lake Louise on August 7th, the outfit, with Bill Peyto as guide, began its trek up the Bow Valley in quest of Balfour. Collie, Dixon and Baker started out after the main party and being new at travel in the wilderness were promptly initiated to "what was for convenience of speech, called 'the trail'." Following Peyto's blazes they first had to deal with fallen timber "piled like spillikins one above the other" and finally emerged from it only to get hopelessly stuck in the endless swamps. Here the horses sank up to their bellies, one getting so deep in a hole "that only with difficulty was he prevented from vanishing altogether," and for a time it appeared that they might have to spend the night in this beleaguered position. Fortunately, Bill had become worried about his patrons' tardiness and returned to find them with the aid of his dog. Leaving the horses under its watchful eye, he led them to the warming fire of his camp.[5]

The following day the going proved easier, and Bow Lake, the site of their base camp was reached. However, they were to be disappointed in their attempt on Mount Balfour as en route "Thompson sought to investigate the lower layers of the ice-sheet that covers Mount Gordon, by falling headfirst down a deep crevasse." Collie, the only unmarried member of the party, made a daring rescue attempt by being lowered down the crevasse on a rope. With some hard work he was able to liberate his shivering comrade from an icy tomb. Because of this mishap the party had to be content with their ascent of Mount Gordon, but from its summit they spied a large mountain to the north, supposed to be Mount Murchison, which roused their interest. Since Dixon and Michael had to return to Banff immediately, Collie and Baker decided to go back with the rest of the group and then re-outfit for an attempt on this northern peak (actually Mount Forbes).

After consulting with Wilson about the area they wished to traverse, Collie, Baker and Sarbach began their journey from Laggan on August 7th. Bill Peyto again acted as guide assisted by two relatively new employees, packer L. Richardson and cook Charlie Black. The trip resulted in the exploration of the Mount Forbes area, a partial ascent of Mount Freshfield and gave Collie cause to reconsider his initial impressions of guides.

On the first day out the weather was oppressively hot and the mosquitoes swarmed in huge black clouds, causing Peyto to call a halt early in the afternoon. Collie, like so many fellow travellers new to the ways of the trail, disagreed and told Bill that such an early stop was unnecessary. It was patiently explained that he had no idea how far a pack horse could travel in a day and that pushing them too hard early in a trip would only cause sore backs and lameness and result in longer delays later on. Not wanting to cause an argument, Collie acquiesced but still harbored some resentment at being, in effect, told off. However, these feelings soon dissipated as the expedition unfolded and he saw the correctness of Peyto's decision.

That Peyto was right was abundantly proved in the sequel; for, owing to the excessively hot weather, we soon had more than one pony with a sore back and ill. This remedied itself, however, for later the weather got cooler and the packs lighter. Moreover, it was no vain boast of Peyto's that he was there to look after the horses; many a time after arriving in camp after a long day's journey, when something to eat and drink was one's first thought, Peyto could be seen driving the sore-backed ponies down to the stream where he carefully washed them and smeared the raw places with bacon-grease to keep off the flies.[6]

Collie's estimation of his guide was further amplified by the way he handled the various situations and obstacles met on the trail. Flooding rivers were one of the worst hazards and when the boiling waters of the Mistaya had to be crossed he marvelled at the way in which Bill, constantly in danger of being swept away with his horse, probed one spot after another until a suitable ford was discovered.

Peyto's mettle was further tested on the trip homeward. It was decided to return via Howse Pass, a route which probably hadn't been travelled since Wilson's trip in 1888 with Calverley and Brearley, and the thick timber and prickly devil's club of the western slope made the going extremely tough. When fallen timber and forest fires finally proved the Blaeberry impassable, he successfully led the pack train over Amiskwi Pass. This route had not previously been traversed by horse and was in rough shape at the time because of a recent heavy snow. From this pass Bill led his now weary party down the Amiskwi River to the Kicking Horse and eventually to Field where the expedition was successfully terminated.

Repairing to Mount Stephen House, Collie and Baker learned of the return of Dr. Jean Habel, a recent guest, from an interesting exploratory trip of his own. Habel, a Berlin-born mathematics teacher in his sixties, was a member of the German-Austrian Alpine Club. He had first visited the Rockies in 1896. At that time, after paying a short visit to Banff and Lake Louise, he travelled on a train to Field and observed a snowy peak at the head of the Yoho Valley. As the mountain kept disappearing and reappearing as the train moved along, he named it Hidden Peak (later Mount Habel and now Mount des Poilus) and resolved to return and attempt to reach it the next year.

At least this was Habel's explanation for the trip. Wilson had a rather contrary opinion claiming that the trip was his idea and that he had been the first one to explore the Yoho Valley on his prospecting trip of 1884. Perhaps on no other issue concerning the early history of the Rockies was he more adamant. In a short summary of the work he had done for the CPR in the early days, he wrote the following concerning Emerald Lake and the Yoho Valley:

In 1895 I tried to get some members of the Appalachian Club to explore and write it up — In 1896 I cut and cleared out the old Indian Trail from Field to the crossing of Emerald Creek, and from there cut a trail to the Lake, and along the North side to the Gravel Flats at the East-end — Then in July 1897 I got Jean Habel to go into the Yoho, photograph it and write it up.[7]

His case was further stated in a series of letters written to J. B. Harkin, Commissioner of Dominion Parks, in the nineteen-twenties:

Jean Habel did not discover the Yoho Valley any more than he discovered the CPR station at Field — I prospected the Yoho Valley in 1884 and the Habel Party saw my cuttings . . .

In 1897 in order to get the CPR interested in this region, I got a German Professor to go in and take photos and write it up in the magazines — I gave him three men . . . and seven head of horses, Provisions, Tents etc. all for

$7.00 per day and it cost me $11.50 per day cash and then the dam German took all the credit![8]

Tom was known to tell his share of tall tales but his repeated and vociferous statements on this issue lead to the suspicion that he had been done out of at least part of the credit due him.

Whatever the truth concerning Habel's exploration of the Yoho, it certainly added materially to the knowledge of the west slope of the Waputiks. It also added a few experiences to the campfire repertoires of the men who Wilson assigned to the trip; guide Ralph Edwards, packer Fred Stephens and cook Frank Wellman. The latter, a broad-shouldered youth with curly red hair, described as being "little more than a schoolboy" was in reality just that as he was only fourteen at the time. Francis Lorn Wellman had been born at Kingston, Ontario in 1883 and had just recently arrived with his widowed mother at Anthracite, the mining community a few miles to the east of Banff, where she was to run a hotel. Of sufficient stature to contribute toward his own livelihood, he had convinced Tom to hire him on for the summer and this was undoubtedly his first trail trip. Even at that he was not at any real disadvantage since neither of his elder compatriots had travelled through the country on the west slope of the Divide where increased moisture made conditions much different from those to which they were accustomed.

Departing Emerald Lake on July 16th in the steady rain which was to plague them most of the journey, the party made its way through the pass to the North Fork (Yoho) Valley and on July 22nd reached the foot of Takakkaw Falls in less than ideal conditions. The men had to drive the horses through a thick carpet of moss on the descent from the pass. So deep was the moss that the heavily-laden pack horses sank completely up to their hocks and were constantly in danger of breaking a leg. Fortunately this didn't occur, but Stephens and Edwards soon found that their problems were just beginning. On reaching the valley floor the vegetation proved so lush that neither Indian nor game trail could be discovered, and they were forced to hack through the thick undergrowth all the way to their destination.

Another complicating factor was the steep-sided valley which often necessitated riding along rather narrow benches up to one hundred feet above the river. These were particularly dangerous for the pack horses, especially when one decided to pass another. Most cayuses, once their order on the trail was established, resented any attempts by those further back to try to pass them. One of Edwards' horses committed just such a breach of etiquette and was promptly kicked and bitten until it lost its balance and plunged over the edge. Incredibly the animal was not injured as about half way down the thirty foot embankment it landed astride a spruce tree growing at a right angle and hung there

Professor Jean Habel.

A camp at the foot of Takakkaw Falls.

balancing precariously. Edwards was confronted with an unenviable situation.

Now I was like the man who had the bull by the tail — he had him, but didn't know what to do with him. I concluded that the first thing to do was to get the pack off. This, after a good deal of difficulty, I was able to do . . . At last an idea struck me. I tied the lash rope around the hocks of his hind legs and, bracing myself against a stout tree, I heaved with all my might. Gradually he slid forward a little at a time on the tree trunk until at last he overbalanced and went crashing to the bottom where he immediately picked himself up and nonchalantly began cropping what grass there was.[9]

While potentially serious, the fall of the pack horse was superseded by a fall of a different sort which could have proved disastrous. After reaching the terminus of the Wapta Icefield, Habel felt that a tour over its surface for the purpose of examining a possible route to the summit of Mount Balfour would be in order. He convinced Edwards and Stephens to accompany him and while crossing a seemingly secure snow bridge Fred suddenly dropped from sight into a yawning crevasse. Fortunately the precaution of roping together had been taken allowing Habel and Edwards to brace themselves and prevent him from falling very far. By heaving in unison they were able to drag the chilled and shaken packer back to the surface, more convinced than ever of the "damn foolishness" of mountaineering. Shortly thereafter, Habel was able to satisfy himself of the inaccessibility of Balfour from the west side and the outfit immediately began to head back towards Field, this time following the Yoho out to its junction with the Kicking Horse.

The continued success of Mount Balfour in avoiding the pick of a mountaineer's ice axe upon its snowy mantle led several adventurers back to Wilson's door in 1898, among them Professor Fay and R. F. Curtis. Discouraged by his own party's failure to reach the peak from Bow Lake and Habel's report of the drawbacks of an attempt from the Yoho Valley, Fay decided on a new route of assault. This would involve a hike on foot up the small valley east from the Yoho bringing them to the foot of the icefield on Balfour's south side. As a porter and third man on the rope, Tom provided a young Banff school teacher, Robert E. "Bob" Campbell.

Born in 1871 in Lanark County, Ontario, the youngest of thirteen children, Campbell had been raised on a farm on the Nottawasaga River close to Wilson's home of Barrie. After attending the school near his farm he went on to study at the Barrie Collegiate Institute and eventually was graduated as a teacher. Intending to ultimately become a lawyer he also studied at the Northern Business College of Owen Sound and then decided to head west in 1893, feeling that his training would land him a job in a law office. Such was not to be. After arriving in Moose Jaw he was talked into taking on the job of

teacher in the new school district of Farewell. But the job was soon eliminated when the community fell on hard times and could not afford to pay him. Moving on to a teaching position in a community near Regina, he remained there until late in 1896 when an invitation came from Wilson to teach at the school in Banff. Tom had recently been elected Chairman of the Banff School Board and in an attempt to find a new teacher had written to the Superintendent of Education in Regina for a recommendation. He suggested Campbell and Bob arrived in Banff to take up his duties on New Year's Eve, 1896. Because he was familiar with horses and available during the summer months the young teacher was a good candidate for a part-time trail hand, and Wilson began to employ him in that capacity in the summer of 1897.

On August 2nd the party of two alpinists and their neophyte guide set out on a handcar which took them from Hector Station to the mouth of Sherbrooke Creek. From there they hiked upstream, past Sherbrooke Lake and around the base of Mount Niles before camp was made. Still four miles distant from their quarry, they made an early start on an exciting day the next morning.

Once under way, we plodded hopefully on over the miles of névé along the Divide. At length the snow became so soft that my stout companion. [Curtis] was sinking almost to his waist. Declaring himself out of it, he urged Campbell and myself to keep on for the now imminent prize. We two were soon on the northern arête and were crossing a well marked notch, when in climbing its farther wall, my ice-axe slipped from my hold and fell a few yards, yet was easily recovered. At this moment "Bob" called my serious attention to the fact that he had a wife and children at Banff, and I looked at my watch. It was 5:30, the very hour, and the day was August 3rd.[10]

Although Fay felt that what lay ahead was no more difficult than what had already been accomplished, Campbell's inexperience and loss of heart made retreat imperative. Fortunately, Bob was able to redeem himself somewhat on August 5th when he accompanied the professor on the first ascent of Mount Niles.

Soon afterward, Fay and Curtis made their way to the chalet at Lake Louise to prepare for an attempt at making the first complete traverse of Abbot Pass to Lake O'Hara. To assist them they hired a stocky, rather bowlegged "lively youth" named Jim Brewster, who was employed as a pony boy and guide at the chalet.

Fay and Curtis found the trip, especially from Abbot Pass down to Lake O'Hara, without scenic equal in the Canadian Rockies. They also found that young Brewster's gymnastic agility made him a valuable companion on the trail. He was able to make his way with ease over the fallen timber and when a small tree was the only bridge spanning a raging torrent he "ran across like a squirrel." However, he also had his drawbacks for when camp was made he immediately "slept the sleep of

Jim Brewster near Abbot Pass, 1898.

the just and the young" while his employers performed the chore of gathering sufficient wood to keep the night fire burning.[11] Later, when writing to Thompson about the trip, Fay offered an assessment of Jim's future possibilities as a guide:

Would make a capital guide with proper training. A little too fresh just now and fond of telling big stories. We learned within two days, to our amazement, that he had saved Curtis's life on the way up to the Pass! C's feet went from under him on a steep snow slope and he slipped fully a yard. No crevasses near.[12]

Despite the traverse proving a success, Fay was soon disappointed to learn that a group of his fellow Appalachianists had finally accomplished the feat that had so recently eluded him — the first ascent of Mount Balfour. Reverend Harry P. Nichols, Reverend Charles L. Noyes, Charles S. Thompson and George M. Weed had accompanied Fay and Curtis on the train from the east to Laggan. Here they approached Wilson who provided them with an outfit, and on July 30th they began making their way up the Pipestone River with Ralph Edwards as guide. As they were on a tight schedule, Tom had suggested they try the Pipestone route as a possible means of saving time and had provided them with a rough sketch map. Through the excellent trail work of Edwards, who took them over the first

recorded crossing of Dolomite Pass, they succeeded in reaching Bow Lake in record time. A few exploratory climbs were made on the Bow Glacier and around Peyto Lake before moving on to Hector Lake for the main assault on Balfour itself. According to Noyes the climb on August 11th "tried tact, agility, and care, but was not difficult or dangerous" and the long sought for summit was reached by four o'clock in the afternoon.[13]

While Wilson was providing the means to allow the Appalachian Club members to test their skills on Balfour, he was also aiding J. Norman Collie in his attempt to reach two other elusive peaks, Mounts Hooker and Brown. Believing that he had seen the mountains from the slopes of Mount Freshfield the previous year, Collie had determined to return and unravel their secrets once and for all in 1898. In the course of the winter he had consulted all available literature on the area and had written to Wilson to plumb his memory for further information.

Collie had been impressed with his outfitter the previous summer and the two had struck up a friendship which was to withstand the test of time, involving an exchange of correspondence until Tom's death over thirty years later. As a token of appreciation for services rendered in 1897, he had sent Tom a copy of the valuable Palliser Journals and had taken the trouble to analyze some mineral samples gathered by him. Although not able to reciprocate immediately, Wilson remembered the favors and in 1931, when Collie was retired on an inadequate pension, gained the permission of the railway to have his friend ride free of charge on any CPR train if he decided to visit the annual Alpine Club of Canada camp. This was, of course, still in the distant future in 1898, but because the two had hit it off so well it was only natural that when Collie returned to the Rockies that year with two English climbing companions, Hermann Woolley and Hugh E. M. Stutfield, he should once more outfit with Tom.

Having had his eyes opened the preceding summer to the ways of the trail and the value of a good guide, Collie was pleased to find upon reaching Laggan that his party had again been assigned to the care of the versatile Bill Peyto. Completing the outfit were packers Nigel Vavasour and Roy Douglas, cook Bill Byers, thirteen horses and three dogs. This entourage set out up the Pipestone a few days behind the Appalachian Club party and as they proceeded Collie, mounted on his perennial favourite "The Grey," had the opportunity to observe and reflect on the hazards the men of the outfit continually faced while journeying through the rugged landscape. He concluded that "Death . . . confronted the backwoods traveller in quite a remarkable variety of shapes; and, even if we did not break our necks on the mountains, we gathered it would be hard lines if some member of the outfit did not die of sunstroke, get burned in bed, starved, slain by falling trees, or drowned while fording rivers."[14]

The correctness of his observation was borne out by the events of the trip. After crossing the Siffleur River they encountered a bad patch of burnt timber and muskeg where the remaining few trees standing proved a constant hazard. With every wayward breeze "there arose a great creaking and groaning among them, like the wailing of lost souls in some arboreal Hades" presaging their toppling over, often narrowly missing horse and rider.

The falling timber soon gave way to the standing variety, and the three mountaineers were forced to wait for hours while the men laboriously axed their way through thick undergrowth. Patiently whiling away the time, they idly mused on the thick haze of smoke drifting in from the north where the country was said to be ablaze through the carelessness of the "wretched folk" making their way to the Klondike. When the trail was finally cleared the party was able to continue across the Kootenay Plains to the banks of the Saskatchewan River under the shadow of the towering cliffs of Mount Wilson, named by Collie for his outfitter. The river was in full flood and Peyto had the misfortune of having four of his horses plunge into its treacherous currents, wetting a good deal of the vital supplies and requiring a dangerous rescue. Next the fast flowing Mistaya had to be forded, and Peyto took a very philosophical view toward its dangers. He felt that it could be crossed quite simply, and if anyone was upset they should be able to struggle ashore somehow, unless, of course, they struck their head on a rock whereupon "one would die easily."

Proceeding up the North Fork Valley proved even more arduous as the heavy timber allowed only three or four miles progress a day. Finally an impenetrable muskeg of several miles barred the way, and as the river was also running high Bill contended that no sane person would attempt to go further. But Collie was not prepared to be denied his objective after coming so far and plied his guide with the only means available. "This called for heroic measures, so I ignored Peyto's picturesque language and suggested whisky. This saved the situation; for when it was carefully argued a little later that the river must be crossed at any cost, Peyto at once agreed, and finally we all got across somehow." [15]

Similar difficulties were each in turn overcome and Collie was eventually rewarded for his persistence. Eighteen days out on the trail brought them to the base of a mountain with an estimated altitude of 12,000 feet which they named Athabasca Peak. On August 18th, while Peyto, Baker and Vavasour went off in quest of some much needed game, Collie and Woolley ascended it and were greeted with an amazing view of "a vast icefield probably never before seen by human eyes and surrounded by entirely unknown, unnamed and unclimbed peaks." One of two particularly magnificent summits that reminded them of "lonely sea-stacks in mid-ocean" they took to be Mount Hooker while to the north-east of it lay a slightly flatter summit they felt sure was Mount

Dr. J. Norman Collie and H. E. M. Stutfield waiting for the trail to be cleared.

Brown. [16] Although Collie was soon to learn that these mountains were not the legendary Hooker and Brown, he and Woolley had unwittingly made a discovery of far greater importance, the Columbia Icefield marking the hydrographic apex of the North American continent.

Bolstered by their initial success, the climbers next made the ascent of Snow Dome. Afterward Peyto moved part of the outfit farther north so that an attempt on what were thought to be Hooker and Brown, but which subsequently would be named Mounts Columbia and Alberta, could be tried. Both proved inaccessible, though, and the three alpinists had to be content with the ascent of the less lofty Diadem Peak.

This accomplished, the dwindling larder demanded their return home. Vavasour and Stutfield had succeeded in killing three sheep while Collie and Woolley were on the heights, but these had now been almost completely consumed. Peyto therefore had to constantly hunt ahead of the pack train as it made its way back towards Laggan, ranging as far afield as the Brazeau River. Recent forest fires made the hunting almost hopeless, and before reaching the Mistaya all seven men were reduced to eating biltong, a form of dried meat. They found it so unappetizing in appearance that "when the first morsel was put before us on the plate we thought that that mad wag, Byers, was serving the outfit the uppers of Peyto's boots, which had recently shown signs of disintegration."[17]

Bill had fortuitously cached a small amount of staple items at the mouth of the Mistaya enabling the party to regain Laggan with body and soul still together. After a hot bath and a few square meals Collie was able to reflect on the trip with satisfaction. One of the foremost memories was the cameraderie which had evolved between trailman and mountaineer as they shared the experiences of the wilderness. Nowhere was this fellowship more evident than in the nightly gatherings around the campfire after the trials and tribulations of the day were past.

The campfire was a great democratizer as it was here that client and employee met on equal terms and engaged in the mutually enjoyable pastime of "swapping tales."

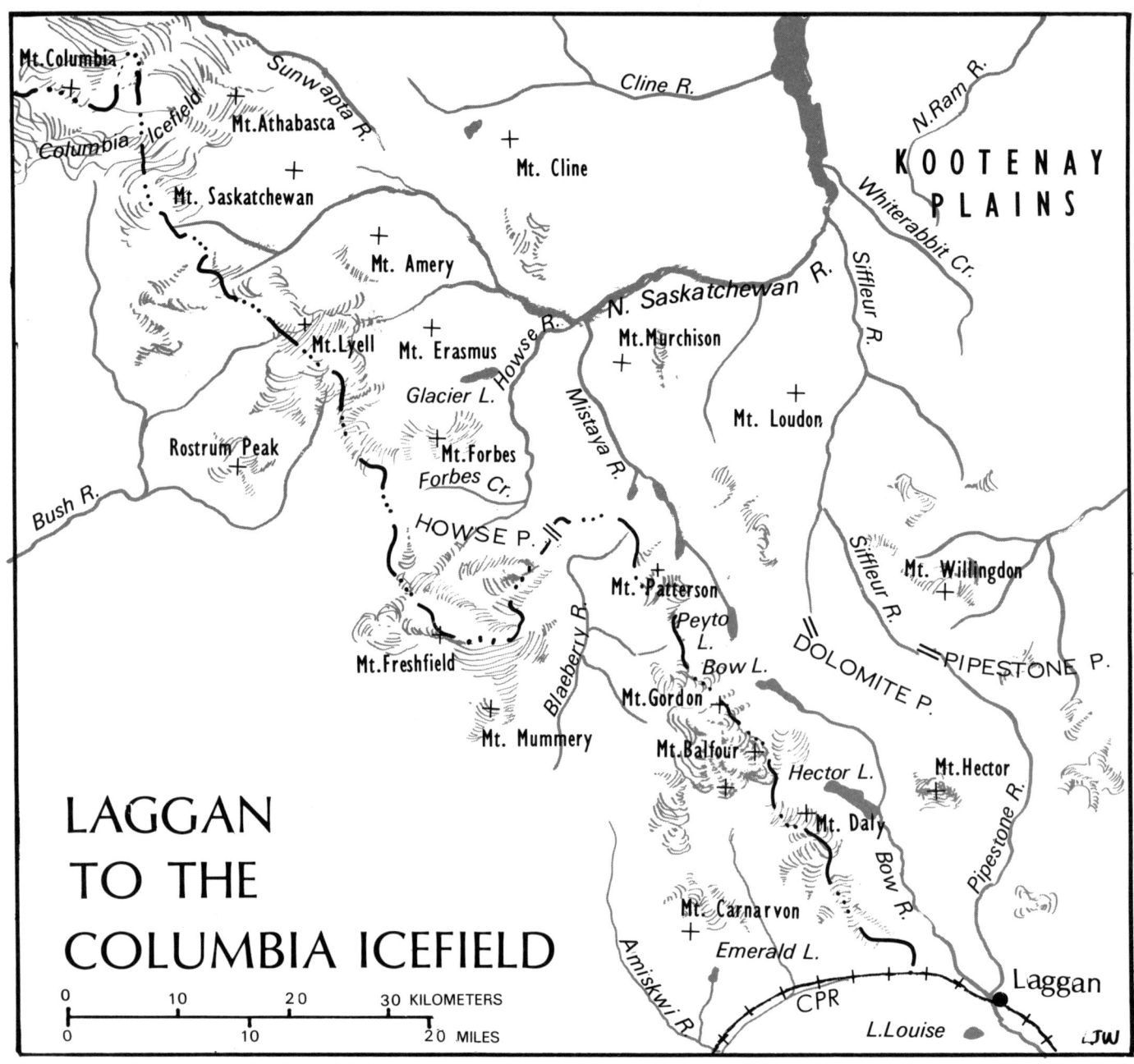

LAGGAN
TO THE
COLUMBIA ICEFIELD

A typical evening gathering around a campfire.

At this time the dudes took the opportunity to tell the assembly of their experiences in distant and exotic countries where they had scaled the giants of the Himalayas, Caucases and Alps. For their part, the guides and packers regaled the eager listeners with stories of wild Indians, dangerous bear hunts and fabulous gold strikes, or instructed them in the exploits of the Sidehill Gouger, that most famous of all mountain creatures. According to legend this elusive beast had been blessed with one leg considerably longer than the other to enable it to more easily make its way around the steep mountainsides so common to the landscape. Never explained was how it navigated when it decided to turn around and go back over the same mountainsides in the opposite direction.

The campfire gabfest also allowed Collie and company to gain an understanding of the simple philosophy of the trailmen, formed through long association with life in closest contact with nature. One particularly noteworthy example of this, which Collie well remembered, occurred at one of the camps made on the North Fork when the subject of conversation fell on the interpretation of certain verses of Genesis:

. . . Byers took the opportunity to pronounce a glowing eulogy upon the scheme of Creation, which in a passage of singular eloquence he described as "a mighty fine outfit". Some rash person venturing to controvert his views, our cook promptly overwhelmed him with a torrent of backwoods satire and invective; and the would-be objector, crushed in argument, took refuge in an outburst of somewhat pointless profanity. Then the tobacco was passed round, and the discussion ended — as such discussions usually do — in smoke.[18]

Collie's feeling for the character and life of his men was soon to draw him into one of the closest relationships of his life. Unable to get to the Rockies in 1899 because of a previous commitment to climb in the Alps, he was still determined to return at some point and make an attempt on some of the newly discovered peaks of the Columbia Icefield. The opportunity came in 1900 when he returned in the company of Stutfield and his friend Sydney Spencer with the intention of climbing Mounts Bryce and Alberta, approaching by way of one of the valleys on the west side of the Divide. Because Peyto was away fighting in the Boer War, Wilson provided Fred Stephens as guide for the expedition. Collie took an immediate liking to Stephens, pronouncing him to be "one of the best fellows it has been our good fortune to meet," and thereafter would consider going out on the trail with no one else. Thus began a lifelong friendship between the famous chemistry professor and the almost illiterate guide.

Although Collie's 1898 trip had tested the patience and endurance of both man and beast alike, it did not even begin to compare with the 1900 outing. Stutfield favored approaching Bryce and Alberta from the Wood River, but Collie pointed out that the Bush River would offer a shorter and more direct route. This was an important consideration as it was realized that the rivers, muskegs and timber would be more formidable than on the eastern side of the Divide. To aid in overcoming some of the expected problems Wilson assigned, in addition to Stephens, another excellent axeman in the person of Charlie Bassett, a recently hired employee. Rounding out the crew were cook Charlie Black and packer Alistair MacAlpine, a young lad newly arrived from Belfast.

Bad luck plagued the expedition from the very beginning. Immediately after hitting the trail, Bassett's horse fell on him causing severe internal injuries, necessitating his return to Banff for medical attention. Replacing him was Harry Lang who, although a good packer, was no match for Bassett with an axe. Once the Bush was reached the water was so high and the undergrowth so dense that making any real headway was virtually impossible. Collie noted in his diary that "the chopping of the axe and the drip of the water from the leaves are the only sounds unless unprintable language is suddenly hurled at some wretched pack animal." [19] He had conservatively estimated that progress might be restricted to three miles a day, but soon even this expectation proved unattainable. The rain poured down in torrents, the mosquitoes hummed in thick clouds, and on some evenings the camp for the night would still be in sight of that left in the morning. Stephens felt that without doubt these were the worst conditions which he had ever experienced and later, in a letter to Wilcox, gave a rather interesting description of them:

Better late than Never so as i Promised you; would Rite and tell you something of our Bush River trip i will just give you a Pointer to Pass it by, we left Donald and followed an trail whitch Led through a Dence forest to the mouth of Bush River we apparently followed the Columbia but was out of sight of it most of the time; never saw sutch undergrowth mud and wet, with mosquitoes that would stop a syclone, the poor Englishmen looked like Plum Puddings walking around with faces swolled up to twice their Natural size well we wanted to get to the head of the bush River But found it in high water to be impossible to follow up the Bank. we took the trail back 6 miles then climbed up over a mountain with the outfit and struck the River 7 or 8 miles up it was raining 7 days out of 6, to make it more pleasant. the Pack horses got covered with Brittish columbia mold, the oat meal soured, the hard tack swelled up so we had to Pack our saddle horses the wood would not burn and a few more things went Rong we finally got up the River far enough so it commenced to get deep and the valley was narrow and filled with Burnt fallen timber we nearly drowned Harry Long because he could not ride a raft of water soaked logs we found it impossible to follow up the valley to the foot of Mt. Bryce and Columbia so we took

to the hills and camped 7000 feet above sea Level and here it snowed for 4 days and the wind blowed so we had to tie down the Pack Saddles to keep them in camp. i suppose this would be Delightfull to you But somehow it don't catch me. this was as far as we got although i could go much farther but the weather was so cloudy that it was useless to go farther. here we turned and came back to Donald. i think we were about Due west of the west Branch whitch comes into the west fork of the Saskatchewan. Well Walter this is a Poor Pen, Poor Paper and the Boy is jerking things around so i will wind this interesting slip to a close; have no Doubt you will find this a very interesting country to go to as the mountains are very high and craggy the whole country is verry Rough and the weather in July will freeze a kyote so i am sure you would call it Grand. [20]

Actually Collie had overestimated how far north the head of the Bush River was and instead of ending up at the foot of Mount Bryce, found himself much further south and at the foot of Bush Peak instead. However, the expedition was not a complete failure as he was able to fill in many blank spaces on his sketch map of the Rockies.

With the numerous expeditions of Appalachian Club members and Collie and friends to the area north of the CPR mainline after 1896, it became obvious to Wilson that the impetus of mountaineering and exploration had shifted away from the once popular country south of Banff. But this region still had a few loyal advocates who called upon his services, and he encouraged them as he felt that it contained some of the finest country in the mountains. Among the enthusiasts was Wilcox, who remained enchanted with the many hidden valleys and lakes of the Lake Louise region and with the possibility of conquering the as yet unclimbed Mount Assiniboine. The year 1899 proved to be his most active beginning in July with a trip to Assiniboine in company with two other alpinists, an American, Henry G. Bryant, and an Englishman, Louis J. Steele.

Outfitting with Tom as usual, Wilcox's party took along Bob Campbell as guide and set out over a new route suggested by their outfitter. This involved a variation on the Simpson Pass trail whereby they would follow a branch of Healy Creek to the summit of the Divide and then continue on to Assiniboine over open meadows which would provide easy travelling and good pasture for the horses. Because of their unfamiliarity with this new path, Campbell and Wilcox were forced to rely on a Topographic Survey map for reference and soon became lost. Only by dogged determination and some excellent trail finding by Campbell was the Simpson River finally reached and with it the now well-known way to their objective. Unfortunately, Wilcox lost a knapsack containing his personal effects and while he and Campbell returned along the trail to search for it, Bryant and Steele attempted an ascent of the 'Matterhorn of the Rockies.'

A Wilson packtrain on Banff Avenue, 1899. Left to right — Louis J. Steele, Ross Peecock, Bob Campbell, Walter Garrett and Walter Wilcox.

They managed to reach the 10,000 foot level before being turned back by a thunderstorm which, much to the mountaineers' chagrin, initiated a long period of rain and snow. The deteriorating weather meant an abandonment of further attempts on the peak and a premature return to civilization via the Spray River and Canmore.

Undaunted by his failure to even gain an attempt on Assiniboine, Wilcox immediately re-outfitted in Banff for further explorations of the Lake Louise region. Wilson provided him with a rather capable young man named Ross Peecock who had recently entered his employ.

Peecock, the son of an English rancher who at one time had business interests in Banff, first came to notice as a result of a ranching venture of his own. Along with fellow Englishman Nigel Vavasour he had hoped to raise cattle in the Banff vicinity in order to supply the beef requirements of the CPR. The site chosen for the venture had been the old railroad construction commissary camp at Hillsdale, where the fairly open nature of the country was thought to provide the best chance for success. Although the pair had begun their project in one of the best Indian summers on record, they soon fell victim to the heavy snows of November, more than four feet falling in one six day stretch. With insufficient supplies of hay, the young ranchers had seen the writing on the wall and had opted to slaughter their forty head of cattle in order to at least break even on their investment. Having no more ambitions to continue in such a risky business both Peecock and Vavasour had decided to throw in their lot

with Wilson in 1897 and had quickly proved themselves to be very valuable additions to his crew.

Wilcox and Peecock started out from Lake Louise on August 13th with the intention of penetrating to Desolation Valley (Valley of the Ten Peaks) where, in the course of their 1894 work, Wilcox and Allen had caught a glimpse of an interesting lake from the slopes of Mount Temple. After a vigorous hike and two days of enforced idleness due to a severe snow storm, the lake was reached and named Moraine Lake, for what was apparently a glacial deposit damming its lower end. From their camp on its shore the entire lake was explored, and on the 19th a stream coming in on the south-east about a mile below the lake was followed to its source in another interesting valley. At Ross's suggestion it was named Consolation Valley to distinguish it from the recently visited Desolation Valley.

Not content with these twin discoveries, Wilcox insisted in pushing on to investigate the Vermilion Pass area, but all progress soon came to a halt when the four horses wandered off and could not be relocated. Peecock made his way on foot to Banff for assistance leaving Wilcox to face the rigors of the wilderness alone. Four days later Ross returned with Tom Lusk and fresh animals only to find the horses which had been lost had just preceded them into camp. The lonely Wilcox was so pleased to see human faces again that he prepared a special meal featuring "a corn-starch blanc mange flavoured with Scotch whiskey," probably much to the delight of that connoisseur of spirits Tom Lusk. Adding the new horses to their old bunch, Wilcox and Peecock continued on their wanderings the next day and succeeded in visiting Boom Lake, Vermilion Pass and Prospector's Valley before returning to Banff.

The failure of Wilcox's party to hang the scalp of Mount Assiniboine at their belts in 1899 led to another assault on the elusive summit the following year. This time the hopefuls were amateurish Chicago climbers, Willoughby and English Walling. Their equally unsuccessful attempt added little of importance except that it marked the first time that Swiss guides were used on Assiniboine and it provided the debut on an extended mountaineering expedition for an interesting young trail cook working for Wilson. The cook was Jimmy Simpson, at that time only a lad of twenty-two but eventually perhaps the most famous of all the Banff outfitters and "the grand old man of the mountains" until his death in 1972.

Justin James McCartney Simpson was born on August 8, 1877 at Stamford, Lincolnshire, and it was there that he grew up and received his early education. His father was a noted authority on Roman coins, and the family had a coat-of-arms which Jim was later reluctant to show in Canada, believing that "most people would think it was an advertisement for Beecham's Pills."

Being somewhat of a rascally lad, Jim got into all kinds of mischief, including poaching on the Marquis of Exeter's estate, and after disgracing his family in church was labelled a black sheep and sent to Canada to go farming in March, 1896. However, after spending one night on a farm near Winnipeg he decided that the sedentary life wasn't for him and removed himself to the city, where he quickly drank up his supply of English sovereigns.

Penniless but happy-go-lucky, Jim stowed away on a west-bound train, getting as far as Laggan before the conductor got wise and kicked him off. With no means of support or method of travelling further, he was forced to hire on for the season with the CPR and went to work with "tools I had never seen before, i. e. pick and shovel." Since he was a rather diminutive youth the hard labour was good for him and helped build up the strength that later complemented his lithe and wiry frame.

Laid off by the railway at the end of the summer he departed for San Francisco with fifty dollars in his pocket. He soon found himself broke and joined a band of a thousand hobos marching on Washington under the leadership of a General Kelly and the California author Jack London. Failing to discover the purpose of the march, he left the group near Albuquerque and worked for the Santa Fe Railway until he returned to the coast at Los Angeles. From there he shipped out on a Victoria, B.C. schooner and put in three months sealing off the California and British Columbia coasts. After being paid off in Victoria he experienced one of the greatest difficulties in life, "how a newly landed sailor learns to pass the first saloon." Once again out of pocket he decided that it was time to return to Banff and go to work on the trail for Wilson, who had offered him a job whenever he wanted it during his previous stay. [21]

Jim's first year on Tom's crew was 1897, and he quickly picked up the tricks of the trade from Tom Lusk and his idol Bill Peyto. But as was the case with most green hands, he was first assigned to the beginner's position in the outfit — trail cook. He may have accompanied Colonel O'Hara on a trip in this capacity during that year, but his real baptism as a culinary artist came the next season when he was delegated to accompany Bob Campbell to Emerald Lake and help cook for a group of fourteen Philadelphians encamped there. Philadelphians were among the most numerous of the early American visitors to the Canadian mountains and in the party were William, George and Mary Vaux, who had been carrying out glacial studies in the Glacier House region, and Dr. and Mrs. Charles Schäffer, who had been doing botanical work in the same vicinity for a number of years. Their acquaintance would lead to many important connections in his future career.

For further training in 1898 Jim was given the task of cooking for a party from Richmond, Virginia under the care of guide Ralph Edwards. The clients consisted of a girl and her young, tubercular brother who visited Badger Pass, the head of the Cascade Valley and Sawback Lake before returning to Banff by way of Forty Mile Creek and Edith Pass. The boy died shortly after returning to the States, and Jim was so unsure of his skills at the time that he claimed he never knew whether it was from the tuberculosis or the effects of his cooking! The year 1899 was mostly spent in cooking for hunting parties north of Banff during which time his artistry improved to the point where he was picked to accompany the Walling party to Assiniboine in 1900.

As he remembered it, this venture proved to be somewhat of a fiasco. After their unsuccessful assault on Assiniboine the brothers and the climbing guides, in an attempt to save time, took one horse and made for Banff by way of the Spray River while the rest of the pack train headed back through Whiteman's Pass and Canmore. Due to the heavy timber on the Spray, the mountaineers found the going rather more than they had bargained for and were forced to kill the horse to keep from starving to death. Little did they realize that they were within fifty yards of a lumber road and only a short hop from the Banff Springs Hotel. The Swiss guides, fed up with their patrons' incompetence, abandoned them at this spot and pushed on ahead to the hotel that evening but did not report that the brothers were lost until the next morning.

Because of their troubles on the Assiniboine expedition, Wilson agreed to send the Wallings on a free week's recovery trip in the Lake Louise area. Along with the services of Tom Lusk as guide and Simpson as cook, he provided a generous supply of blackberry brandy, known to be the brothers' favorite. But in so doing he forgot to

Jim Simpson.

reckon with Lusk's famous thirst. While Jim had the pair out hunting on the first day of the excursion Tom got into the brandy and one thing soon led to another. When they returned to camp the thirsty hunters found only several empty brandy bottles and one "well-baked" guide.

Simpson was not the only trail hand hired on by Wilson at this time who was later to make a name for himself as an outfitter and guide in his own right. The expansion of Tom's bases of operation obviously required the employment of considerably more men and among those he hired were a few who really excelled at their work. One of these was a young Ontarian named Jack Otto who would later go on to successes equal to those of his confrere Simpson. Otto, born into a family of six boys and three girls at Haliburton, Ontario, very early in life went to work in the local lumber camps. In addition, he worked in the mines and spent his winters trapping, finding the latter particularly to his liking. As a result, when he arrived at Golden, B.C., sometime in the late nineties, he set up one of the longest traplines in the district and soon achieved quite a reputation. This was undoubtedly what brought him to the attention of Wilson, who convinced him to join his crew at Field during the summer trapping doldrums.

Like Simpson, Otto's first assignments were to the post of trail cook. Although he had a booming voice which, it was said, could be heard for miles, he was usually a very quiet individual and not one to complain.

However, while out with one particular party he found that their remarks about his cooking were just too much to endure. He immediately informed the party's leader that he was through and only agreed to reconsider when the leader informed the other members that if there were any more complaints they would have to cook for themselves. After that Jack received only compliments, but to find out to what lengths the clients would go to avoid doing their own cooking he devised a somewhat fiendish test.

. . . I came into camp early, got supper started and baked a pan of biscuits. When the meal started the soup was perfect, the roast was good, the food was fit for any king etc. etc. Meanwhile I opened up 2 or 3 biscuits and filled them with salt. The first man bit into one and said "Food for the Gods", the second agreed and said "Nectarine for the Angels." The third man bit into the salt. He stood up spluttered, spat, waved his arms wildly and with red face he pounded the table and roared "Just as I like 'em." [22]

Although the reaction of these three when they learned of the trick played on them went unrecorded, most dudes accepted such antics good naturedly. As for Jack, his sense of humor, as illustrated on this and many more occasions, soon made him one of the most popular members of Tom's staff.

Chief Hector Crawler and Tom Wilson at the first Banff Indian Days, 1894.

4 Contracts and Competition

As his operations developed, Wilson found that problems like those experienced with the Wallings were bound to occur in outfitting and accepted such setbacks philosophically. He could not expect that everyone would find the life of the trail, with its frequent hardships and discomforts, to their liking, and was not surprised when many did not come back for a second trip. At any rate, by the turn of the century he had as much business as he could effectively handle. A more important concern was how to make it profitable.

Replacing the business from the parties which did not return were new customers who were being referred to him through the efforts of the CPR. His relationship with the railway had been growing closer throughout the eighteen-nineties as the company continued to expand its program of attracting tourists to its hotels in the Rockies and Selkirks. Van Horne's policy of importing the tourist to the scenery had resulted in the organization of group excursions, the opening up of new trails and carriage drives and even CPR and federal government cooperation in the development of Banff and its hot sulphur springs. These measures were, of course, good for the outfitting business, but perhaps one of the most significant and gratifying steps taken by the railway was the decision to supply Swiss climbing guides for prospective mountaineering parties. The lack of qualified climbing guides in the region had proved to be one of its drawbacks as far as mountaineers were concerned and in 1899 this situation was remedied when two Swiss guides, Edward Feuz and Christian Häsler, were brought from Interlaken and stationed at Glacier House for the summer. They proved so popular that soon guides were situated at other of the company's mountain hotels as well.

Tom was able to, at least in part, reciprocate for these beneficial policies by continuing to provide excellent service to the parties sent his way and by performing several public relations functions for the company. One of his major contributions was the initiation of Banff Indian Days in 1894. During June of that year high water on the Bow River washed out several miles of track along its banks causing a large number of tourists to be stranded at the Banff Springs Hotel. At a loss as to how to entertain his soon bored and disgruntled guests, manager Mathews approached Tom and asked him for ideas. His suggestion was that some of the Stoney Indians be approached and asked to participate in a series of athletic contests for prizes put up by the CPR. Personally travelling to the Stoney reserve at Morley as the company's emissary, he succeeded in convincing the Indians of the benefits of his plan and brought back a large contingent to a camp near Banff's animal paddock. The next day the Stoneys, decked out in their full regalia, paraded through town to the Banff Springs and made the delighted guests aware of their presence. Then everyone proceeded back to the animal paddock where the braves staged horse races, bucking and roping contests, and bow and arrow demonstrations while the squaws competed against each other in teepee pitching, horse packing, and other accomplishments of the trail. The initial event proved so popular that it was decided to make it an annual attraction, and for many years thereafter Tom remained its organizer, assisted by such other local businessmen as Dave White and Norman Luxton.

Other CPR public relations activities included the telegraphing of matters of local interest to the Manager of Passenger Traffic to be used in advertising campaigns and the securing of specimens of native animals which were often requested of the CPR by American scientific and wildlife institutions. During 1900-01, the American

Museum of Natural History offered Tom from $30 to $50 each for caribou hides, and the International Forest, Fish and Game Association of Chicago promised $250 a pair for bighorn sheep and mountain goats. But perhaps his most interesting function in the public relations field was his handling of many of the V.I.P.s who visited the mountains under the auspices of the railway. For example, in 1900 he provided men to take the famous author-historian Agnes Laut and two companions over a new trail which he had cleared to the shore of Moraine Lake, allowing them the distinction of being the first ladies to lay eyes on the spot. Even more noteworthy was the provision of his services to Edward Whymper, the day's most celebrated mountaineer, during his widely heralded visits to the Rockies beginning in 1901.

Whymper, the London-born son of a noted wood carver and engraver Josiah Wood Whymper, was regarded as the foremost product of mountaineering's Golden Age during the mid-nineteenth century. First visiting the Alps in 1860 he had become infatuated with the as yet unclimbed Matterhorn and set his sights on being the one to destroy its almost mythical invincibility. Seven unsuccessful attempts were mounted between 1861 and 1865 until finally, in the latter year, he had succeeded in leading a party of seven to the conquest. However, the achievement had been tragically marred when a rope broke on the descent, and for the rest of his life Whymper was haunted by the vision of four of his companions sliding off the edge of a cliff, arms outstretched, to their deaths below.

By the time Whymper visited the Rockies the spark of youth that had driven him to great accomplishments in the past was no longer evident, and he was rumored to be an alcoholic and past his mountaineering prime. Yet at sixty-two he was still a very imposing figure and a somewhat awestruck reporter for the *Calgary Daily Herald* described him in rather admiring terms on making his acquaintance: "He is an Englishman 62 years old, very active and aggressive, smooth-faced, of medium height, and showing traces of a pretty hard life away from the luxuries of civilization. It is only necessary to see him and hear him talk to be convinced that he possesses that British bulldog tenacity which stops at no obstacle and that he belongs to the strong type of humanity that does things." [1]

Apparently bulldog tenacity was a prominent feature of his personality as it was also commented on in later years by Jim Simpson, who spent a day with him in a pastime enjoyed equally by both men:

Whymper was peculiar, possibly because he had been lionized too much, but he was so determined an individual and such a strong character that he resembled a bulldog very much like the cartoons of that dog standing astride the Union Jack ready to devour anyone who touched it.

Edward Whymper.

He got me very drunk at the old Field Hotel after the camp was over and confided that he had a very clever brother who drank himself to death and said he, "Yes Simpson, very clever and I often used to say to him 'George, why don't you take it in moderation the same as I do'". You know what moderation he used . . . [2]

Whymper's visit to the mountains in 1901 resulted from a coast to coast rail trip the year before, after which he had convinced the CPR to accept a proposal that would see him climb and explore in the Rockies at their expense. He would be given all his own travelling and lodging costs as well as those for his entourage of four Swiss guides and in return would attempt to advertise the Rockies through newspaper reports and written accounts in English publications. Wilson's assignment was to see to it that he was provided with the best guides and packers available to ensure the smooth running of his summer's campaign.

Upon his arrival at Banff in early June, Whymper requested that he be given Bill Peyto, recently returned from the Boer War, on the recommendation of a comrade-in-arms of Bill's who he had met on the train coming west. The choice, in some respects, proved to be an unfortunate one. First of all, Bill was no longer in Tom's employ as he was attempting to establish an outfitting and guiding business of his own. In addition, Bill's temperament was such that it was not likely he would be able to effectively deal with Whymper's stubbornness and omniscient attitude for any length of time. However, Tom's instructions were to provide the great man with what he wanted and he had no trouble in convincing Peyto, anxious to test his independence, to accept.

Whymper's first objective was to do some preliminary exploration in the Vermilion Pass vicinity and on June 18th, with his four Swiss guides and photographer W. G. Francklyn, he met Peyto and the pack train at Castle Mountain. Assisting with the packing was Jack Sinclair, an Australian who lived in the cabin next to Bill's along the Bow River in Banff and was a partner with him in a copper mining venture. From their rendezvous the party proceeded into the Vermilion River valley and established a base camp from which a number of worthy peaks were ascended and some interesting side valleys examined during the later part of June. Despite rather adverse weather conditions, Whymper's famous temper seemed particularly serene at this early stage in the season and, although he found numerous faults with the Swiss, conceded that Peyto "properly executed his commission."

Such amicable relations were not to remain in evidence for long, and on a further excursion to the Yoho Valley in July the situation deteriorated rapidly. Matters were complicated by continuing bad weather, by numerous misunderstandings between Whymper and the Swiss, who felt that they were being treated as porters rather than climbing guides, and by a strange malady which laid Bill low for several days. Whymper was led to comment in his diary that "instead of being roused by my example (I am always at work), the more I do the less they seem inclined to do." [3] Finally Bill lost his temper when berated for coming back to camp too early from some trail clearing and for attempting to get into one of the cook boxes which Whymper didn't want opened. A few days later, after moving the camp from Yoho Pass to the upper Yoho Valley, Bill insisted on returning to Banff with the excuse that two sick horses needed replacing, but probably, as much as anything, to regain his composure.

Left somewhat in a lurch, Whymper went down to Field and fortunately found Wilson there. Tom took immediate steps to rectify Peyto's temporary desertion by providing Tom Martin, one of his men stationed at Field, to help find a more direct route than that via Emerald Lake between the upper Yoho Valley and Field. He also introduced Whymper to a fellow English mountaineer, Reverend James Outram, who was looking for climbing companions. Outram was invited to join the party which, under Martin's direction, set out on August 5th to

attempt to find the valley which Whymper believed would prove the key to the direct route. They were unsuccessful, but on August 8th Wilson himself joined them and was able to lead Whymper and Klucker, one of the Swiss guides, over a previously untried pass (Kiwetinok Pass), through an unexplored valley (Amiskwi Valley) and eventually out to the town. Whymper pronounced this day's work "the hitherto best accomplished" and admitted that "our success was very much due to Wilson." [4] Although Tom had to immediately hurry back to Banff, Whymper decided that he would prefer to have the outfitter's personal attention whenever possible and quickly sent him a note both requesting this and paying him a high compliment:

I shall be very glad if you can find it possible to join us in the Yoho Valley at any time. We shall not be difficult to find. I have no very appropriate name to suggest for the valley we discovered yesterday on account of its natural features and if you have no objections I will propose that it will be called Wilson's Valley . . . [5]

A wag's memorium to Edward Whymper.

Whymper's camp in the Little Yoho Valley, August 1, 1901.

Whymper was unable to elicit the immediate return of Wilson and he soon wanted him more than ever as relations with Peyto deteriorated even further. On returning to his camp in the upper Yoho he found that Bill and Sinclair had returned from Banff and he promptly ordered them to find a direct route between the upper and main Yoho Valleys. Again he found cause to disagree with their performance, and for the next two weeks Bill's temper once more verged on the boiling point. The last straw came at Field on August 24th when Bill requested his pay, and an argument about the amount owing developed which only ended when he threatened Whymper with legal action. An agreement was reached and Bill gladly took his leave, but Whymper, who had been planning a trip to the Ice River Valley, was once more left without a trail guide and horse transport. Again Wilson came to the rescue. Although he could not accompany Whymper personally for the whole length of his expedition, Tom agreed to provide two of his best men, Campbell and Martin, to be at his service.

An initial reconnaissance of the Ice River Valley was made by Whymper in Campbell's company in the early part of September, and for a few days they were joined by Wilson, who pointed out some interesting mineral deposits. Later this trip was followed by a more extensive exploration with both Campbell and Martin taking part. In the course of the second trip an incident occurred which served to show that Whymper's crustiness was, at least sometimes, only a facade. Martin, a tall, thin American who one acquaintance described as "that dry, humourous old stick," was resting while his patron paced up and down the trail, as was Whymper's custom when thinking things out. On this particular stretch of trail there was a fallen log which he had to step over on each of his passings to and fro. Eventually it got on his nerves and he called, "Martin! come here and cut that log." The peacefully reclining guide gazed at the obstruction reflectively for a few moments and then replied, "Wall! Mr. Whymper, I've been up and down this valley many times and everytime that log has been there, and I'm thinking,

Mr. Whymper, that if you want that log cut you'll have to cut it yourself." The flabbergasted Whymper retorted, "Martin! you're fired" and haughtily stalked off to his tent. Martin was by this time used to being fired for such presumed insolence and when a short while later he heard another shout, "Martin! come here," he casually wandered over to the tent. There appeared Whymper with a bottle in one hand and a mug in the other and in exactly the same tone he ordered, "Martin! have a mug of beer."

Before long Whymper was glad that he had patched things up in his own inimitable fashion for he found Martin to be one of Wilson's most capable men. Soon he began referring to him as "Long Tom" in his diary, and by the time the trip was ended had named a creek in the upper Ice River Valley for him. Campbell's service was likewise found to be of a high order and he was similarly honored.

The Ice River explorations concluded Whymper's work for 1901, but he was to return in other years for further exploits. Wilson handled the outfitting of the trips of 1903 and 1904, but they proved much less tumultuous and demanding than the 1901 outings. In 1903 he was only called upon to supply a man to accompany Whymper on a walk over the CPR line from the Gap to Revelstoke. However, in 1904 Tom again personally accompanied him for a time, going as far afield as the Crowsnest Pass area in the extreme south-western part of Alberta. There he and two Swiss guides accomplished the first recorded ascent of Crowsnest Mountain while Whymper remained "indisposed" on terra firma, probably from the effects of overindulgence.

With the passage of the years and time for reflection on his association with the CPR, Tom ultimately determined that his connection with the company was not always as beneficial as it had seemed earlier. Particularly galling was the fact that he was never fully reimbursed for many of the jobs carried out on their behalf. But at the conclusion of the 1901 season these hindsights were still in the distant future, and he was well satisfied by his relationship with them. Despite a long period spent working closely with the company, in what he termed an "arrangement," he had never entered into any formal agreement. By the turn of the century, though, the railway's management was becoming increasingly adamant about having securely contracted services available to it. In order to further this end, Tom was offered a concession on some of the CPR's livery and outfitting business in return for signing an agreement specifying certain obligations on his part. Choosing Field and Laggan as his locations, he finally signed a contract in 1902 by which he guaranteed "to accommodate and supply the requirements of the Company and its guests in connection with the transfer and conveyance of baggage and passengers and furnishing and supplying of horses, conveyances, drivers and attendants at the said stations and in connection with their said Hotel at Field and their

said Chalet at Emerald Lake and also between Laggan and their said Chalet at Lake Louise upon the terms and conditions hereinafter contained."

Among the conditions were maintenance of "a sufficient number of Democrat wagons, buggies, pack saddles and workhorses"; agreement to "meet the regular trains and special trains to convey the passengers to the three hotels"; employment of "only such men in the conduct of such business as shall be sober, competent men of good character and shall in the performance of their duties conduct themselves courteously"; and finally agreement to "carry Company employees and provisions and equipment free of charge." In return the railroad agreed to carry feed and the necessary supplies for the maintenance of the stables without charge and to collect the following fares on his behalf:

Conveyance from Field to Emerald Lake and return (1 or 2 persons), $4.00 — for each additional person, $2.00. Conveyance from Laggan to Chalet at Lake Louise (single fare) for each passenger including hand luggage, 50c — for each piece of baggage additional, 50c. Hire for each saddle horse or pack horse per day or part, $2.00. Hire for each Packer or man per day or part, $2.00.[7]

Since pack horses, saddle horses and outfitting equipment were his stock-in-trade, Tom had to begin his livery operations with only one wagon, but was soon able to rectify this situation by acquiring the necessary conveyances, some of them from the CPR itself.

Several possibilities present themselves for Tom's choice to contract at Field and Laggan instead of Banff. One obvious one was that the Banff concession might not have been offered to him, the livery part, at least, being operated by the CPR themselves at the time. An equally likely explanation, though, was Tom's belief that the more lucrative business was to be found in the "long trail" rather than in livery work and touring sightseers on bridle paths in close proximity to the hotels. As pointed out, it had been the growing popularity of the country north of the CPR main line that had led him to establish at Field and Lake Louise in the first place, and he continued to believe in the area's future. This was particularly true with regard to hunting which continued to provide a good portion of his business. It was probably not coincidental that the year he contracted was the same one in which the former 250 square mile Rocky Mountains Park and the 51 square mile Lake Louise Reservation made in 1891 were included in the new 4900 square mile Rocky Mountains Park. Now the North Saskatchewan River had to be crossed before any legal hunting could begin.

After receiving the CPR concession it quickly became apparent that the work load it was going to impose would be too much for one man to effectively handle. This realization led Tom to consider a partner. His eye fell on Bob Campbell who had already purchased a small share

Wilson's buildings at Field stand in the background as a special train carrying the Duke and Duchess of York passes by, 1901.

of the business in 1898 and with his sound financial mind had begun to work as Tom's bookkeeper. By the fall of 1901 Campbell had retired from his teaching position, and early in the spring of 1902 a deal was concluded forming a partnership under the title of "Wilson and Campbell." To ensure the smooth running of their business it was agreed that Tom would be responsible for the operations at Laggan and Lake Louise while Bob handled those at Field and Emerald Lake. A contemporary description of the set-up at Field mentioned "a little shop on the north of the river where curios are for sale including sheep's heads, bark canoes, sweet grass blankets etc." as well as "extensive and expensive equipment in horse saddles, tents, buggies, democrats, pack saddles etc."[8]

While Wilson's contract with the CPR effectively put most of the business at Field and Laggan in his and Campbell's hands, there remained some leeway for rivals at these locales and, of course, a wide open field for competition at Banff. Until near the turn of the century Tom's supremacy in the entire Banff-Lake Louise-Field region had remained virtually unchallenged, but by 1902 this situation was rapidly changing. Interestingly, with one exception all the competitors had at some time worked for him. They were, in fact, several of his best men including Fred Stephens, Jim Simpson and, as already noted, Bill Peyto. The exception began as a partnership of two individuals whose shoestring operation was eventually to develop into the largest transportation enterprise in the entire Canadian Rockies and was even to extend as far as Hawaii. These two were Jim Brewster, Curtis and Fay's agile young guide of 1898, and his elder brother Bill.

The sons of John and Bella Brewster, William A. and James I. Brewster were born at Kingston, Ontario on July 15, 1880 and February 10, 1882 respectively. Their father, of Irish descent, had apprenticed as a blacksmith but rarely practised the trade, preferring veterinary work instead. Sometime in 1882 he fell victim to the lure of the West and moved to Winnipeg where, among other jobs, he worked as one of the first drivers on the newly created Winnipeg street railway. With the exception of part of

1883, when he went to Medicine Hat as the foreman of a crew sent to install boilers in a river boat, he remained in Winnipeg with his family, swelled by the addition of two more sons, Fred and George, until 1886. In that year his brother, who had been sent to help construct the first permanent buildings at the Cave and Basin, advised him that there was a need for a dairy in the Banff vicinity to service the town, the railway's dining cars and undoubtedly soon the Banff Springs Hotel. Since the economic situation in Winnipeg was somewhat unfavorable at the time he decided to test his luck as a dairyman, and, after arriving in Banff on October 6, 1886, acquired a piece of land near the corner of Banff Avenue and Moose Street.

For a year and a half Brewster spent his time acquiring milchcows and constructing a log house on his lot. On March 17, 1888, the rest of the family arrived to take up residence in the new home, and soon their numbers were again increased with the birth of two sons, Jack and Forrest (Pat), and a daughter, Pearl. Meanwhile the dairy began to prove more successful than the elder Brewster had dared hope, and it was not long before the need to expand required a move to a new location across the CPR tracks on Whiskey Creek. By 1892 his dairy herd had increased to the point where he found it necessary to register a brand (written x), and by 1898 he was paying as much as $100 a year to the government for rent of pasture lands around the Vermilion Lakes and at Hillsdale.

Shortly after their arrival in Banff, Bill and Jim began attending the town's first school classes which were held in part of Superintendent Stewart's office. Then in 1892 they were sent to Saint John's College in Winnipeg, although this more formalized education ended rather abruptly in 1893 when the college was closed by an epidemic of scarlet fever. Thereafter, for the few remaining years of their education, they went to the newly built school in Banff, their attendance being somewhat spotty since they preferred to spend their time out hunting and fishing in the mountains with William Twin, a Stoney who had befriended the family. At the same time they were frequently called on to help their father with his milk deliveries, especially to the Banff Springs Hotel which had become by far his best customer. Soon they were on familiar terms with Mathews and their knowledge of the area so impressed him that, even though they were mere boys, he began to ask them to guide the odd fishing party out from the hotel. After these initial trips they often spent their summers working as guides for the CPR. Jim, as pointed out, was attached to the Lake Louise Chalet in 1898.

Meanwhile, Bill began to spend the winter months tending bar for his uncle, James I. Brewster, at the Russell House Hotel in Golden. This occupation was not without its attendant hazards. In the course of one of the frequent bar room brawls he found himself acting as the floor for a particularly large lumberjack dancing a jig in

his spiked boots. He was to bear scars as a constant reminder of the incident for the rest of his days. The job helped to keep him well-occupied until 1898 when he got restless and decided to take a string of horses north to sell to the thousands of foot-weary souls heading for the Klondike. He got as far as the headwaters of the Liard River before deciding to call it quits. Fortunately he was able to trade horses for some furs which fetched a good price when he reached Edmonton in October.

After playing hockey for Edmonton's Thistle Club during the winter of 1898-99, Bill found his wanderlust at least temporarily cured and he returned to Banff. There he and Jim decided that it would be to their advantage to go into the outfitting and guiding business on a full-time basis. The summer of 1899 was mainly spent securing additional horses and equipment, with the aid of their father, and in taking a few short outings. By the spring of 1900 they were eager to get firmly established and began to advertise their services as "W. & J. Brewster, Guides and Packers" in the columns of a recently initiated local newspaper, *The National Park Gazette*. But assisted only by William Twin, the boys were limited in the number of parties that could be guided in any one summer. Another drawback was the fact that their customers continued to be almost exclusively short trip sightseers and fishermen from the Banff Springs Hotel while the more extensive mountaineering, exploring and hunting parties fell into Wilson's hands. As a result, other sources of income were needed, and Bill became the park's first fire guardian in 1901. This job paid him a respectable $50 a month for patrolling the railroad's right-of-way to extinguish small fires and for checking locomotives to see that they had proper fire screens.

Finally, early in 1902, Bill and Jim agreed to take part in an experiment which was to quickly remedy their business difficulties. The experiment was the CPR's offer

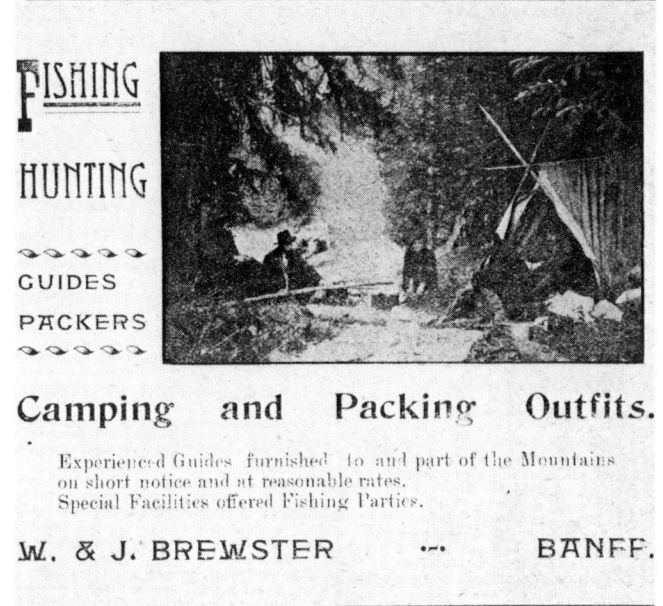

Bill Brewster saddling a horse at the Brewster Dairy corrals, ca. 1904.

to pay their way to New York in order that they could appear at the annual Sportsman's Show in Madison Square Garden to advertise the railroad and the beauties of the Rockies as well as their own services. Only with the continued assistance of their father, who helped defray expenses, were they able to accept the offer, but they soon found that any costs incurred were well worthwhile. Their authentic depiction of trail life in the mountains, complete with teepee, proved a tremendous drawing card. What started as a one time effort soon developed into an annual event supplying them with many new and wealthy customers. The financial assurance that these customers provided allowed them to expand their operations, and by the end of 1903 they had amassed a string of 75 pack horses and were employing a considerable number of men.

Forming the nucleus of their guides and packers were those who had previous experience on the trail in the vicinity. When looking for manpower Bill and Jim naturally wanted to obtain the best available and they were to be found in Wilson's corps of well-trained men. Several of their original employees came from this source, including Tom Lusk, Frank Wellman, Fred Tabuteau, Bert Sibbald and Bob Logan, the latter two from ranches in the foothills country east of the mountains. Added to these were the younger Brewster sons, Fred, George, Jack and Pat, who aided their brothers whenever possible, and several as yet inexperienced but capable men who would eventually establish excellent reputations for themselves. Among the most noteworthy of these were Bill Potts and George Harrison.

Potts, born at Plattsburg, New York around 1885, moved west when quite young to live with his grandparents Mr. and Mrs. James Potts, an elderly Scots couple who had come to the Morley district to homestead. His father, William J. Potts, was a partner in the Alberta Hotel at Banff prior to 1903, and young Bill attended school in the town during the winter of 1901-02. After an abortive attempt to reach the Klondike and some time spent cow-punching at Morley, he came to Banff permanently in 1903 and hired on with the Brewsters, whose acquaintance he had made during his school days.

Harrison, born at Sibley, Iowa in 1887, spent part of his youth in Billings, Montana before coming to Canada at the age of thirteen. He first went to work on a ranch in the Cochrane district, but eventually found employment on a horse ranch which the Brewsters were establishing on the Red Deer River. Because of his obvious horse sense, he was quickly invited to come to Banff to serve on their trail crew, and in 1903 spent his first summer in that capacity.

As the Brewsters' business expanded they gradually began entering into a more formal relationship with the CPR. Because of their early work for Mathews and the success of the Sportsman's Show concept, they were soon on familiar terms with many of the company's top officials. This, combined with their solid support of the then governing Liberal party, soon led the railway to consider granting them a concession. The plum, of course, was Banff, and in the spring of 1904 the sole rights to out-

fit parties from the Banff Springs Hotel were allotted them, the terms apparently being the payment to the company of ten percent of all monies collected in return for the privilege. At the same time they were reorganized and refinanced, and in May, 1904 began advertising themselves as "Brewster Brothers, Guides and Packers to the Canadian Pacific Railway Co." The refinancing was largely accomplished through the inclusion of two American partners, Philip A. Moore and Frederick B. Hussey, in the new organization.

Moore and Hussey were classmates at Princeton University in the class of 1902. Moore had been born at Bayonne, New Jersey in 1879, his family being heirs to the Old Crow Whisky Distilleries fortune. Hussey was a native of Pittsburg, where his family were involved in Hussey, Howe and Company, the country's pioneer manufacturer of crucible steel. At school the two were drawn into a close friendship by their shared love of athletics and the outdoors, both becoming members of several university teams. Moore in particular excelled,

Philip Moore and Fred Hussey.

tying for the United States intercollegiate championship in pole vaulting in 1901 and winning the championship on the parallel bars in 1902.

During the 1902 term the pair's interest in the outdoors led them to the Sportsman's Show in New York where they met the Brewster brothers and talked with them of the excellent hunting to be had in the Rockies. Deciding that they must go and see for themselves, they were able to convince their respective parents to make such a trip the reward for successful graduation. Fortunately both managed to pass their examinations and that fall, under Jim Brewster's personal guidance, were treated to one of the most exciting experiences either had ever enjoyed. The friendship which evolved on this occasion brought the two back for a further hunting trip the following year, at which time they expressed an interest in investing in the Brewsters' business if the opportunity presented itself. The offer was taken seriously, and when it became obvious that the CPR concession was about to be obtained Bill and Jim contacted them and worked out an agreement.

In order to celebrate their newly founded partnership a particularly strenuous trip was planned for Moore and Hussey's visit of 1904. Beginning early in July, an advance party with eighteen pack horses under the direction of Bill Potts was sent north through Wilcox Pass and then down the Sunwapta and Athabasca as far as Athabasca Falls. Here Potts awaited the rest of the party, which included not only Moore and Hussey but also Halsey Williams, a Princeton classmate, and Dr. Stearns, a well-known manufacturer of patent medicines from Detroit. Guiding them was Jim Brewster assisted by packers George Harrison, Fred Tabuteau and Bob Logan and cook Sid Collins, an Englishman living in Banff.

On rendezvousing with Potts near the end of July, the party continued on down the Athabasca to the vicinity of the mouth of the Miette River where a permanent hunting camp was set up. For two months this camp served as a base for several excursions, including a trip by Brewster and Hussey back to Banff and then on to the Ice River where the company had another large party out for a six week trip. Near the end of September, Bill Brewster and Bert Sibbald arrived at the hunting camp to help Potts bring Dr. Stearns and his trophies back to Banff. However, Jim Brewster and the rest of the party pushed on to the Yellowhead Pass, over to the headwaters of the Canoe River, down it to Boat Encampment and then down the Columbia to Donald and finally returned to Banff. Although little was thought of it at the time, this circuitous trip proved to be a very historic journey for it marked the first recorded occasion that a party starting out from Banff had succeeded in reaching the Yellowhead district.

Moore and Hussey both returned to the States at the end of this exhausting summer, but when they arrived

The Brewster party on its way to the Yellowhead in 1904. Standing (left to right) are Bob Logan, Sid Collins, Phil Moore, George Harrison and Jim Brewster. Seated (left to right) are Fred Tabuteau and Halsey Williams.

Brewsters' livery stable and store on Banff Avenue.

again the following spring it was with the intention of staying. Along with Bill Brewster they became involved in the construction of a large residence across Banff Avenue from John Brewster's original lease. Known as the Brewster Bungalow, it soon became a notorious bachelor's haven housing many a wild and woolly guest. Despite his earlier plans, Hussey did not remain an occupant for long, preferring to spend most of his time in the States and becoming more or less a silent partner in Brewster Brothers. Not so Moore who became a permanent resident of Banff involved in all facets of the company's interests. In fact his close association with the Brewster family soon became even further cemented when, in January, 1907, he and Pearl Brewster were married.

Stimulated by the capture of the outfitting concession and its restructuring and refinancing, the company immediately began to diversify itself. The preliminary step taken in 1904 was the investment of $5000 in a livery service, known originally as Banff Livery but later as Brewster Brothers Livery. During the same year the construction of a large general store next to the King Edward Hotel on Banff Avenue was initiated. Another interesting project was the building of a combination boarding house-bakery on a lot behind the same hotel. The boarding part of the structure, quickly dubbed "The Birdcage," became the abode of the Brewster guides and packers when they were in off the trail, and if its walls

could have spoken they soon would have been able to tell many a tale about all night card games, drinking bouts and sundry other carouses.

Perhaps the most impressive enterprise taken on by Brewster Brothers at this time, though, was the erection of a large entertainment hall to serve the needs of the town's growing population. Originally known as the Brewster Opera House, the commodious structure was first located on Bear Street, but in 1913 the building was moved to a new site on Caribou Street and renamed Brewster Hall. It opened its doors to the Banff populace for its premiere performance on June 1, 1905, when Dale's English Opera Singers, a troupe of travelling entertainers, gave a concert.

Investment funds required for its new projects were so extensive that when a new and tantalizing proposition was presented to the company the partners were at first unable to accept. When granting the outfitting concession to the Brewsters in 1904, the CPR's officials had decided to retain the rights to the livery service. However, by the spring of 1905 they were finding it so burdensome that they wished to divest themselves of it entirely. The most logical successors were, of course, Brewster Brothers, but they could not raise the capital required to purchase the CPR's equipment. Finally, the management proved so anxious to unload the business that they themselves agreed to lend the necessary funds, with liberal terms of repayment. The deal was completed in

June, 1905, and with it went the sole right to solicit conveyance at the Banff Springs Hotel and on the platform of the Banff station. As in the case of the outfitting concession, Brewster Brothers had to pay for the privilege. For the first year the price was $1500 for the combined outfitting and livery contract. In addition to this they had to supply livery free of charge to CPR officials and be prepared to carry any number of passengers, no matter how few or many, upon demand. Among the equipment turned over in the agreement was the hotel's famous four horse tally-ho (multiple passenger buggy) which had made its maiden appearance on the road between the Banff Springs and the station the previous year.

With their new and time-consuming interests to look after, by 1905 Bill and Jim had little time to devote to the personal guiding of the parties which they outfitted. Therefore they constantly needed to be on the look-out to find new and able trailmen. Many colorful characters thereby found their way into the ranks of the company's corps of guides and packers, some of whom remained for only a short period and others who found the life of their liking and stayed on. Two of the latter variety, who became recognized as a pair of the most interesting individuals ever to trail the Rockies, were Herbert Alonzo "Soapy" Smith and Nello "Tex" Vernon-Wood.

Soapy Smith, named after the famous character of Yukon fame, was born in Vermont and first came to Canada in 1904. After working briefly for the pioneer rancher Frank Ricks near Morley, he had his half brother Fred Scott established their own ranch in the Jumping Pound district. Quickly tiring of spending the entire year on the range, Soapy appeared at Banff in the summer of 1905 and was hired on as a harnessmaker by Brewster Brothers. Although happy in this job, he was always anxious for the opportunity to get out on the trail. Finally Bill Brewster relented and allowed him to accompany a party as cook. This marked the inauguration of a twenty-four year career as cook, packer, guide and outfitter combined with his winter occupation of ranching.

With wire-rimmed glasses and a visage somewhat like "a combination between a walrus and Teddy Roosevelt," as one dude later put it, Soapy was a rather droll individual who rarely cracked a smile. Yet his reputation as a humorist and practical joker was unsurpassed in the annals of the Canadian Rockies. He could add a light note to even the most glum of situations, a talent witnessed by a group of fellow trailmen who visited him at his ranch one wintry Christmas eve. The rather downcast group was sitting around the fireplace drinking and swapping lies while a blizzard howled outside when Soapy suddenly got up and announced he was going outside to clean the barn. The guests were somewhat surprised that he should pick that particular moment to perform the chore but said nothing as he disappeared into the swirling wind without. A short time later he returned and sitting down to resume his drink remarked offhandly, "Well, if Jesus Christ wants to be born tonight the stable's ready."[9] Un-

Soapy Smith at rest.

doubtedly the remark helped to buoy his visitors' spirits considerably.

Tex Vernon-Wood was cut from much the same mold as Soapy Smith. Coming from Haddon Hall, England around the turn of the century, he lived at Medicine Hat with his mother until her death in 1905. He then went to work on a ranch near Gleichen where, during the round-up of 1906, a horse fell on him badly injuring his leg. A cure in the famous hot springs at Banff was suggested and so, with only three dollars in his pockets, he set out for the mountains. The second day in town he disposed of the three dollars in the King Edward Hotel bar where fortune quickly led him into an acquaintance with the smooth-talking Jim Brewster. It was a fairly simple matter for Jim to convince him to go back exactly where he wasn't supposed to be — on top of a horse. Shortly after joining Brewster Brothers it became apparent that a handle like Nello Vernon-Wood was going to cause him no end of grief working with their rough-and-ready bunch, and he was soon telling his dudes that his name was simply Wood. However, when he returned to Banff wearing a pair of Texas bat-wing chaps after a trip south of the line, fellow guide Jim McLeod tagged him with "Tex".

Tex worked eight summers with Brewsters before joining the warden service and later going into outfitting on his own. Most of his time was spent as a guide at Lake Louise. There he lived in a teepee which never ceased to be a source of amazement to new clients. On more than one occasion his uninitiated eastern guests adamantly demanded that their precious gear be moved outside if he was going to insist on incinerating himself by lighting a campfire in the structure. They usually returned sheepishly to the warmth of the fire a short time later musing on how such a thing was possible. These and numerous other anecdotes about his "Pilgrims," as Tex referred to the dudes, provided a wealth of material for the highly amusing articles he would begin writing for several American sporting magazines in the nineteen-thirties. The most successful of these was a series known as "Pipestone Letters" which started appearing in *Hunting and Fishing* in June, 1935.

Prior to the granting of the CPR concession to Brewster Brothers in 1904 their main competitor for the outfitting business of the Banff Springs Hotel was Bill Peyto. Peyto had remained Wilson's most knowledgeable and popular guide until 1900 when he left Banff to take part in the Boer War. This interlude in his life came about as a result of rather odd circumstances. He and Jack Sinclair were sitting around one evening in Bill's cabin drinking and discussing the war when it was decided that, both of them being loyal subjects of the British Empire, one should volunteer while the other stayed home to work their copper claim. To determine the lucky participant a coin was flipped and Bill was the winner. He immediately enlisted in Lord Strathcona's Horse under the command of General Sam Steele.

Peyto's experiences on the veldt fighting the wily Boer were later to make excellent fodder for the nightly tale swapping around the campfire. One of the most popular stories, as first related by Steele himself, was about Bill's assignment to draw fire:

Somewhere Bill 'salvaged' an umbrella. He tied it to his saddle and carried it wherever he went. What for? Well, we'd be riding over the veldt and come to a kopje. Bill would dismount and open up the 'brolly' [and] parade up and down just within long rifle range. If someone took a pot at him the inference was that the boer were concealed in the hills.[10]

Bill's bravery in these and other hazardous circumstances resulted in two horses being shot out from under him and soon led to a promotion to corporal. It was to be short-lived. To celebrate his success he felt a spot of liquor was called for and was moved to 'borrow' an officer's cape coat containing several bottles. General Steele promptly learned of the incident and immediately ordered the return of the coat and its valuables. Back came the garment but considerably lightened of its contents and before long Corporal Peyto was stripped of his new rank and two months pay.

Bill returned from the war early in 1901 to a hero's welcome at Banff, whereupon he made his decision to go it alone in the outfitting business. Although somewhat short on horseflesh and equipment for his first year's endeavors, he was able to borrow what was needed from

Wilson. By 1902 the shortages had been rectified and he had completed the construction of a corral on his lot as well as expanding his land holdings near Cochrane for winter pasturage. Putting his business on a firm basis was not his only major accomplishment of that year, as on January 9th the taciturn and elusive bachelor was married. His bride was Emily Wood, a sister of fellow guide Jim Wood, from Eburne, B.C. where her father was a merchant and later mayor. The marriage, which tragically ended with Emily's premature death in 1906, resulted in the birth of one son, Robin. The boy so caught his father's fancy that his picture dominated Bill's 1906 advertising calendar while he relegated himself to a much smaller photograph in the lower corner.

When entering into outfitting in 1901, Bill was fortunate in being able to capitalize on the contacts and excellent reputation which he had established during his years with Wilson. This he did in his advertisements, citing as references "Members of the American and English Alpine Clubs." Also, his acquaintance with the powers in the CPR allowed him to advertise as "Guide for the CPR hotel" until the Brewster concession put an end to the privilege. Both these ploys ultimately led to the attraction of many new customers, but at the outset his major parties were composed of those he had already taken out on the trail and had impressed with his abilities. Such was the case with his first "long trail" expedition as an independent outfitter, that of James Outram in 1902.

Outram and Peyto's first trip together had been a whirlwind affair the previous fall after they had completed their respective time with Whymper. The former Vicar of St. Peter's, Ipswich, Outram had first come to Canada for reasons of health in 1900. Later he would become involved in a land company, the Northern and Vermilion Development Company, which had considerable interests in northern Alberta but which, like so many similar ventures, would eventually go bankrupt after the First World War. In the meantime, though, he would inherit a baronetcy and retire to Calgary from where he would continue to make frequent visits to his beloved mountains.

During his 1900 trip with his brother, Outram accomplished several ascents in the Lake Louise and Field areas and also caught a glimpse of Mount Assiniboine from the summit of Cascade Mountain. This peak he made his main objective for the 1901 season but held little hope of achieving it because his financial position would not allow the expense of outfitting an attempt on his own. However, while climbing and exploring with Whymper, word reached camp of the failure of Wilcox and Bryant to conquer Assiniboine on a recent attempt. As the failure was being discussed around the campfire and Outram was lamenting his inability to even attempt the mountain, Peyto unabashedly asserted that from his knowledge of the peak it should present no serious difficulties for the experienced mountaineer. Furthermore, if the occasion should ever arise he would guarantee to get a party from Banff to Assiniboine in two days and back in less, thereby making the trip of little expense to his client. The abrupt termination of his employment with Whymper allowed him the opportunity to make good on this boast.

As it transpired, Bill was to prove as good as his word. Meeting Outram and his two Swiss guides at Banff, he set out on August 31st with a four horse pack train assisted by Jack Sinclair. Following the trail pioneered by Campbell and Wilcox in 1899, he delivered his party to the base of Assiniboine on September 1st, easily establishing a record for the short duration of the trip. The next day he accompanied Outram and his guides to a high altitude on the south-western side before leaving them to their own devices while he prospected for minerals. Due to poor visibility the climbers reached only a secondary summit on the first attempt, but on September 3rd almost exactly the same route was followed to the true summit.

Returning to base camp from where Peyto and Sinclair had seen them reach their goal, the summit party was greeted with congratulatory shouts and "strains of martial music from the latter's violin," a famous instrument which Sinclair had constructed from the remains of a round cheese box scrounged from Dave White's store. The trip back to Banff proved even more hurried than the outward journey, and Outram re-entered the town only five days and five hours after his initial departure, anxious to tell the world of his grand conquest.

Success in tackling Assiniboine in 1901 was responsible for leading Outram's gaze in the direction of some of the exciting peaks north of the Saskatchewan River for 1902's adventure. As his financial situation had improved the trip he planned was a lengthy one, and Peyto was at first at a loss as to who to send out with it. Jack Sinclair had decided to test his fortune in the gold fields of South Africa, and since Bill had to give his new business constant attention he could not afford to spend too much time away from his headquarters. Luckily he was able to find two of Wilson's former men who were at loose ends and convinced them to take on the job. The two were Jim Simpson and Fred Ballard.

Ballard had much the same kind of background as Fred Stephens, coming to Banff around 1900 with his brother Jack from the Michigan woods where he had virtually been raised with an axe in his hands. Working with Wilson for a short time, his first trip had been in 1901 when he acted as cook on Habel's second expedition in the Rockies. This was an attempt by the zealous professor to reach Athabasca Pass and to study the region between the Bush and Wood Rivers, but the effort had fallen short of the mark and turned out to be mainly an exploration of the Fortress Lake area.

Habel had tried to get Fred Stephens as guide, but since he was elsewhere occupied the party had been put in the charge of Dan Campbell, Bob Campbell's brother, assisted by Joe Barker and Ballard. Habel and Ballard did not see eye to eye and had locked horns frequently while on the trail, especially since Ballard always referred to Germans as Dutchmen. When constantly reminded by Habel that "Shermans are not Dutchmen" Fred's standard reply was that they were all "squareheads" anyway, and the perturbed professor could do nothing but throw up his hands in disgust and mutter, "ach, such arrogance."

While making a detailed examination of the Fortress Lake area, Habel had been searching constantly for the trail blazes of the A. P. Coleman party, which had penetrated to the same vicinity in 1892. Shortly after returning to Europe from the trip he died unexpectedly, and upon being informed of his death Ballard was heard to mutter, "Good, he can see the blazes now."[11]

The Outram party set out from Laggan on July 8th with fourteen horses to carry the abundant provisions brought along to prevent the suffering of "privations more or less severe" that had to date been the lot of those venturing north. Because of the need for his presence at Banff, Peyto accompanied the party only as far as the Saskatchewan before turning over responsibility to Simpson and Ballard. Thereafter, the two were to prove equal to the tasks facing them north of the river where, as

Fred Ballard.

usual, the trail needed constant clearing. On the few afternoons that such was not the case or Outram and his Swiss guide Christian Kaufmann were on the heights, they busied themselves building rough cabins which they expected to use while trapping the next winter.

Outram's primary objective was to climb the peaks and map the Divide between the Freshfield Group on the south and the Columbia Icefield on the north. He decided to begin in the north with Mount Columbia, one of the most striking peaks in the Rockies. Simpson requested permission to accompany him on the first ascent on July 19th, but to his surprise was abruptly turned down. However, he was able to gain his revenge a few days later when Outram asked for his help in carrying some heavy survey equipment to the top of Mount Lyell and he flatly refused. Eventually, Jim was to have his day on Columbia for twenty-one years later he took part in the second ascent with Dr. J. Monroe Thorington of Philadelphia.

After the ascents of Columbia and Lyell were completed, Outram had the pack train move on to the Mount Forbes region where, by prearrangement, he was to take part in a stint of climbing with Collie's party. After his misbegotten adventure on the Bush River in 1900, Collie had spent the 1901 season climbing in Norway and the Lofoten Islands. But at Stutfield's instigation it was decided to return to the Rockies in 1902 and lay seige to much the same group of mountains as Outram had

designs upon. Although the latter had written to Collie early in March, 1902, hinting at a combination of forces, the professor was at first reluctant to agree. As Collie put it, he preferred that "the people who first started the mountaineering out in the Rockies get some of the scalps," and that as an "interloper" Outram should be circumvented. By June, though, he had come to the realization that a temporary joint effort might be mutually beneficial and laid the appropriate plans to bring it about. For purposes of a guide, he confided to his companions, "I must have Fred" and wrote to Wilson to make the arrangements.[12]

Collie was quickly to learn that his old outfitter could not comply with the request as Stephens, like Peyto, had decided to go his own way in the outfitting and guiding business. Apparently he and Wilson had had some sort of disagreement as Fred later wrote Collie that "Tom is no longer a friend" and this had led to his decision to strike out on his own. Fred was by this time married, had a small son, and was living near Lacombe, Alberta. There he was to make his headquarters for the next few years, recruiting most of the men needed for his outfit from among the many new settlers appearing in the district at the time. When eventually contacted personally by Collie for the 1902 trip, he decided to employ Dave Tewksbury and Clarence Murray, two recent American immigrants, and Jack Robson, his close friend from Banff.

Meeting Collie, Stutfield, Woolley and the American George M. Weed at Laggan on July 23rd, Fred was astounded to see what his clients expected him to pack. Because of the disappearance of substantial amounts of their baggage, the Englishmen had been forced to borrow what they could in Banff, including a large mattress. "What's this blamed truck?" questioned the disbelieving guide while Robson inquired if they should await the wardrobe and the rest of the bedroom suite before proceeding. Upon being provided with an explanation, Fred agreed to attempt to pack the monstrosity, which with considerable sweat and vituperation he succeeded in doing. However, it would remain for the entire trip the butt of many jibes and a source of constant irritation since the cayuse assigned to carry it would vent his displeasure by depositing it unceremoniously in the middle of the trail at every opportunity.

On their way northward the climbers tested their skills by conquering Mount Murchison, which had defeated them in 1898, while the as yet green packers took wonder and delight in the unfamiliar mountain scenery which unfolded before them. En route a visit was also made to Simpson and Ballard's trapping cabin on the Mistaya River, giving Collie cause to cogitate on the "grit and endurance" that a man must possess to deal with such wild country during the frigid winter trapping season.

Joining Outram at the junction of the streams emanating from Mount Forbes and the Freshfield Glacier on July 31st, the party was surprised and

Launching "The Glacier Belle" on Glacier Lake, 1902.

somewhat chagrined to learn of his recent successes on Columbia and Lyell. But despite the barely concealed undercurrent of resentment, the combined group spent what all admitted was a truly glorious eleven days together. Mount Freshfield was ascended on August 4th, and after three days of trail cutting by Simpson, Ballard and Stephens to get to the base of Mount Forbes, the magnificent 11,852 foot peak guarding the headwaters of the Howse River was captured.

At that point the two groups split up and went their own separate ways. Outram returned to the West Branch (Alexandra) River and made the first ascents of Mounts Bryce and Alexandra before completing the first traverse of Mount Wilson on the journey back to Laggan. The Collie party moved at a more leisurely pace, ascending Howse Peak and then continuing on to Glacier Lake in order to explore the nearby Lyell Glacier. Since the undergrowth around the lake made passage virtually impossible, Fred was once again called upon to demonstrate his skill with an axe in the building of a raft. According to

Collie, the finished product and its navigational conduct proved to be quite a sight:

It was a large and very fine specimen of naval architecture made of good sized logs lashed together with cinches (pack ropes), and wooden cross-pieces and branches laid thereon to raise our goodly pile of baggage above the water. She was named "The Glacier Belle", but we had no liquor to waste on her christening. The baggage was brought down on the horses, and piled up and lashed securely on the raised portions of the raft, the edifice being fitly crowned by the colossal form of the mattress amid jeers from the packers. Punting poles were fashioned out of pine saplings; Fred sang out, "All Aboard" and with everybody pushing and shoving with poles and chattering a strange medley of railway and nautical jargon, we committed ourselves to the deep.[13]

As it transpired, the planned examination of the Lyell Glacier had to be curtailed because of a raging forest fire that suspiciously seemed to originate from one of Outram's former camping places. The return trip to Laggan was therefore soon begun and was completed in five days, with a brief stopover to complete the first ascent of Mount Noyes.

All in all, the Outram and Collie expeditions made 1902 the most productive year ever in the Canadian Rockies from a mountaineering standpoint. Outram alone was involved in first ascents of ten major peaks while Collie's party participated in five, allowing him to substantially complete his map of the southern portion of the Rockies. The successes of the respective parties also reflected well on both Peyto and Stephens in their quest to establish reputations as outfitters. In addition, the season helped set the stage for their colleague Jim Simpson.

Simpson had remained in Wilson's employ at least until 1900 and probably right to the end of 1901. In 1898 he had passed his twenty-first birthday and "immediately cabled our English lawyers . . . to get the legacy coming to me on that date from some relative I never knew who, in a moment of weakness, left it thus."[14] With the money he had begun to buy some horses and saddlery with a view toward eventually going out on his own. The impetus was provided by the trip in 1902 for Peyto when it became apparent that Simpson could probably outfit such a party himself. Unlike Peyto and Stephens, though, he did not believe in spreading himself too thin merely for the sake of independence and accordingly began to scout around for a suitable partner. He managed to find one in the person of George Taylor, a Yorkshireman who had been a rancher prior to becoming chief packer for A. O. Wheeler's Selkirk Range topographic survey in 1902.

Since Taylor had been able to secure the CPR concession at Glacier House, he preferred to work out of that location; Simpson found the surroundings of Banff more to his liking. An arrangement was therefore formulated in the spring of 1904 allowing Taylor to handle the Glacier end of the business while Jim took care of the Banff end. Soon the partners had two excellent men working for them: Ernest Brearley, a former stockbrokers' clerk from Yorkshire, and Sydney Baker, an apprentice surveyor from Suffolk, both of whom had come to Canada after returning from the Boer War. Some of Simpson and Taylor's work continued to be provided by surveys, but a few private clients also began to come their way. The most notable of these were Professor W. H. Schulyer of Ypsilanti, Michigan and Mary de la Beach-Nichol of England. Schulyer was taken out from Glacier House by Taylor and Brearley to make scientific observations on the Asulkan and Illecillewaet Glaciers while Mrs. Beach-Nichol was guided from Banff by Simpson and Baker to engage in entomological studies in the Yoho Valley.

Syd Baker and his family at Glacier House.

Although the 1904 season proved to be a successful one, Taylor decided that ranching, not outfitting, was his true calling. Determining to dispose of his interest in the business, early in 1905 he found an eager purchaser in the person of his affable and educated employee Syd Baker. Simpson and Baker continued the partnership for three years until Syd bought out Jim's interest in the Glacier operation.

For a number of years Baker continued to provide horses and guides to those interested in visiting the popular tourist spots of the region, including the Illecillewaet Glacier, Avalanche and Glacier Crests and the spectacular caves in the Cougar Valley. In addition, he established a curio and photographic tent near Glacier House which became a favorite place for both hotel guests and train passengers to browse. Eventually, though, his mind was affected by the altitude, and after a period of rather strange behavior he sold his outfitting concession to Jim Brewster in 1915. He then moved his family from their permanent residence in Banff to Vancouver, where he became established in the photography business and ultimately developed a highly successful bookstore. As for Simpson, the disposal of his Glacier interest finally left him completely independent as an outfitter, a position he was to maintain for more than four decades.

Phil Moore, Bill Potts, George Harrison and Bob Logan at Ya Ha Tinda Ranch, ca.
1907.

5 Enter the Alpine Club

The proliferation of outfitting and guiding businesses along the CPR line through the Rockies at the turn of the century proved to have both positive and negative aspects. On the plus side, the increasing influx of tourists into the area were provided with the means to pursue their particular interests, be they climbing, hunting and fishing, scientific investigation, exploration or merely sightseeing. Of course, satisfied customers theoretically provided economic well-being for both the outfitters and their employees and for other tourist-oriented businessmen as well. But detracting from these benefits were two very real considerations: firstly, the implications that the seasonal nature of the business had for those engaged in it; secondly, the possibility that increased competition might eventually force some outfitters entirely out of business.

The seasonal nature of outfitting caused unemployment or the necessity of finding supplemental income for most of those who chose to remain in the mountains for the winter months. Beginning in April with the first spring bear hunt, the trail season built to its peak in July and August with fishing, climbing, exploring and scientific parties and culminated with the final sheep or goat hunt in October. At that point it was the custom for the men coming in off the trail to gather at Banff for the annual Packer's Ball. Initiated in 1902, the ball soon became the social event of the year for the Banff population, featuring dancing till dawn and "huge punch and claret bowls [which] were kept well replenished." Huge was an apt description for the punch bowls as some of the participants at these functions later remembered them to be brimfull washtubs placed at convenient locations on the stage of the Brewster Opera House. While in town, many of those in whose honor the event was staged bunked in at "The Birdcage," thereby annually adding another chapter to its already notorious reputation.

Unfortunately, though, the gala affair marked the last date that most outfitters were able to keep their guides, packers and cooks on the payroll. Prior to 1900, when Wilson employed only a relatively small number of men, the fall layoff did not prove any real problem, but after the nearly simultaneous appearance of several competitors there was a large increase of manpower that had to be dealt with. In fact, even the outfitters themselves, unless they had other enterprises such as Brewster Brothers, had to face the prospect of having no income from their business for a minimum of six months and had to search elsewhere for employment. Most of the men, unwilling or unable to sit idly by for such an extended period, became involved in a variety of winter livelihoods.

In some respects, perhaps, the most fortunate individuals were those who worked for Brewster Brothers as they at least had some chance of being kept on over the period. Although they might be assigned to any of a number of jobs, the most common occupations were those of watching over the large herd of horses on their winter range or working on the ice harvest.

Because of their almost overnight success, Brewsters' stock had increased rapidly, numbering some 250 head in 1905 compared with only 75 in 1903. Even in the earlier years the problem of finding suitable winter pasturage had been a perplexing one but had been temporarily solved by keeping the stock on an excellent range along the upper reaches of the Red Deer River. In 1904 a formal application for a grazing lease on one township of this land was made to the superintendent of the park, but it was refused. However, the next year upon reapplication their request was approved at a cost of $100 per year, and the subsequently famous Yaha Tinda (Mountain Prairie) Ranch officially came into existence. By 1907 a few buildings had been erected on the ranch, and it became customary for two or three men to spend the winter months there seeing to the horses' welfare. Despite it being a rather lonely occupation, there were those who welcomed the opportunity to have a secure job over the difficult winter stretch.

Lasting some six weeks to two months, the ice harvest did not keep men employed for as long a period as did ranch work, but it utilized many more of them. The harvest was the result of a contract by which Brewster Brothers agreed to supply the refrigeration needs of the CPR in Western Canada with ice cut from the Bow River. The harvest began around the middle of January when the ice had reached a thickness of about two feet and often required as many as fifty men and twenty teams of horses to carry it out. The men were engaged either in the actual cutting of the 700 to 800 pound blocks or in hauling them to the waiting boxcars for shipment to ice storage houses. In a good year the contract might call for the filling of up to 700 boxcars and was a major employer of otherwise idle manpower.

Apart from the foregoing, those trailmen seeking winter jobs were often able to find work in either the mining or lumbering industries, activities which were allowed in the park prior to the enactment of more stringent conservation regulations. Probably the least favored of the two was mining, but due to the relatively high wages to be made and the close proximity of the mines to Banff several men were eventually attracted there.

As early as the mid-eighties coal mines had gone into production a few miles east of Banff at Anthracite, and in 1904 the CPR established more extensive mines at Bankhead on the Cascade River, a few miles south of Lake Minnewanka. But coal mining proved to be a very hazardous occupation, even for those conditioned to the hardships of the trail. For example, in the fall of 1904, it was reported that Jim Wood, fresh from a season of guiding, had badly crushed his foot on his first shift in the Bankhead mines. Similarly, a few years later, the popular Joe Barker was killed at Bankhead when some mining timbers he was unloading fell from a railway car knocking his head against the rails.

Logging was carried out mainly in the numerous timber berths let by the government along the Bow River and its tributaries, the Eau Claire and Bow River Lumber Company being the largest leaseholders. This company engaged in major cutting at several sites on the Spray River, and the trailmen's experience with horses enabled them to find work hauling out logs with two and four horse teams. Others preferred to cut timber for themselves. In the spring of 1900 the citizens of Banff were treated to the sight of Jim Simpson and Ross Peecock driving their logs down the river after a fruitful winter's cutting in the upper Bow Valley. A few years later Jack Otto and Tom Martin began to take out timber near Field for use in making railroad ties which they sold to the CPR.

Another related job, favored by many over the actual cutting and hauling of logs, was the choice and estimation of timber limits for large lumber companies. Timber-cruising, as it was known, attracted many trailmen at one time or another, but one of the most interesting trips experienced by any of them was that taken by Jim Simpson to the vicinity of Fortress Lake for a Revelstoke firm. Starting out with a pack train in the fall of 1907, he found the North Saskatchewan in full flood from recent rains and, unable to get the horses safely across, decided to continue the journey on foot. After rafting the torrent he completed the amazing feat of covering the seventy-five miles to the lake in two and a half days and staked out eleven sections of timber before a party coming up the Wood River from Golden could beat him to it. When he completed the staking he immediately started back for the Saskatchewan, hoping to be home before the snow fell. However, his tight schedule had allowed little chance for eating, and by the time he reached Wilcox Pass the hunger pangs were becoming acute. As the area contained an abundance of grouse he easily managed to kill five and then proceeded to eat them all at one sitting. After a brief halt for rest and disgestion, he continued without stopping to Kootenay Plains, where he felt his pack horses would have by then made their way. As luck would have it, the lumber company ultimately failed to properly register the sections and Jim's payment, which was to have been a commission on the sale of timber, never materialized.

While employment in the mines or in some aspect of the lumber industry provided a means to take up the slack for some, the most popular off-season exploits were undoubtedly prospecting and trapping. Given their individualism, it is not surprising that these men of the trail were attracted to rather singular endeavors which allowed them to work for themselves rather than someone else. Prospecting, of course, was not entirely limited to the winter season. Many times interesting formations were discovered during summer trips but were not re-visited until the late fall when time allowed for more thorough examination and, hopefully, claim staking. After this the winter months were usually spent in the rather onerous chore of developing the claim. On the other hand, trapping was strictly limited to the coldest part of the year when the fur-bearing animals were in their prime and rapid travel over the trapline was made possible by the use of snowshoes.

Wilson, one of the more avid prospectors, had begun his prospecting during 1884 in the regions of Mount Stephen, the Yoho Valley and Quartz Creek. After entering full-time into outfitting he had much less time to devote to it, although he continued to dabble whenever a particularly interesting opportunity presented itself. His favorite locale was in the Ice River Valley where, around 1897, he found traces of two minerals which he was unable to identify. Providing samples to Collie and Dr. Dawson for analysis, he soon learned that they were varieties of sodalite and garnet. But being unable to in-

Bill Peyto at one of his mining cabins near Simpson Pass, 1913.

terest anyone in financing the mining of either mineral, because of their rather inferior quality, he did not bother to register any claims.

Eventually though interest in the sodalite did come from a most unexpected source, Edward Whymper. During the course of his visits to the Ice River in 1901, Whymper examined Wilson's find and took back samples to England with him. Feeling that it would be economically feasible to mine, he had Tom stake a claim in 1903. Over the next few years Whymper launched an elaborate selling campaign through his wide connections in Europe and had several orders in hand early in 1905 when he sent for the first shipment. Inexplicably it did not arrive and Whymper was angry.

I think you know that I am a little sore about the way in which this matter has gone along. You staked a claim, and I understood that it was to be our joint property. A considerable amount was got out, at my expense. I sent for it, and did not get it and was rather led to suppose that it had been annexed by someone else, who had taken possession of our claim. I want my stuff, and want possession of the claim . . .[1]

Although it is unclear what actually did happen, a likely explanation is that when the time came to ship the sodalite the expense was found to be higher than its market value. Whatever the explanation, no further reference to it was made in Whymper's letters to Wilson and they remained good friends.

Bill Peyto, another inveterate prospector, was little more successful than Wilson. Bill's interest in minerals pre-dated his arrival at Banff, and it is quite possible that he spent a few years before going to work for Tom in search of the ever elusive motherlode. Even though he was never formally educated in geology, his enthusiasm for it quickly led him to become self-trained, and he amassed a considerable library on the subject. On countless occasions while out with some mountaineering party, he forsook invitations to scale the heights in favor of prospecting while they were occupied with their climbing.

Peyto's interest lay primarily in the country near Simpson Pass where he staked several copper claims, one of them in conjunction with Jack Sinclair, and near the head of Red Earth Creek where some interesting talc deposits were discovered. Cabins were constructed in both locales, and at the end of the season he would leave Banff to spend most of the winter working the claims. The copper never amounted to much, but the talc offered possibilities provided that a market for it could be secured. However, he was prevented from putting a mine into production by the government's contention that his claim lay within the park boundaries and was therefore subject to stricter rules regarding mining after 1911. Bill disagreed with this, believing his claim lay just outside the boundary and was thereby exempt from park regulations. The adamancy of the park officials soon left him extremely bitter and for the rest of his days he had "no use for the government." In time the claim was taken over by the National Talc Company and during the twenties they did succeed in extracting some talc from it and other claims in the vicinity. Although Peyto's right to the claim was mentioned in company correspondence, there is no record of him having been paid for it.

Fortunately some aspects of Bill's prospecting activities did bear fruit. While searching for minerals he often ran across Indian arrowheads which he eagerly collected. They were later to form one of the most extensive collections ever made in the Canadian Rockies. His interest in geology also extended into the field of paleontology, and fossil remains were likewise collected whenever the opportunity arose. One particularly interesting specimen was discovered near the mouth of Johnston's Creek. This was an almost perfectly preserved specimen of a hitherto unkown species of rhomboid-shaped fossil fish *(Platysomus canadensis)* which was sent to Ottawa to permanently reside in the National Museum.

While prospecting offered little return for time and effort expended, such was not necessarily the case with trapping. There were a few locations left in the mountains where sufficient fur-bearing animal populations remained to make a trapline worthwhile. One of these was the vast extent of country between Bow Lake and Alexandra River where Jim Simpson spent many of his winters. The major attraction was the fairly abundant marten, or Canadian sable, but other species such as mink, lynx, muskrat, fox and bear were present as well.

Beginning in 1901, Jim and his companion Fred Ballard began to construct rough trapping shelters throughout the region and, as mentioned, continued to do so while escorting Outram's party of 1902. Their main headquarters was a well-constructed cabin near the mouth of the Mistaya which was described by Collie on his visit to it the same year: "The interior, which smelt very fusty and damp, was filled with skins, horns, traps of all kinds and sizes — conspicuous among them being two bear traps, cruel-looking instruments like gigantic rabbit-traps, and requiring a force of nearly 400 lbs. to open the jaws when closed — tools of various sorts, and other trappers' implements."[2] Some time later another traveller making his way down the Mistaya also visited this cabin and found a poem pencilled by Simpson on a slab of wood attached to the door:

These few lines are dedicated to the low lived sucker who is in the habit of breaking in here.

*If you look for excitement, be ye here
When the owner hereof is standing near.
Proceed at the game of breaking in,
But mutter farewell to all your kin.*

*You son of a gun(?), you've not the nerve
To let the owner of this observe
The way in which the deed is done
Or, Jesus Christ, we'd have some fun.*[3]

As Collie had noted, trapping in this rugged landscape required "grit and endurance" on the part of those involved, but it also had its lighter side as well. The trapline was invariably a lengthy one requiring several days travel on snowshoes in extremes of weather varying from -50°F. in the midst of a blinding blizzard to +40°F with the onset of a warm chinook wind. Famous for the speed and distance he could make on snowshoes in such conditions, Jim soon earned the name of "Nashan-esen" (wolverine-go-quick) from the Stoney Indians. His partner Ballard, being short of leg and always choosing a wide pair of snowshoes, was not quite so adept. As a consequence of his physical limitations and poor choice of equipment, he was forever stepping on one foot with the other creating what he termed "a buffalo waller" in the snow.

His troubles extended to other types of footwear as well. On particularly warm days when there was little snow the snowshoes were discarded in favor of oil-tanned shoepacks which, according to Simpson, were "slippery as a cable of bannana skins over a cavern in Hell." On one occasion, descending a steep grade from Mount Sarbach, Jim slid on both feet creating a track followed by Fred coming behind. Half-way down the latter's instep caught on a pine pole and he fell head first into a pile of logs. The air turned blue with bad language, and Jim thought it best to hurry on ahead to the cabin and await his partner's appearance. Soon Fred came storming in. He threw his shoepacks in a corner, jammed a cartridge in his rifle and pointed it at his footwear yelling "Move once, just once, you sons of bitches." Roaring with laughter, Jim ducked outside to prevent getting caught in a barrage, but Fred soon cooled off and decided to let his shoepacks live to slip another day.[4]

As spring approached the partners often ran short of supplies, something Jim attributed to Fred's voracious appetite. Early in 1903, with no flour left to bake the ever-popular bannock, it was decided that one of them would have to snowshoe into Laggan to restock the larder. Because Jim could make it faster and knew his partner's penchant for carrying food in his stomach rather than on his back, he volunteered to go. The

Fred Ballard at one of his and Simpson's trapping cabins, 1903.

journey took several days and on his way back he laid over at a little cabin north of Bow Pass in order to hunt goat. While sitting at the cabin's doorway in the evening he heard a crashing in the woods and grabbed his rifle, expecting to see an early spring bear. But soon the night air carried the unmistakable sound of a human voice bellowing "Jesus Christ, lend me your wings." It was Ballard who, feeling the familiar grumbling in his stomach, had set out on broken snowshoes from the mouth of the Mistaya to find Jim and, more importantly, the grub. Floundering through the snow he finally reached the cabin completely exhausted, but was able to summon up enough strength to lay seige to the new foodstuffs. Without a word of greeting he emptied the contents of the pack and went to work until Jim had to stop him or make preparations to go back to Laggan for more.[5]

In the early years of trapping in the Rockies a good winter would see a man clear around $800 for his efforts, but as time went on this proved to be the exception rather than the rule. That and the extreme loneliness of the life soon led Fred to abandon it in favor of the townsman's lot. His last season with Jim was 1903 after which he trapped for one more winter with his brother Jack at For-

tress Lake and then opened a small upholstery and carpentry shop in Banff. Later he went on to become Banff's most proficient house builder due to his innovative use of power tools, the first seen in the town.

After Ballard's departure Simpson carried on the trapline even though such an enterprise was one that was fraught with considerable danger. A man alone in the wilderness had to rely solely on his own knowledge and instincts for survival and could afford to make few mistakes. As Jim himself once put it, if one should seriously injure himself many miles from civilization in deep snow and sub-zero temperatures there was only one recourse,

"Load your rifle and look down the barrel to see if it is clean." A certain element of fatalism was an integral part of every trailman's psyche for they realized that in both their summer and winter activities death was a constant possibility.

Although the problem of winter employment was a major one, it was not as complex as that resulting from the increased number of outfitters and guides working along the CPR after the turn of the century — the potential which existed for the overexpansion of services. If visitors continued to arrive in increasing numbers no hardships would exist, but the tourist trade was subject to yearly fluctuations, caused primarily by the economic situation and the weather. Another related factor was the capability of the various outfitters to handle their finances. Ability on the trail and business acumen by no means went hand in hand, and all too often just the opposite was the case. Even such seemingly secure operators as Brewster Brothers found there were times when they didn't know where their next dollar was coming from. Suprisingly enough, though, the first to feel the squeeze of competition and the pinch of finances sufficiently to abandon the outfitter's life was Tom Wilson.

When coming in from his 1902 expedition, James Outram saw several of Wilson's parties heading north and commented that if his good fortune continued he should undoubtedly soon become a wealthy man. Unfortunately, the observation could not have been further from the truth. Although Tom seemingly had all the work he could handle, he didn't possess a good sense of business and suffered accordingly. His basic weakness stemmed from an easy-going nature which led him not to press too hard for the collection of unpaid bills. Despite the wealth of many of his customers, some were notoriously tardy in paying their debts. On the other hand, they often drove tremendously hard bargains in negotiating the cost of a trip. Sometimes in his early days, not knowing what the future held, he was forced to accept a party at very little profit to himself simply to en-

sure that he could meet the high expense of keeping sufficient numbers of men and horses available in the event of a good season. The CPR concession should have and did remove some of these problems, but even the railway was not noted for being particularly prompt in paying its bills. For example, in January, 1903, Bob Campbell informed Tom that they still had not been paid for several CPR parties from the previous year and that he was having problems meeting their accounts.

Tom had first contemplated retirement from the trail as early as 1898. Upon hearing the rumor, the mountaineering fraternity had been appalled and Professor Fay quickly sent off a missive appealing for him to consider:

. . . I earnestly hope that such is not the case for at first glance (and even on thinking it over) I find it hard to conceive of the region as a field for mountaineering and exploration without you. All this side of tourist interest is so closely connected with yourself in my mind, that I find myself at a loss to see how you could possibly be spared . . . . Who could replace you? [6]

Campbell's purchase of a small share in his business had probably saved the day, and the following few years proved to be the most lucrative Tom ever experienced. By 1904, though, some of his perennial problems were being

John Wilson and Tom Wilson at the Kootenay Plains cabin, 1906.

exacerbated by the appearance of widespread competition. On returning from his foray to the Crowsnest Pass with Whymper, he announced his intention to sell out, and this time no appeal for reconsideration came from any quarter. The logical buyer for his interest was Campbell, and a deal was completed which saw Bob receive full ownership of the business but Tom retain many of the horses and some of the equipment. The horses soon found a home at his ranch on the Kootenay Plains.

Situated on the upper North Saskatchewan River in the area between the mouths of the Siffleur River and Cline Creek, the Kootenay Plains were formed by a series of shingle terraces varying from one to four miles in width and were almost completely ringed by mountains. Having received their name from the Kootenay Indians, who in pre-historic times had annually crossed the Howse Pass from the interior plateau of British Columbia in quest of the plentiful wood buffalo of the region, they eventually became a favorite hunting territory of the Stoney Indians. Game was attracted by the thick "bunch grass," the plains being a true short grass prairie, and by the remarkable winter weather conditions which left the ground virtually free of snow. Such circumstances later made the plains attractive as a site for winter horse pasturage and they ultimately attracted Tom's attention for that reason.

Although he had undoubtedly discovered them early in his mountain rambles, it was not until the winter of 1902-03 that Tom had some Stoneys construct a rough cabin and corrals near the mouth of White Rabbit Creek, where he wintered about forty head of horses. He found the location much to his liking, and his attraction to the area could have been an added consideration in his abandonment of outfitting. Certainly some of the money received from Campbell was put into a stock of trade goods, including rifles, ammunition, flour, tobacco and even a few cattle, which were exchanged for pelts with the Stoneys.

For the next several years Tom spent about ten months of the year trading from his cabin and caring for his increasingly large herd of horses. The practice only came to an end in the winter of 1908 when he almost fell victim to the harsh environment which, despite his long experience, he once regarded too lightly.

The incident occurred near Christmas when the desire to spend the festive season with his family at Banff led him to set off on snowshoes in less than ideal conditions. Beset by a blizzard with plummeting temperatures, he had the misfortune of breaking a snowshoe, and for several days he struggled through waist-deep snow down the Pipestone in a desperate attempt to reach the railroad. Nearing his destination fate once more struck him a cruel blow when he broke through an ice bridge and fell into the river's numbing water. Normally Tom would have built a fire to dry himself out in such circumstances, but exposure had dulled his mind and he

Tom Wilson on snowshoes in heavy snow.

stumbled onward in frozen clothes. Several hours later he had all but resigned himself to his fate when he heard the welcome sound of the whistle from the daily passenger train pulling into Laggan. As close as he was, he barely made it to the station, and had to be immediately transported to the hospital at Banff.

Examination showed that Tom's extremities were severely frostbitten, and eventually four of his toes and a part of each foot had to be amputated. With typical dry humor he later remarked that at least the doctor had enough sense to take the same amount from each foot so that he wouldn't become unbalanced. But even with an optimistic outlook, his convalescence proved to be a lengthy one, and it was not until the summer of 1910 that he was once more fit for travel on the trail.

Before this painful and almost tragic event occurred there were some interesting developments on the Kootenay Plains. During the spring of 1905, Elliott C. Barnes put in an appearance at a location across the river from Wilson's range. Barnes, somewhat of a "rolling stone," came from Bismarck, North Dakota and was in his early thirties when he arrived from Red Deer with a string of horses. Following Wilson's example, he built a cabin and corrals and turned out his horses on what

Elliott Barnes in his cabin at Kootenay Plains.

became known as the Kadoona Tinda (Windy Plains) Ranch. Early in July, 1905, his wife and two young sons arrived to join him at Banff, and he began a small rather short-lived outfitting operation in conjunction with Reggie Holmes, an Englishman recently arrived in the vicinity.

In addition to his trail stock, Barnes also attempted to raise Clydesdales on the ranch, but he soon realized that these heavier work horses were not taking to the surroundings. This setback and his peripatetic nature led him to sell out to Wilson for $450 in August, 1908.

Tom, in the meantime, had begun an attempt to turn his own original squatter's rights into a true lease. Corresponding with Minister of the Interior Frank Oliver, he was informed that since the area had not yet been officially surveyed no lease could be granted. Almost as an afterthought, Oliver added that "hopefully your interests will not be materially affected whether you are covered by lease or not."[7] Such were Tom's hopes as well, but time was to prove them vain ones indeed.

Wilson's departure from outfitting in 1904 was a significant development in the history of the Canadian Rockies. He had personally provided the means whereby

almost every important climbing, exploring or hunting party had penetrated the unknown reaches of the mountains away from the CPR line and, in the process, had become a virtual encyclopedia on the area. In addition, with the exceptions of Bill and Jim Brewster, every individual employed in the outfitting business in a major way had got their start and learned the trade working for him. Now the question was whether his decision to abandon the trail would be emulated by others.

Certainly some of his compatriots must have contemplated the thought in the next few years with the increasingly tight grip of the CPR concessionaires on the cream of the tourist crop. But they all seemed to be able to keep their heads above water, and a few additional competitors even appeared on the scene. Then, in 1906, a new factor came into play — one that for a few years at least was to materially aid the non-CPR people. This was the Alpine Club of Canada, the brainchild of an aggressive and extremely active Irishman who was ultimately to hold a large place in the annals of the Canadian Rockies, Arthur Oliver Wheeler.

Wheeler was a Dominion Land Surveyor who had served his apprenticeship surveying Indian reservations and CPR townsites at various locations in Western Canada prior to 1885. After serving in the Surveyor's Intelligence Corps during the Riel Rebellion, he went into private practice for a few years, but by 1893 was back with the Surveys Branch employed mainly on irrigation work. However, earlier in his career he had been trained by Surveyor-General Edouard Deville in photogrammetry, the method of camera-assisted surveying then being utilized in the Rockies, and it was here that his interest lay. As a result, in 1900, he was assigned to the survey of the Crowsnest coal mining area, and in 1901 was scheduled to participate in surveys along the rail line through the Rockies. But due to the impending arrival of Whymper in the same region, the government decided to shift the survey to the Selkirk Range. Wheeler was placed in charge for both the 1901 and 1902 seasons and by necessity soon became adept at climbing the many and varied peaks of the range. The challenge of these climbs and the inspiration of the views obtained on them convinced him that he wished to spend as much time as possible in the mountains. Happily, after the completion of the Selkirk work, the results of which were later published in his book *The Selkirk Range,* he was assigned to the recommencement of the survey in the Rockies.

Wheeler's appreciation of climbing soon led him into contact with some of the area's foremost mountaineers, in particular Professor Fay. Fay was in the process of resurrecting Philip Abbot's idea of creating an American Alpine Club, and Wheeler discussed with him the possibility of forming a Canadian club at the same time. The professor supported the concept, but Wheeler met with "scepticism and indifference" from all but a few of the Canadians he contacted. Fay then offered an alternative, the inclusion of a Canadian section in the American club.

Attempting to gain support for this new scheme, Wheeler sent letters to many leading newspapers, among them the *Manitoba Free Press.* Immediately he received a copy of that paper with an article in it, signed "M.T," taking him to task for being unpatriotic in even suggesting the idea. Interested by this response he wrote to "M.T." and found, to his surprise, it was a woman writer for the paper, Mrs. Elizabeth Parker of Winnipeg, herself a one time resident and a lover of the mountains. Soon the two had joined forces and were able to convince J. W. Dafoe, the editor of the *Manitoba Free Press,* to open the paper's columns for the promotion of a strictly Canadian club.

Support gradually came from a number of other newspapers and, among others, the CPR and the Banff outfitters, both of whom could see the potential benefits that such an organization could have for their respective interests. However, it was not until February, 1906, that Wheeler felt secure enough in his support to present a plan to the railway. Attending an executive meeting of the Western Division heads held at Mount Stephen

A. O. Wheeler surveying in the Rockies.

House on February 14th, he took the opportunity to approach William Whyte, the Second Vice-President of the CPR, on the subject. His approach took the form of a request for twenty passes to and from Winnipeg from any point on the line to enable delegates to take part in the formation of an alpine club. Whyte readily agreed.

Immediately afterward, Wheeler began pondering a list of names in order to determine who should be invited to the founding meeting. He quickly decided to place a high priority on outfitters. As he saw it, the focal point of the club's activities should be an annual climbing camp in the mountains, and to ensure its success the best guiding and packing services available were absolutely vital. Thus the list ultimately included: Syd Baker, of Simpson and Baker; Bill Brewster, of Brewster Brothers; Bob Campbell and his brother Dan who had joined him in his business; Tom Wilson; and Tom Martin, who had gone into partnership with Jack Otto at Field, Glacier and

Participants at the founding meeting of the Alpine Club of Canada in Winnipeg, March, 1906. Back row — Tom Martin (second from left), A. O. Wheeler (third from left), Tom Wilson (fourth from left) and Bob Campbell (far right). Front row — Dan Campbell (far left) and Syd Baker (second from left).

Leanchoil at the time of the dissolution of the Wilson and Campbell partnership.

All these men were actively engaged in outfitting with the exception of Wilson who was asked because of his wide knowledge of the mountains, his considerable herd of stock that might possibly be placed at the club's disposal, and, not least of all, his reputation as the foremost guide in the Rockies. Wheeler was quick to capitalize on this reputation, arranging a newspaper interview in which Tom could extoll the virtues of the mountains and the concept of a solely Canadian climbing club:

That Canadian mountains surpass in beauty the wider famed beauty spots of Italy, Switzerland and the Himalayas is the opinion held by Tom Wilson, for years a guide in the Canadian Rockies, who has come to Winnipeg to tell of the wonders of the mountains he loves to the delegates to the alpine club . . .

It makes the blood of the old guide boil to realize that English and wealthy Canadians are touring the Alps and the mountains of other countries while the mountains at

home are neglected . . . "It is a sad fact that the beauties of the Canadian Rockies are being discovered and toured by other than the Canadian," said Mr. Wilson. "Tourists from France, Italy and Switzerland have been touring the Canadian mountains while Canadians have been oblivious to the scenery lying in the recesses and valleys of their own mountains. It is for the purpose of securing the interest of the Canadian people in their own beautiful scenic spots that many other men besides myself have come to attend the meeting of the Alpine Club."[8]

Above all, though, Tom deserved a part in the creation of the club because he had been one of the original enthusiasts for Wheeler's idea and had done all he could to foster it. Wheeler, in a letter to Mrs. Wilson at the time of Tom's death, freely acknowledged this fact: "Personally, I feel that it was in a large measure due to Tom's support that I was able to found the Alpine Club of Canada and I always think of him in that regard."[9]

The founding meeting commenced at the Y.M.C.A. building in Winnipeg on March 27, 1906, with all twenty delegates in attendance. Committees, appointed to draw up a constitution and to provide for an election of officers, reported the next day, and the club was formally organized. Wilson was elected to membership on the three man Advisory Committee, and a further committee, comprised of A. O. Wheeler, H. G. Wheeler, M. P. Bridgland and all the outfitters, was appointed to complete arrangements for the first annual camp.

The site chosen for the camp was a little lake on the summit of Yoho Pass, first visited by the Habel party on their way from Emerald Lake into the Yoho Valley in 1897. The spot was an excellent one from the point of view of initiating those unfamiliar with the arts of climbing, the comparatively easy Mounts President, Vice-President, Collie and Burgess being close at hand. But from the packing viewpoint it was not nearly so ideal as it required a trip of approximately twenty miles from the nearest railway depot and an ascent to an altitude of some 6,000 feet at the top of the pass. The prospect was therefore not greeted with a great deal of enthusiasm by the outfitters, particularly since they were not to be paid for their efforts. The extremely limited funds of the club at its inception left no room for payment of horse transport, and Wheeler was fortunate that the outfitters agreed to volunteer their services at the founding meeting.

Given these circumstances, it is not surprising that as the time for the camp approached there began to be a few who had second thoughts about their commitments. Primary among these were Brewster Brothers. At the Winnipeg meeting Bill Brewster agreed to supply ten horses and saddles, but by the end of May he had withdrawn both from the agreement and from the club itself. Reasons for the decision, other than those mentioned, were either simply a case of economics or the even more likely probability of a personality conflict with Wheeler. At any rate, the withdrawal left Wheeler ten horses short and he turned to Wilson to fill the gap, offering him a few added incentives:

Can you arrange to supply ten more than you were booked for. Think we had you down for 8 but I think you will see by referring to the letter I sent you on the subject we will be in a position to pay for these at so much per day. Pack and Riding saddles will be required with them.

I wonder if you heard that you would be in charge of the packing between Mt. Stephen Ho. and camp. Tom Martin is in charge beyond the camp.[10]

Tom complied with the request for the additional horses and saddlery but could not take charge of the packing. The stock and the trading post at Kootenay Plains demanded his full attention during the course of the summer and he made no appearance at the first annual camp. Fortunately, Wheeler was able to convince Elliott Barnes to take his place.

The long awaited event was scheduled to get underway on July 8, 1906, with a rendezvous of the participants at Mount Stephen House in preparation for the trek to the campsite. Some days previously the outfitters and their men began the task of packing in the tents, provisions and equipment necessary to care for the needs and comfort of an expected 112 people. Most of the essentials had been donated — the canvas dining canopy from the CPR, the tents from the Royal North West Mounted Police, Campbell and Baker, and the bunting from Superintendent Howard Douglas. In addition, the CPR had volunteered the services of two Swiss guides, Edward Feuz Jr. and Gottfried Feuz, and the cooks stationed at its now flourishing Yoho Valley camp.

After completing the erection of the camp the men returned to Field with the horses to bring in the neophyte alpinists, and upon arriving at the hotel were greeted by an amazing scene. The circular advertising the camp had specifically outlined the criteria of dress for those in attendance:

Those climbing require heavily soled leather boots, well set with Hungarian nails. Knickerbockers, puttees, sweater and knockabout hat furnish the most serviceable costume.

No lady climbing, who wears skirts, will be allowed to take a place on a rope, as they are a distinct source of danger to the entire party. Knickerbockers or bloomers with puttees or gaiters and sweater will be found serviceable and safe.[11]

Obviously most of the enthusiasts had failed to read the literature as one observer noted that while the costumes were not nearly so stylish as those worn in the Easter Day parade at Atlantic City, they possessed infinitely more variety. Many of the ladies had long skirts and straw hats decorated with flowers, while some of the men wore Derby hats and carried umbrellas. Tom Martin, never one to let such a choice situation slip by without comment, remarked to Wheeler in his humorous drawl, "Say Boss! Git yer eye on them thar outfits what's comin: They're fierce!"[12]

Despite the almost total lack of preparedness and experience of those attending, the week long camp proved surprisingly successful. In all a total of eight peaks were scaled, the qualifying climb for active membership being Mount Vice-President, and several side trips were made, including a two day circuit of Yoho Valley and an expedition to initiate measurement of the Yoho Glacier. The Yoho Valley excursion was particularly well-enjoyed, and the outfitters added to the occasion with their colourful tales around the campfire: "I would like the space to tell of that night in the Yoho around our campfire, of the tales told by Jack Otto — honest Jack Otto — of the bear stories that fell from his lips till the sight or sound of a fat old porcupine made us believe that we were face to face with a grizzly!"[13]

All present at the camp realized that its success was

Participants at the initial Alpine Club of Canada camp at Summit Lake, 1906.

almost entirely attributable to the capabilities of "the men in buckskin." Without their freely offered services and their skill and determination it would not have been possible, a fact commented upon by Wheeler in his rather flowery address to the assembled congregation:

That the first camp has been a possibility is almost entirely due to the loyal patriotism and keen love of the mountains of a number of the prominent outfitters. If you do not know what an outfitter is I can only advise you to make their acquaintance right now. They will tell you more you ought to know in five minutes than otherwise you would learn in a life time. They have placed their resources at the disposal of the camp free of charge and are giving their personal assistance to show us the glories of this mountain world and the wonder of it, in order that you may spread the fame of them the length and breadth of Canada, and make known to our fellow citizens the superb birthright of which we are in posses-

sion. I think it proper that you know the names of the gentlemen to whom we are so greatly indebted, as I feel that all would possibly like to confess their thanks. They are: Mr. R. E. Campbell of Laggan and Field; Mr. Tom Martin and Jack Otto of Field and Leanchoil; Mr. S. H. Baker of Glacier; Mr. E. C. Barnes of Banff.[14]

As it turned out, the club was able to express its appreciation in a more tangible way since the larger than expected attendance put the budget in the black. Among them the outfitters received a "bonus" of $239.

In spite of the meagre returns from the first camp, the outfitters realized the potential of the situation if similar gatherings were held in the future. There was bound to be some benefit for them in the form of private parties after the main camp if the popularity of mountaineering continued to grow. This eventually happened and the annual camp itself soon became a much more lucrative proposition.

The 1907 event was held in the Paradise Valley where the little horse transport required was provided exclusively by Elliott Barnes. But the 1908 Rogers Pass camp was an entirely different proposition. Although the campsite itself was located close to the railroad, the area offered much of interest for those willing to sign up for one of the several two-day excursions offered. These included trips to the Asulkan Valley, where an auxiliary camp was set up, the Illecillewaet Glacier and the Deutschman Caves in the Cougar Valley. All these excursions required both horses and guides making for an excellent pay day for the outfitters involved. Out of a total budget of $2,368 for the camp, $400 was paid for the use of horses, $273 for wages and $138 in the form of a bonus.

The main beneficiaries of this windfall were Simpson and Baker and Otto Brothers, a new organization created by Jack Otto and his brothers Bruce and Closson. The latter two had arrived on the scene from Ontario around 1904 and, like their brother, had gone to work for Wilson. In fact Bruce Otto had been involved in a rather interesting scheme of Tom's. At the instigation of Whymper and several other of his clients, Tom had experimented with the idea of offering boat trips down the North Saskatchewan River from Kootenay Plains to Edmonton. In July, 1904, after the peak of the run-off had subsided, he and Bruce had constructed a canvas boat and made the maiden voyage, experiencing difficulty handling the light craft in the strong current. Because of this Tom decided that a canvas boat was not suitable for the job and, realizing it would not be feasible to use heavier boats because of the expense of shipping them back by rail each time, abandoned the idea. At the end of 1904, with the instigation of their brother's partnership with Tom Martin, both Bruce and Closson went to work for the new company. They remained with it until they themselves joined with Jack to form Otto Brothers in 1907.

Undoubtedly, Simpson and Baker and the Ottos were chosen to handle the outfitting for the 1908 camp because of the proximity of their bases at Glacier to Rogers Pass and because of Wheeler's familiarity with them through survey work. Simpson had been with Wheeler on the Topographic Survey for a time in 1904 and probably again in 1905 while the Ottos had been employed in the same capacity from 1906 onward. During this period Wheeler honored them with the naming of Otto Pass and Creek, part of the watershed of the Amiskwi River.

Wheeler's rather difficult personality, which sometimes bordered on the dictatorial, did not make working for him an easy chore, but those who could handle it were well-rewarded. In his annual address at the 1908 camp he made reference to his desire that there be organized "a corps of reliable guides and outfitters, who shall be available in connection with the work of the Club." In other words, he wanted a club outfitter whose services could always be relied on, thereby eliminating the possibility that all outfits might be tied up when

Bruce Otto at the remains of Rocky Mountain House, 1904.

needed. Because of their excellent service at the 1908 camp, discussions were held with the Otto brothers during the winter, and, in 1909, they secured the valuable appointment of "Official Outfitters to the Alpine Club of Canada." To Jim Simpson went the position of "equerry", their assistant in charge of the horses.

This combination handled the 1909 camp placed on a beautiful meadow near the shore of Lake O'Hara, a camp which saw 190 participants in attendance. The large numbers present demanded a considerable body of men to deal with the transport, and for the first time the outfitters and packers were allotted a separate section of the campsite solely for their own use. Another innovation, also much appreciated, was the organization of a six-day expedition into the Yoho Valley after the completion of the camp proper. Thirty-three took part in the circuit of the valley with packers and horses accompanying them as far as Sherbrooke Lake and then rejoining them at the foot of the Yoho Glacier. The expedition appreciably increased the amount paid for horses and outfitting and helped to point out the wiseness of the Ottos' and Simpson's determination to remain on good terms with "the Old Man."

Wheeler himself was highly pleased with the orderliness and dispatch shown by the outfitters in carrying out their duties and was firmly convinced that his decision to appoint an official outfitter was a good one. This point of view seemed particularly valid in light of what had been transpiring with the CPR concessions.

In 1908 Bob Campbell's contract with the company had expired and instead of renewing it he decided to move on to some other, possibly more lucrative, means of earning a livelihood. A purchaser for the concession was found in Brewster Brothers, a company constantly on the lookout to expand its already considerable interests. The bid was supported by the western officials of the CPR who had close contacts with Brewster Brothers and were not at all averse to seeing the firm secure a complete outfitting and livery monopoly at the mountain hotels. A deal struck during the winter of 1907-08 saw the contract pass into Brewster hands, but Campbell retained control of most of his horses and equipment. These he kept until May, 1909, when, having no further use for them, he sold the lot to Jim Brewster as well. After selling out, Bob moved to Calgary and entered the grain and flour trade, eventually becoming a highly successful businessman. His contacts with friends and acquaintances in the mountains were kept up, though, and by 1913 both Liberals and Conservatives were approaching him to run in the provincial election for Rocky Mountain constituency. He chose to run under the Conservative banner and won the seat by eighty-one votes, holding it for a number of years.

Although the Brewster interests did not achieve a complete monopoly at the CPR mountain hotels until 1915, when they bought out Syd Baker at Glacier, by 1909 it certainly seemed they were about to. There were those who feared for the fate of the independent outfit-

ters in such circumstances, and Wheeler led the opposition to their being forced out. Part of his consideration, of course, may have stemmed from animosity toward Brewster Brothers from their having left him in the lurch before the 1906 camp. In any event, he took every opportunity to speak out against the CPR's movement toward allowing a complete monopoly in this field, which presented an interesting dichotomy, for at the same time he was forced to acknowledge the railway's help and support of the Canadian Alpine Club. His address at the annual camp of 1909 was a good example:

I now wish to call attention to a matter connected with our alpine regions that bids fair to becoming a serious abuse. I feel that it is one against which the Alpine Club, in loyalty to its propaganda, is bound to throw all its weight to prevent so crying an evil. I refer to the determined attempt now being made to create a monopoly of the guide and outfitting business for the mountain centres along the line of the Canadian Pacific Railway. When that railway first opened up the alpine regions of the main range to the mountaineer, the nature lover, the art seeker and the incidental tourist, there was formed in connection with the business a corps of men who were accustomed to wrestle successfully with the forces of nature and who could safely lead the traveller through the mazes of the virgin forest, across the dangerous leaps of the rushing torrent and over the snow-clad passes. These were men who could do things, who knew how to make you as comfortable in a mountain camp as in a palatial hotel, and far happier. The object of the present attempted monopoly is to drive these men out of the field by bringing to bear against them the weight of the huge corporation of the Canadian Pacific Railway Company. Wilson has gone, Stephens has gone, Martin, Peyto, Campbell and others have gone, driven out by the usual methods of monopoly. And the guides of whom Canada's mountain regions were so proud are now only a name. What have we instead? A service of boy youths imported during the holiday season from schools and colleges in the East, on whom is clapped a brand new suit of buckskin and they are dubbed "guides". God save the mark! They remind me of babes in the woods, and the sooner the robins come and cover them up with leaves the better. . . . That minor officials are in sympathy is apparent, and the cry is "We must protect our livery privileges". That is alright so long as such privileges do not infringe the rights of Canadians. The Canadian people have given certain rights to the Canadian Pacific Railway Company . . . but it cannot be that any such privileges were given for the purpose of preventing competent and reliable men from plying a legitimate business in a legitimate way, and from reaping a fair share of the mountain business. . . .

I now wish to make acknowledgement of the valuable assistance given to us at the present camp by the several departments of the C.P.R. — consisting of the loan of two guides for the camp, transportation facilities and sundry other privileges.[15]

As it turned out, Wheeler was hoist on his own petard. The 1910 camp was planned for the Consolation Valley, and, in addition, it was decided to establish a permanent camp in the Yoho Valley on an experimental basis. A double camp demanded additional men, horses and equipment along with careful planning to ensure success. During the winter Wheeler was able to convince the Ottos and Simpson to take on the added responsibility and matters proceeded apace until the very eve of the camp. Then the roof fell in. Without warning the Otto brothers decided to pull up stakes and re-establish themselves in the Jasper district. As usual, Jim Brewster was first on the scene to purchase their business, and with the sale went the contract to handle the Alpine Club's 1910 camps. Wheeler thus found himself in the unenviable position of being forced to rely on the services of a company with whom he was completely at odds. Although Jim Brewster reached an agreement with the Ottos to superintend the outfitting from the Consolation camp, his company handled the transportation into this camp and all the services connected with the Yoho Valley camp. Wheeler found much to be desired in their performance stating that at the Yoho camp the result was "a most indifferent service" and that at the Consolation camp "the service was bungled by incompetent subordinates, causing annoyance to many of our visitors."[16]

The bad experience of 1910 reinforced Wheeler's feelings about the necessity of using independent outfitters. Although it was several years before another official club outfitter was appointed, he continued to use one of the independent outfitters along the CPR line, mainly Jim Simpson, when a camp was held in that region. As a result, the Alpine Club continued to remain an important factor in the financial security of the area's outfitters. But after 1910 it also began to play a role in the new country to the north — Jasper National Park.

An early camp at Swift's in the Athabasca Valley.

6 Away to the North Country

If not for a trick of fate the country around Jasper and not that in the vicinity of Banff would have become the mecca for tourists, sportsmen and climbers in the years immediately after 1885. Historically and geographically the Jasper area held all the advantages. As mentioned, the earliest fur traders had used the Howse Pass to surmount the Rockies on their way to the Pacific slope, but after David Thompson's discovery of the Athabasca Pass in 1811 it became the favored passage connecting Edmonton House on the North Saskatchewan with the Big Bend of the Columbia. Situated astride the transcontinental fur trade route, the Athabasca Valley naturally saw an early development which the Bow Valley was denied. To aid in provisioning the fur brigades a Northwest Company post was established at the north end of Brûlé Lake around 1813. Later relocated on a site at Jasper Lake, the post, which originally was known as Rocky Mountain House, was renamed Jasper House after Jasper Hawse, the trader placed in charge. Complementing Jasper House was a second, somewhat smaller post known as Henry House, which seems to have occupied at different times several locales near the junction of the Miette and Athabasca Rivers. Iroquois Indians, first brought west by the Northwest Company as canoemen, gradually settled in the surrounding area, earning a livelihood working on the fur brigades, trapping and trading with the company.

In addition to those connected with the fur trade, the area was also visited by a variety of other travellers during the three and a half decades between 1835 and 1870. Among others, these included the artist Paul Kane and the Belgian Jesuit Father Pierre J. DeSmet in 1846, Dr. James Hector of the Palliser Expedition in 1859, the Overlanders of 1862 and the Milton and Cheadle expedition of 1863.

Following close on their heels were early surveyors for the CPR. Beginning around 1830 some of the attention which formerly had been exclusively focused on Athabasca Pass had shifted to the lower, more easily traversed Leather or Yellowhead Pass at the head of the Miette River, and the CPR, anxious to find a suitable route through the barrier of the Rockies, was intent upon examining its feasibility for the proposed line. After the exploration of it and numerous other passes by Marcus Smith, Walter Moberly, Henry McLeod and several other CPR surveyors between 1871 and 1880, the Yellowhead was indeed found to be the most practicable pass, and it seemed as though the area would once again enter a new era of development.

However, two factors combined to plunge the Jasper area into relative obscurity for the next thirty years. These were the unexpected and controversial decision by the CPR in 1881 to abandon its proposed route by the Yellowhead in favor of a more southerly line via the Kicking Horse, and the final closure of Jasper House by the Hudson's Bay Company in 1884. After these events the area was to be left for many years solely to its few inhabitants. The ancestors of the original Iroquois, their half-breed relatives, and Lewis Swift, an American who married a Métis and started a small farm in the mid-nineties at the Palisades, were all who stayed.

Among the outfitters along the CPR line there was only very limited knowledge of the country north of the confluence of the Sunwapta with the Athabasca as late as about 1906. The only one of them known to have visited the Yellowhead region from Banff was Jim Brewster, who had guided the Moore-Hussey party of 1904. There was some information available from the Stoney Indians, and a few outfitters had come in contact with Coleman's reports, which pointed out that the Whirlpool River flowing from Athabasca Pass was accessible by proceeding downstream from Athabasca Falls. Unfortunately most of them were only familiar with the upper reaches of the Athabasca, since all the parties they had outfitted who were attempting to reach Athabasca Pass, including Wilcox, Collie and Habel, had fallen short of the mark. Despite their lack of knowledge of the Jasper area, though, it was not long before the pressure of competition began to turn some individuals' eyes toward this undeveloped region as a scene for their activities. The Otto brothers were among them, but they were not the first. That distinction went to Fred Stephens.

The impetus for Stephens' first attempt to reach the Jasper-Yellowhead country was provided by his good friend and frequent client Stanley Washburn. While at college Washburn had done a great deal of reading and research on the mountains of Western Canada and he was puzzled by the blank spaces north of the CPR on most maps. Unable to find any information on the area, he soon decided to examine it for himself. Contacting Stephens in early 1901 to arrange for an outfit, he received a rather sceptical reception as Fred maintained that the country was "out of his beat." Nevertheless he agreed to go, and along with two helpers and a fifteen horse pack train met Washburn at Laggan.

If Stephens had a fault as an outfitter and guide it was that he often failed to take along enough supplies, relying too heavily on the killing of game en route. On this particular outing the grub pile was already low soon after crossing the Saskatchewan, and the party had to lay over in order to hunt sheep. They were able to kill five, but in the process Washburn badly twisted his ankle and had to rest in camp for almost two weeks before being fit for the trail. The shortage of food and the forced delay made any further attempt to proceed northward out of the question and the party returned, ingloriously, to Laggan.

But failure in 1901 only whetted Washburn's desire to achieve his objective, and when he approached Stephens again in 1903, Fred expressed a keen desire in seeing it fulfilled. Again a party set out from Laggan and again delays and shortages of supplies intervened to throw the trip off schedule. This time Wilcox Pass was reached before Washburn's companions decided they wished no more of horses or trails, and the pack string was, once more, turned around.

In spite of the complete lack of success of these two trips, they did awaken within Fred the determination to visit and examine the Yellowhead country for himself. Around 1905 he finally succeeded in doing so after setting out from his home at Lacombe, and he was so impressed with the area he began making yearly visits.

Since there weren't any parties immediately available to outfit in the vicinity, Fred filled his time cruising timber and prospecting around the headwaters of the Fraser River. In the summer of 1907 he paid a short visit to Tete Jaune Cache and there made the acquaintance of Bill and Mort Teare, two veteran prospectors, and Ted

Fred Stephens.

Abrams, their young understudy. Some sixty-five years later Abrams was able to clearly recall the event, as while camped with them Fred made the biggest Saskatoon berry pie he had ever laid eyes on, two inches deep and a full fourteen by seven inches across. The chance meeting with the Teares resulted in the forming of a close friendship, and thereafter Fred spent much of his time in their company.

At the same moment, the long dormant Jasper area was once more on the verge of coming to life with the decision of two new transcontinental railways, the Grand Trunk Pacific and the Canadian Northern, to utilize the Yellowhead Pass for their lines and with the creation of Jasper Forest Park (later Jasper National Park) in September, 1907. This meant that outfitting and guiding was soon likely to become a viable occupation in the district, and Fred prepared himself by learning as much as possible about the areas which would prove attractive from a tourist point of view. As his permanent home was still at Lacombe he would have to bring in his parties from that point, but he had now travelled the mountain trails between the two places on several occasions and was convinced that it was feasible. Not surprisingly his first customer was Washburn in 1909.

Fred had made plans the previous fall to meet the Teare brothers at their mining claim some sixty miles down the Fraser from Tete Jaune Cache and his client eagerly fell in with the idea. The party included a young mining engineer named Sawyer, a cook, and Fred's brother Nick. Nick Stephens had worked throughout the western United States as a lumberjack before returning to the family homestead in Michigan, from where he came once every few years to join his brother on a pack trip. Washburn immediately took a liking to him, describing him as "a day-in-and-day-out, smile-in-the-rain, stick-with-you-in-trouble kind of companion."

The journey turned out to be an epic one lasting from June to October and covering a vast extent of territory. Beginning at Lacombe, they proceeded to the Saskatchewan and then north via the Front Ranges to a tributary of the Brazeau River, which was followed for several days through extensive muskegs. Leaving it and finally gaining the main river, they met a mining engineer prospecting the Brazeau basin for coal. This was probably D. B. Dowling of the Geological Survey of Canada, who inspected the area north of the Brazeau in 1909 under the guidance of Tom Lusk, now outfitting on his own at Morley.

Fred had hoped to reach the Athabasca by crossing the little used Jonas Pass, but a landslide blocked the trail and necessitated heading south over Nigel Pass at the head of the Brazeau to the North Fork of the Saskatchewan and then north by the more conventional route of Wilcox Pass. On reaching the Athabasca it was found to be in full flood, and ten days were spent laboriously cutting fallen timber and fording torrential streams before arriving at the GTP survey line near the Miette.

During this, the most trying stretch of the summer's odyssey, the evening campfires seemed to bring out the best in Fred as he entertained the assembly not only with tall tales but also with dissertations on Darwin, international politics, religion and countless other matters which Washburn never expected to hear coming from the lips of an unschooled guide. Fred also expounded on his philosophy of life, which was fairly typical for one guiding, trapping and prospecting in the wildest reaches of the mountains:

Life is too short to worry about money. If I lose all I have tomorrow, I can get a couple of bear traps and by next spring I'll be on my feet again. The mountains are always here, and I know where there's a bunch of bear and a colony of beaver, and I can get along out here and live like a prince, while Morgan, Rockefeller, and these other poor millionaires are lying awake nights lest someone come and steal their money.[1]

After crossing the Athabasca, six days of recuperation were taken at Swift's homestead before pressing onward to Tete Jaune Cache, eighty miles westward through the Yellowhead Pass. Following a well-worn path, which in parts vied with the early CPR pack trail through the Kicking Horse in treacherousness, the summit of the Yellowhead was crossed. Once over it Fred proposed to examine a reportedly excellent stand of timber in the upper Fraser Valley, but it was quickly found to be completely burnt over and the party was soon once again on its way to a rendezvous with the Teares.

The brothers were eventually encountered at Tete Jaune Cache, and the combined group then boated down the Fraser to the Beaver River, where the mineral claim lay. However, it was now late August, and as Washburn was soon due back at his office desk, little time could be alloted to prospecting. The party quickly returned to Tete Jaune and then set out at a hectic pace back toward the Athabasca. Then, with time of the essence, it was decided to follow the old fur trade trail from Henry House and deliver Washburn to the railhead of the GTP, now some sixty-six miles west of Edmonton at Entwhistle.

The dash eastward proved easy going in comparison to the experiences of some of the summer's other trails, particularly after striking the wagon road and eventually the newly prepared grade for the railroad. On the first of October Washburn was safely deposited in the caboose of a construction train, content at last that he had achieved his eight year dream of experiencing the wilds of the Yellowhead country before the encroachment of civilization.

Retracing the route homeward after leaving Washburn, Fred could not foresee that it would be his second to last journey over that piece of ground for some time. While he had every intention of outfitting from Lacombe again the next season, unforeseen circumstances intervened to make it impossible.

In the course of the winter of 1909-10 Fred and his wife were separated, and she was awarded custody of their young son Jesse. The decision did not sit well with Fred, and one moonlit night in the early spring he kidnapped the boy from his brother-in-law's ranch on the Medicine River west of Lacombe, tied him securely on a pack saddle and set out for the Brazeau River. The police followed in hot pursuit, but once into the mountains he had no trouble eluding them while striking north for his old haunts. The next summer he left the lad in the care of friends while he was on the trail, but in future years often took the boy along on some of his trips. Eventually he left Jesse to stay with an acquaintance in Centralia, Washington where he was able to pursue his interest in music, becoming an accomplished pianist and violinist. Meanwhile, Fred, unable for obvious reasons to return to Lacombe, had decided to make the Jasper-Yellowhead region his permanent headquarters. For the next few years he spent his time timber-cruising and prospecting with his friends the Teares around Tete Jaune Cache and outfitting from a location near Entrance.

At the same time, some important developments had been transpiring in connection with the two competing transcontinental railways that were planning to use the Yellowhead as their route to the coast. The Canadian Northern had been able to get the jump on its rival as its rails reached Edmonton in November, 1905, while the Grand Trunk Pacific's were still several hundred miles to the east. From Edmonton the CNR had pushed on as far as Stony Plain, twenty-five miles westward, by the spring of 1907, but then main line construction had come to a halt while its surveyors and engineers concentrated on laying out various branch lines. The long delay allowed the GTP, whose tracks had not even reached Edmonton until the summer of 1909, to forge ahead and begin the laying out of preliminary survey lines up the Athabasca and Miette Valleys.

As with the earlier construction of the CPR, the beginning of this work brought with it a large influx of manpower from the east. Of course, the surveying and later the construction lifeline past the railhead depended on the horse, and horses naturally meant that a good

many of the men who came were packers. Again, as with the CPR, the majority of them made only a transitory appearance and then moved on, but a few found the Jasper country to their liking and decided to remain and engage in guiding and outfitting. Among their number were Alex Wylie, James Shand-Harvey and John Yates, all of whom eventually acquired excellent reputations working with the tourist-explorers venturing into the region. The first of them to do so was that rather colorful individual John Yates.

Yates was a tall, angular young man who had been born in Blackburn, England in 1880 but had emigrated to California with his parents and their five other children while only a lad of four. He had then been raised on a ranch near San Diego and after completing high school had received $500 from his father to help make a beginning in life. Eventually he followed his older brother Bill to Alberta and, around 1906, joined him on a homestead that had been taken out with a partner, Allan McConnochie, on the west side of Lac Ste. Anne some forty-five miles west of Edmonton.

The homestead quickly became known as the Hobo Ranch because of the partners' generosity in providing a

John Yates packing up camp.

temporary home for footloose young men who were coming into the area trying to find land of their own. In addition to their work on the homestead, the partners were involved in packing supplies for the railroad survey. John's original trip in this capacity was to Prairie Creek in the fall of 1906. However, he first came into real prominence early in 1907 when he was able to outmaneuver, outdrink and outride his opponents in a contest for the contract to carry the mail to the railroad construction camps between Edmonton and Tete Jaune Cache. The mail contract required John to regularly traverse the trail to and from Tete Jaune Cache, and while doing so in the fall of 1907 he chanced to meet the A. P. Coleman party in retreat from Mount Robson.

Coleman, his brother Lucius, and the Reverend George B. Kinney of Victoria had been convinced by A. O. Wheeler at the founding meeting of the Alpine Club of Canada to attempt the capture of Robson, the highest peak in the Canadian Rockies at 12,972 feet, as a fitting inauguration of the club's mountaineering activities. Unable to proceed with their plans until 1907, the party had succeeded in making the difficult journey from Laggan to the Yellowhead only to arrive too late in the season to make a determined bid on their objective. Due to the fast approaching snows of winter a return via Edmonton was imperative, but as they went along some of their pack horses, worn out by the hardships of the summer's trails, were of necessity left behind. The trio was therefore in rather dire straits by the time they happened upon Yates at the Big Eddy camp on the McLeod River. Since Coleman's immediate return to his teaching post in Toronto was imperative, and John was bound for Edmonton on the mail run anyway, he agreed to lend the professor a horse and take him along. Coleman much appreciated the favor and was so impressed with John's abilities that he requested his services as an outfitter and guide for a renewed attempt on Robson the following year. Yates graciously accepted.

On August 4, 1908, the previous year's party regrouped at the Hobo and set out for the Yellowhead complete with "an obstreperous set of ponies" and Hoodoo, the ranch's pet bulldog. Before travelling far it became obvious to Coleman that his decision to employ Yates had been a wise one as "he was the most resourceful man with horses and in the general conduct of camp life in the wilderness imaginable: strong, courageous, and alert in all emergencies of a life made up of major or minor emergencies. His skill in packing a horse so as to avoid a sore back on the trail was only equalled by his versatility in turning dried goat meat, smoked fish, desicated potatoes, and odds and ends of rice, oatmeal and bannocks into flavoursome 'bouillon' or 'Mulligan'."[2]

The approach to the massive bulk of Mount Robson was made by way of the Moose River, a tributary of the Fraser, over Moose Pass at the head of its east fork, onto the headwaters of the Smoky River via Calumet Creek,

Adolphus Moberly

and finally over Robson Pass to the foot of Robson Glacier. This route was followed on the advice and with the assistance of Adolphus Moberly — one of the numerous half-breed descendants of one time Jasper House trader Henry Moberly. As a tribute to his valuable help, the picturesque lake on the north side of the pass was named Adolphus. And on reaching the summit of Robson Pass, the view of a crystal clear lake to the south with an iceberg afloat in it provided the inspiration for another piece of nomenclature, Berg Lake.

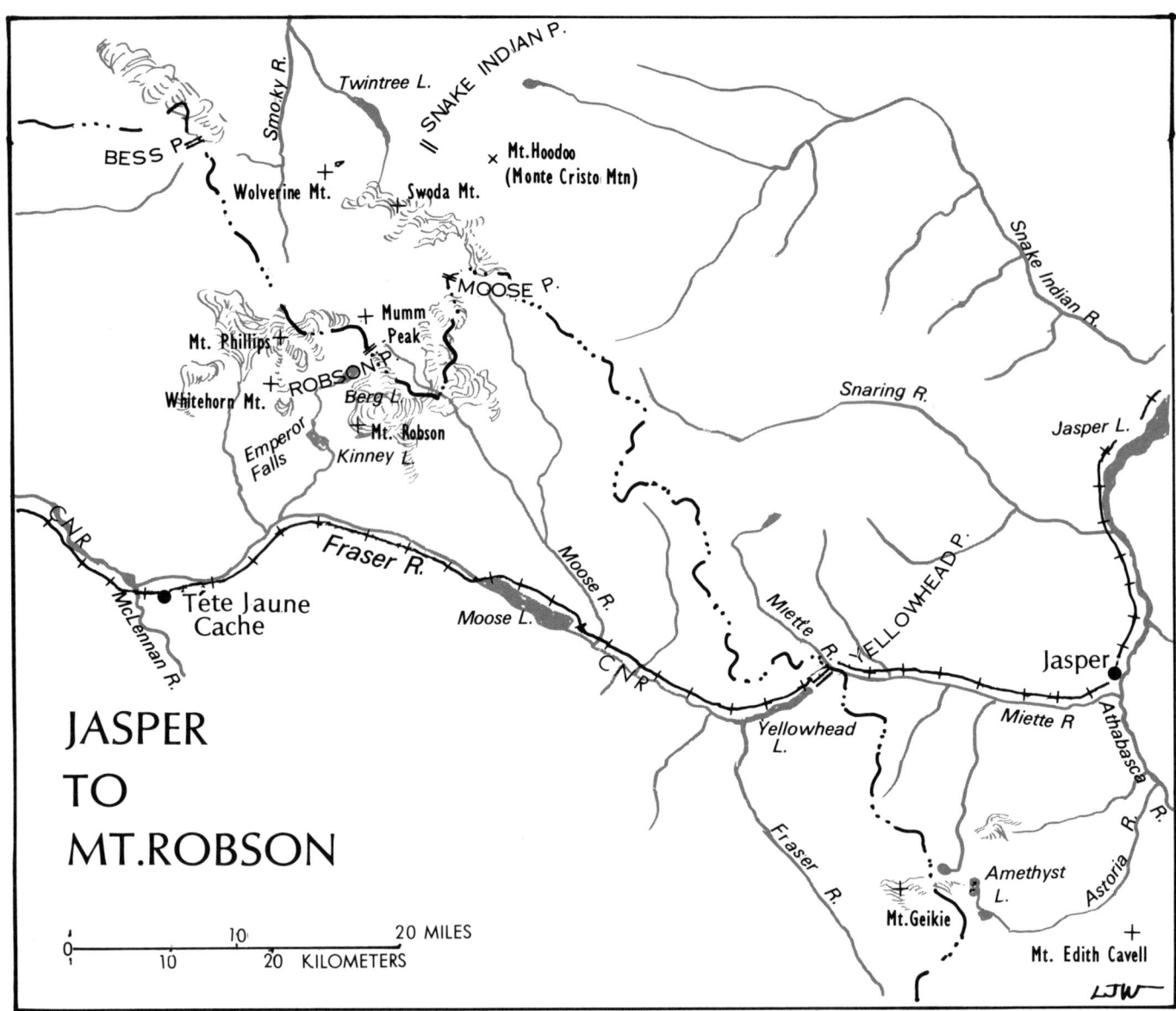

JASPER
TO
MT.ROBSON

0   10   20 MILES
0   10   20 KILOMETERS

Unfortunately the party was already more than a week behind schedule when it gained the foot of Robson Glacier on August 29th, and then continuous rain and snow made an immediate assault out of the question. Five days of impatient waiting ensued, during which it became apparent that the food would only hold out for another week. John was dispatched back to the Athabasca in order to replenish the larder, a mission which undoubtedly would have taken an entire week except for another chance meeting with Moberly's band of half-breeds a day's journey down the Moose Valley. Moberly's people had just completed a successful goat hunt and were able to supply a sufficient quantity of meat and other necessities to temporarily alleviate the food problem. By September 4th John was back in camp eager to discover what his clients found so exhilirating about climbing a mountain. His opportunity came the next day.

Yates's eager, almost light-hearted approach to mountaineering was quickly replaced by a rather stark realization of its rigors. He lacked all the essential equip-

ment, being shod only in thinly soled boots into which he had inserted hobnails and using an alpenstock roughly fashioned from a pole and a heavy wire nail. Proceeding across the glacier was a long, tiring grind but caused few difficulties until a steep snow slope was encountered at its upper end. The snow required step-cutting, and as A. P. Coleman had injured his knee, John had to take his turn at hacking out the rather fragile-looking footholds while clinging precariously to the fifty degree slope.

Soon John's makeshift climbing boots began to prove more of a hindrance than a help, the hobnails acting as heat conductors taking away all warmth from his feet. By the time the climbers reached the next obstacle, an almost vertical cliff at the top of the snow slope, his feet were completely numbed. Because of this and the unexpected length of time taken to reach the 10,000 foot level, Coleman decided that discretion was the better part of valor. After a short break for food and photographs, the dispirited and weary group began an equally painful and hazardous descent. Several hours later the main camp was regained, and as John thawed out his toes beside a roaring fire the party's spirits revived to the point where they were able to make some half-hearted jokes about his having got "cold feet" on his maiden mountaineering venture.

The experience led John to realize that, for the time being at least, his place was with the horses not the climbers, and when invited to participate in a second attempt he understandably showed little enthusiasm. As for the rest of the party, they mounted two more assaults, and then Kinney, the most accomplished alpinist among them, tried a completely solo attempt. All proved fruitless, mainly because of the inclement weather. Of the twenty-one days spent in Robson's shadow only twice were there two in succession that proved suitable for climbing. On September 18th the weather at last seemed to be clearing, but the advanced season and the continually dwindling food stocks forced a return to civilization. A record time for the 250 mile return trip over the trail to Lac Ste. Anne was accomplished before switching to a wagon for the remainder of the journey to Edmonton. Here John saw his people safely boarded on trains for their particular destinations before setting out once more for the Yellowhead on the mail run.

Experience gained outfitting and guiding the Coleman party in 1908 stood Yates in good stead the following year. Kinney, determined to be the first to reach Robson's lofty summit, contacted him during the winter with plans to launch a new expedition the next summer. However, early in the spring Kinney heard rumors that "foreign parties" also had designs on the peak and decided to move his timetable forward to ensure an attempt ahead of them. Telegraphing his guide to prepare for an early June departure, he left Victoria bound for Edmonton. Upon arrival he found a letter from Yates in which his guide outlined his refusal to go because it was too early in the season after the particularly heavy snowfall of the past winter. Dismayed but undaunted, Kinney set out on his own while John busied himself packing for a survey party working on the 15th Base Line.

Quite unexpectedly, at the end of July, John received word that there was a party who had specifically requested his services en route by buggy for Wolf Creek, where they hoped to rendezvous with him. Leaving the survey he was unable to reach Wolf Creek at the appointed time, but another packer brought the party as far west as the Athabasca where he caught up to them. On making their acquaintance he realized that this was probably the "foreign party" who Kinney had so feared, consisting of three members of the Alpine Club (London), Arnold Mumm, Leopold Amery and Geoffrey Hastings, as well as Hasting's friend A. G. Priestley and Mumm's personal Swiss guide Moritz Inderbinen.

The British had been among a group from the Alpine Club who had been specifically invited by the Alpine Club of Canada to attend their annual camp held at Lake O'Hara in 1909. Amery and Mumm decided that the

The Mumm party in camp, 1909. Back row (left to right) — A. L. Mumm, L. S. Amery, Moritz Inderbinen and John Yates. Front row — Geoffrey Hastings (second from left) and James Shand-Harvey (second from right).

camp would only serve as a preamble to a more extensive expedition to Robson, and while discussing this with Hastings on their voyage overseas he too expressed a desire to have a crack at the giant. In order to make the proper arrangements for an outfit, Amery paid a brief visit to Edmonton before joining his companions at O'Hara. Contacting an acquaintance, Harry Evans of the Hudson's Bay Company, he was told that something could probably be worked out with Yates, and Amery was pleased to agree when he heard that John had been Coleman's guide. But when the entire party returned to Edmonton on August 7th, Evans informed them that he had been unable to contact Yates and that he was making arrangements for another guide. Amery insisted that he must have the man who had been found so efficient by Coleman, and Evans agreed to send a messenger to see if John could be convinced to join the party.

After their meeting on the Athabasca, Mumm immediately became aware that his insistence had been well rewarded, commenting that "we could not be in better hands." Under Yates's able guidance he expected the party to have no trouble reaching the base of Robson from where the first ascent could be launched. However, at that time he was unaware that an unwelcome surprise awaited them further up the river. At the ferry above Jasper Lake on August 23rd they encountered a highly excited George Kinney who claimed to have just completed the conquest in the company of a young guide he

had met on the trail. The guide, Donald Phillips, was unknown to Yates at the time but was not to remain so for long. In fact, within a few years he would be acknowledged as one of the foremost outfitters and guides of the entire Jasper-Yellowhead region.

Phillips, nicknamed "Curly" because of his mop of brown hair, was a stocky, rather baby-faced youth of twenty-four when he first arrived in the area in 1909. A native of the heavy bush country around Dorset, Ontario, he had learned as a boy all the secrets of hunting, trapping and canoe work from his father, Daniel Phillips, an experienced backwoodsman. As early as 1902 he had begun trapping both on his own and in the company of his future brother-in-law Bert Wilkins in the vicinity of Temagami, and later began working with his close friend Ed Britton on a trapline out of Biscotasing. In the winter of 1907-08 he and Britton decided to set out in search of adventure, and on April 15th, Curly's birthday, they boarded a train bound for the west. After making several brief stops en route the pair eventually arrived at Calgary where they parted company, Curly heading for the mountains.

On reaching Field, Curly was able to secure a job with the CPR on the construction of the Spiral Tunnels, but after one look at the damp and dangerous working conditions decided that it was not for him. Returning to Banff for a brief stopover, he had a discussion with Bill Brewster, possibly with regard to employment as a guide,

Donald "Curly" Phillips.

but quickly came to the conclusion that the country was too crowded for his liking. He soon departed for Edmonton and spent the winter of 1908-09 working on the GTP line for George Kaywood, a tie contractor. With the coming of spring he bought a few horses and set out for the Yellowhead in the hope of discovering suitable trapping grounds and perhaps even picking up the occasional hunting party to guide. His experience with horses was limited, but he had done some guiding by canoe in his Ontario days and felt that he could adjust to the new circumstances. He soon had a chance to prove himself for fate brought him into the company of the Reverend Kinney.

As previously mentioned, Kinney's almost paranoic fear of being beaten to the summit of Robson had led him to head out on his own. On June 17th he left Edmonton with three pack horses, three months provisions and a few dollars in his pocket hoping to meet someone on the trail willing to share fortune. Struggling through to the McLeod River he encountered an old prospector named McBride who agreed to join forces, whereupon Kinney sold him a horse and half of his provisions. The partnership proved short-lived for, as Yates had predicted, the Athabasca tributaries were found to be in full flood and after almost drowning in the Rocky River, McBride made for safer ground.

Kinney pressed on, losing more of his food and equipment in other flooding streams and finally being forced to seek refuge on a small island when the Athabasca itself rose to unprecedented heights. As the water began to recede he discovered a high water trail which led him to the home of John Moberly, about seven miles above Jasper Lake. There, on July 11th, he found Phillips, who like himself had been marooned on an island in the Athabasca for six days before heading for the higher ground at Moberly's. Soon after their meeting the persistent Kinney had the young greenhorn convinced to accompany him to Robson.

As it turned out, Kinney had taken advantage of Phillips' inexperience to dupe him into participating in the venture. Curly was himself rather short on supplies and had been planning to return to Edmonton for a restocking, but Kinney glibly assured him that he had plenty for both of them. By the time the pair reached Yellowhead Pass, Curly had sized up Kinney's grub pile and it was apparent that he had been, at best, stretching the truth. According to his calculations they had scarcely enough for one month and was only willing to continue because he felt Kinney's rifle would enable him to kill sufficient game to ward off starvation. Once more his faith proved misplaced as he found, after firing nine successive misses at a caribou only fifty yards distant, that the barrel was bent about a quarter of an inch out of line. The drawbacks made chances for success appear rather slim, but their proximity to Robson and the reverend gentleman's grim determination to have his day persuaded Curly to make some sort of an attempt,

Curly Phillips and the Reverend Kinney packing.

however brief. Arriving at the foot of Robson's north shoulder, Kinney's silk tent was erected on a bench of land overlooking the river and preparations were made for the assault.

The next afternoon when they began the ascent Curly's situation was much the same as Yates's had been the year before. Except for his visit to Field he had never even been in the mountains, much less climbed one, and his equipment was of the crudest variety. He wore light, unnailed boots, a pair of thin gloves over which were pulled woollen socks for extra warmth, and carried a five-foot branch as an improvised alpenstock. Only ignorance of what was entailed in scaling a peak of Robson's immensity would lead a man to undertake such an adventure and, of course, Kinney was not about to enlighten him. Even the latter might have had some second thoughts about his plan if he could have foreseen what lay ahead. No ascent in the history of the Canadian Rockies demanded more sheer guts and determination in the face of hair-raising brushes with death by avalanche, exposure and starvation.

Beginning by establishing what was named "Camp High Up" at the 9,500 foot level, two tortuous but unsuccessful bids were launched on July 27th and 29th. While attempting these the pair alternately returned to the main camp to restock their rucksacks or slept covered with the thinnest of blankets at their fly camp on a ledge so narrow that a little wall of stones had to be piled up to prevent them from rolling off into the abyss. After the second attempt the weather turned sour, and Curly took the opportunity to do some hunting and fishing to try to fill out the perilously scant larder. Seven days of effort

Curly Phillips on Mount Robson.

earned him no more than two spindly grouse and a few marmots for the stew pot, and it was apparent that if success was going to crown their efforts it would have to be soon. This seemed doubly so after a third foray on August 9th was turned back at 10,000 feet by heavy snows and avalanches tearing past at frequent intervals.

Finally, on August 12th, the weather appeared to be lifting, and for the fourth time they toiled up towards the fly camp. Quite obviously this was to be the last ditch effort, and in order to get a jump on their objective they decided to forsake the fly camp in favor of a bivouac at the highest possible altitude. This turned out to be the 10,500 foot level where an impromptu ledge was hacked out of the snow and lined with flat pieces of cold grey slate.

Dawning cold and clear, the morning of Friday the 13th seemed to offer tolerable possibilities for success, although these soon dimmed as telltale storm clouds began to gather in the south. As they made their way up the steep cliffs of the west slope from the bivouac, the

storm overtook them and for a time it appeared as though further progress would be impossible. But soon the storm abated somewhat and one by one the treacherous series of cliffs leading to the summit, many sloping over sixty degrees, were scaled by ice-coated hands and feet. On the summit ridge the wind had heavily corniced the snow, but, according to Kinney's later report, this too was overcome and victory finally achieved.

Kinney, his long sought for ambition seemingly fulfilled, treated the moment with suitable reverence for a man of the cloth: "I was on a needle peak that rose so abruptly that even cornices cannot build very far out on it. Baring my head I said, 'In the name of Almighty God, by whose strength I have climbed here, I capture this peak, Mount Robson, for my own country and for the Alpine Club of Canada!'."[3] However, the joys of conquest soon had to give way to the perils of descent as it was already five o'clock in the afternoon. Due to a late-arriving chinook the temperatures had risen drastically and had all but erased their laboriously cut steps. This misfortune demanded an additional seven hours work to bring them safely to the upper camp. Here the remaining bits of marmot were ravenously consumed and a short rest taken before returning to the main camp, completing a twenty-hour day of continual climbing.

Because there were only three or four days of half rations left and it was seven days journey to Swift's where more food could be procured, no rest could be allowed the next day. Proceeding towards Moose Pass, Curly's luck at hunting improved marginally as he secured a few grouse, ptarmigan and ground squirrels for the interminable stews. Unfortunately any advantage gained by the extra game was wiped out the next day when Kinney, who insisted on leading on the trail as well as the mountain, guided them into muskeg and heavy timber, and in the wrong direction as well. Curly thereupon demanded to do the guiding and luckily was able to put them back on the right track. Good fortune again smiled a few days later when they happened on a trail party heading in the same direction who offered to share their food and company. After crossing the Athabasca near Jasper Lake and informing the British party of their triumph, a few necessities were purchased at John Moberly's and the trail eastward resumed. Arriving at Medicine Lodge on the McLeod River on September 1st, Kinney sold Curly the few remaining bits of his outfit and then bade him farewell.

Within a few years the question of whether Kinney and Phillips had actually gained the true summit of Robson was being actively discussed by various members of the alpine fraternity. Kinney steadfastly maintained that they did, and had probably experienced little difficulty in convincing Curly, who at the early date of 1909 was completely unfamiliar with mountaineering etiquette, that a matter of a few feet made no appreciable difference. A joint account of the expedition and the ascent appeared in the 1910 edition of the *Canadian Alpine Journal*, but in it Curly's remarks were restricted mainly to a description of the trails and camp life while Kinney related the details of the actual climbing. Strangely, during the next few years Curly was not called upon to confirm or deny reaching the top as no one took the trouble to ask him. However, at the 1913 Mount Robson Alpine Club camp which he helped to outfit, his close friend Conrad Kain, the Austrian climbing guide, took part in what was thought to be the second ascent of the mountain. On returning victoriously to camp, Kain was informed by a now older and wiser Phillips that it was, in effect, the first ascent since he and Kinney had fallen short of their goal: "We reached, on our ascent (in mist and storm), an ice dome fifty or sixty feet high, which we took for the peak. The danger was too great to ascend the dome."[4]

Despite this later revelation, a great deal of credit was due Curly for the pluck and determination he showed as a rank amateur in the face of such formidable conditions as those encountered on Robson. Kinney reported that throughout the whole ordeal he never heard a word of discouragement, and this was soon to become the mark of the man in many other trying circumstances. All in all, the ascent was a feather in the cap for a young guide attempting to establish a reputation for himself, particularly when news of it reached the ears of other mountaineers and explorers anxious to come to grips with the little known country north of the great peak. Certainly it must have gone a long way toward convincing him to remain in the area and to attempt to earn his livelihood from outfitting and guiding.

At any rate, remain he did, spending the next two winters working for railroad timber contractors between Obed and Brûlé and picking up guiding jobs during the summer and fall. In 1911 Curly ran his pack trains from Edson, but by 1912 was well established at Fitzhugh (renamed Jasper in 1913) with corrals, a cabin and a rather unique two-storey pack and saddle shed along the trail that would one day become Pyramid Drive.

The site of his headquarters in the town was no accident. It conformed to a newly enacted government regulation which had resulted from experience with the stables at Banff, where they tended to be spread all over the main business area causing tourists to complain of the noxious odors. Starting with a clean slate at Jasper, the government decided to "debar from the townsite all stables and their attendant smells and flies."[5] To compensate for this ruling, steps were taken to have six sites surveyed near the foot of the hill at the back of the town, one lot of two acres for a government corral and stables and five of one acre each to be apportioned to outfitters as the need arose. Phillips, being first on the scene, was given his choice and took the second plot northeast of the government site.

When the outfitters along the CPR learned of the ascent of Robson, it was only the most current in a series of exciting reports emanating from the more northerly region. By 1909 Fred Stephens' activities were well-known to his old friends at Banff, Lake Louise and Field, and every month brought fresh news of the supposed great opportunities provided by the building of the GTP and its rival the CNR. It was undoubtedly the lure of these opportunities, in combination with the interest of some of their steady clients and the continuing pressure of competition, which were the major considerations in the decision of the Ottos to abandon their apparently secure foothold at Field in favor of the Jasper area. Within a short time some of these considerations would also play an important part in the appearance in the same locale of another well-known outfitting name — Brewster. However, in this case it was not Jim and Bill Brewster but their younger brothers Fred and Jack, who were intent on striking out on their own.

Oddly enough, the Ottos' announced intentions of departing from Field and the sale of their interests just before the 1910 Alpine Club camp did not result in an immediate move to the north. They handled the outfitting from the Consolation Valley camp and in addition continued to outfit some parties from Field during the 1910 season. This was probably by arrangement with Jim Brewster as the Ottos were already committed to taking out parties with whom it was too late to make other plans. One of these was a rather cosmopolitan group headed by J. E. C. Eaton, a colleague of Collie's in the Alpine Club, and including his Italian cousin Captain Marocco and the Swiss guide Heinrich Burgener. Eaton had previously corresponded with Jack Otto about setting up the trip which he had decided, after consulting Collie, should be destined for the Freshfield Group. Bruce Otto was assigned to them as guide and within a short time Eaton was able to pronounce "I do not think the British Empire contains a better fellow."[6] After leaving Field on July 15th with Otto, a cook and ten horses, the climbers succeeded in conquering Mounts Pilkington, Walker, Dent and Freshfield before returning to Laggan on August 5th.

Meanwhile Jack and Closson Otto had delivered forty-seven head of horses with saddles and a few carriages to Jim Brewster per their agreement and had then gone to Moberly where a few pack animals were purchased for their trip through the mountains. Picking up Bruce, fresh from his exploits with the Eaton party, they headed north by way of Wilcox Pass and the Athabasca, arriving at its junction with the Miette some twenty-one days later. Being unfamiliar with the terrain they were unsure of their bearings, so Jack climbed part way up Signal Mountain and, with the aid of his spy glass, was able to pick out the Swift children playing in their yard several miles downstream. After visiting at Swift's for two days and learning something of the lay of the land, they continued eastward down the Athabasca. At the mouth of Solomon Creek they stopped and set up a temporary headquarters before pushing on to Edmonton, where they spent the balance of the winter.

While in Edmonton the brothers accepted an interesting proposition put to them by Howard Douglas, the former Superintendent at Banff who had just taken on the new position of Commissioner of Dominion Parks. At the request of D. B. Dowling, Douglas had agreed to have a thirty mile stretch of trail cleared from the proposed rail line into Maligne Lake. The trail was required for the impending visit of a party intent on surveying the lake at Dowling's request. Composing the party were two intrepid women and a young boy: Mary T. S. Schäffer, who in 1908 had made the only recorded visit by a white person to the lake since the CPR surveyor Henry McLeod in 1875, her sister-in-law Mrs. H. H. Sharples, and her nephew Paul Sharples. Mrs. Schäffer had become well acquainted with Jack Otto during his days at Field, and since the contract for trail clearing also included guiding the party, the Ottos were the logical choice for the job.

Early in the spring of 1911, the brothers acquired more horses in Edmonton and shipped their outfit to the railhead at Hinton. On reaching Solomon Creek they re-established their former camp, hired a few men and then headed out to begin the task of clearing the trail. It proved slow work as the route to be followed went through heavy timber from the future site of Jasper to Buffalo Prairie on the Athabasca near the mouth of the Whirlpool and then over a high, un-named pass into Maligne Lake. The additional handicap of late spring storms resulted in the work being far from completed when Jack Otto met the ladies and Sid Unwin, a guide from Banff, at Hinton on June 7th. Nevertheless, after a night spent at Prairie Creek, Jack began leading them over the GTP tote road, which was in such poor condition that a horse and an ox had recently been reported to have drowned in the mud while attempting to negotiate it. A few days later, after reaching the part of the trail his men had cleared, the going proved easier for a time. But a constant irritation was caused by several sixteen foot pieces of cedar that one of the pack horses, Jonas, was forced to carry in order that a boat might be constructed. "His burden had been lashed to his unprotesting sides, a rope had been looped across the front end of the boards, Jack had assumed the position of steering gear, and with Jonas acting as propellor the pair had taken the lead of the small procession. . . . The sight of him under the best of conditions was trying, for when the boards were not striking the inoffensive horse in the cheek, or nearly knocking the steersman down, they were slipping from their guiding ropes, going fore and aft according to the lay of the land, and having to be shifted back into place."[7]

Additional hardships were encountered when ten feet of fresh snow was found on the pass. A day's halt was called while Jack's crew broke a path through it, but upon travelling it the next day it proved so narrow that one of the packers had to walk ahead of poor Jonas and hold the lumber vertically to enable him to gain passage through some stretches. Coming to the top of the pass two objects thought to be goats were spotted by the ladies, but on closer inspection they proved to be snow shovels fashioned from trees and left behind by the trail clearers. Understandably the height of land was immediately dubbed Shovel Pass.

Difficulties continued to plague the pack train until June 20th when Maligne's shore was finally reached. Immediately the three brothers set to work constructing the boat, which was completed just in time to coincide with the start of a further two week period of rain and snow. Also, it was discovered that a spool of wire needed for the survey was missing, and when Bruce returned to Hinton to fetch it he found that it had not even left Toronto. This misfortune meant almost a three week delay, although the time was put to good use in a thorough exploration of the lake and its surrounding peaks and valleys.

During this period Jack was not found to be wanting in any of the skills demanded of a good and faithful

Jack Otto as steering gear and Jonas as propellor.

guide. Rowing the boat for up to twelve hours or exploring on foot for an equal length of time did not dampen his spirits. In addition, he found time to do the odd jobs that maintenance of a camp in the wilderness required, from baking bread in the campfire to mending Mrs. Schäffer's broken glasses with tools fashioned by hand. Food stocks had to be replenished by hunting after other chores were completed, yet by six o'clock the next morning he was awake with a cheery fire burning to greet the ladies when they arose.

Work was finally completed on July 25th, and Jack quickly packed up, took his charges back to the railhead and then accompanied them to Edmonton. Although the survey had taken much longer than expected, permitting him and his brothers little time to outfit other parties that summer, it was ultimately to prove highly beneficial for them. As in the case of Phillips' work with Kinney, word of the excellent service provided by the well-known Mrs. Schäffer would stand them in good stead with future parties desiring to outfit in the region. Soon the Ottos had an

excellent foothold in Jasper with corrals located on the site between those of Phillips and the government.

Fred and Jack Brewster's arrival at Jasper resulted from somewhat different circumstances than did the Ottos'. Frederick Archibald Brewster, the third son of John Brewster, was born on December 21, 1884 at Kildonan, Manitoba, and like his two elder brothers received his early education at Saint John's College, Winnipeg. On completing his course in 1905, he was not yet sure what he wished to do with his life, but while thinking about it accepted an invitation from his uncle George Brewster to accompany him on an exploration trip.

Starting from Ashcroft, 160 miles east of Vancouver on the CPR line, the pair travelled with pack horses by way of Quesnel, Fort St. James, Omineca River and Babine Lake to Hazleton. Here the horses were abandoned in favor of a canoe, which took them the rest of the way down the Omineca to the Finlay River and then to its headwaters where the winter was spent. Early the next spring the Finlay was followed its full length and Edmon-

Fred Brewster.

ton finally reached via Peace River Crossing and Athabasca Landing, requiring the building of three different boats in the process. When he reached Edmonton in June, Fred had been on the trail for almost a year, yet within a few days, this time in the company of Fred Hussey, departed for the coast to do it all over again. After he arrived back in Edmonton three and a half months later, he felt that he had experienced enough of trail life to last quite some time. Accordingly, he decided to turn his mind to more academic pursuits. Beginning in the fall of 1906, he attended Queen's University, Kingston from which he was granted a B.Sc. in Mining Engineering in 1909.

During the summer of 1908, while on holiday from university, Fred had received his first practical mining experience working for the Consolidated Mining and Smelting Company examining some copper and silver claims on Vancouver Island and the Queen Charlotte Islands. After graduation he returned to do more prospecting in these regions on his own, but the good claims were already tied up and by the late fall of 1909 he was once more back at Banff.

Undecided as to what to do next, Fred spent some time on his uncle James Brewster's ranch near Bowden, south of Red Deer, before returning home to work on the trail. This he continued to do until 1910 when he was approached by his brother-in-law Phil Moore, who had severed his connection with Brewster Brothers, about forming a partnership. Fred agreed, and along with his brother Jack Walker Brewster, only a lad of seventeen at

the time, a company known as Brewster and Moore was created.

The company's initial endeavor was working on the construction of a branch line from the Calgary and Edmonton Railway into the Nordegg coal fields during the winter of 1910-11. Working out of Red Deer, they were mainly involved in the freighting of ties and other supplies to the railhead, although they briefly ran a stagecoach to Rocky Mountain House, and Moore operated a store near Nordegg for a period. Meanwhile, Fred began to hear of the possibilities along the GTP line, probably from his uncle's acquaintances Pres and Charlie Berry, who had begun to make yearly pack trips to the Yellowhead region from their ranch at Raven, west of Innisfail.

In February, 1911, Fred took a trip as far as Edson and prospects in the area appeared so bright that in the spring the company's horses and freighting equipment were moved by way of Edmonton to Bickerdike on the GTP. Few problems were encountered in finding work, and before long they were freighting and packing on the construction of a branch line into the Coal Branch district and were also hauling coal for British American Colleries. Headquarters were quickly moved on to the end of steel at the rough-and-ready town of Prairie Creek where temporary corrals were erected and tents put up to serve as living quarters. Soon Fred and Jack were joined by their brothers Pat and George, who helped supply some much needed manpower.

Although construction and freighting work took up most of their time, Fred felt that outfitting tourists would eventually provide the bulk of their business, as it had for his brothers in the early days at Banff. With this in mind he took measures to learn as much as possible about the area. Early in the summer of 1911 he set out to explore the country north of the proposed railroad line, travelling over Moose Pass, down the Moose River and then up the Fraser and through Yellowhead Pass. From that point he headed eastward down the Miette and met his brother Jack at the future Jasper townsite. This he described as "a boulder strewn flat with a second growth of Lodgepole Pine about four feet high."[8] Even though he did not realize it at the time, this unlikely seeming spot was soon to become his home.

Prairie Creek was maintained as the centre of the Brewster and Moore operations until late in 1912 when, falling in line with most of the other outfitters, their headquarters were moved on to Fitzhugh. After the growing clan of Brewsters was joined by Moore and his wife Pearl, construction was started on a stable and corrals on one of the plots northeast of those of Phillips and Otto. Conforming to a government request for a rustic style of architecture, using either logs or boulders, their structure was designed "on the lines of old Fort David Thompson [sic] of the Hudson's Bay Company" and was thought to be "a decided acquisition to the beauty of the townsite."[9]

Jack Brewster herding horses in the Brewster and Moore corrals at Jasper, 1914.

Alpine Club climbers on the summit of Mount Resplendent during the 1913 Robson Camp.

7 Partnerships and Prosperity

The outfitters working in the Jasper-Yellowhead region after 1909 were, in one respect, initially quite different from those plying their trade along the CPR. Basically their operations were smaller in size. There were a number of reasons for this, the most obvious being that at the outset there were far fewer tourist parties demanding their services. The southern businesses had developed as a consequence of the tourist traffic generated by the railway while the northern ones began development simultaneously with the building of the lines. This meant that more attention would be devoted to work on the numerous contracts that were readily obtainable from the railroad contractors for that particular section of the Grand Trunk Pacific and later the Canadian Northern. Because these contracts mainly involved the cutting and hauling of bridge timbers and ties, this work demanded the use of heavy wagons and teams rather than the stock-in-trade of the outfitter, cayuses and pack saddles. Both Brewster and Moore and Phillips relied extensively on such activities for their livelihoods and soon the Ottos did as well, working with a tie cutting outfit up the Moose River Valley.

Stephens and Yates, not directly associated with railroad construction, also tended to be small operators, but in their particular cases it was largely by choice. Stephens preferred to spend much of his time timber-cruising and prospecting, while Yates soon had a homestead of his own and a coal mining lease near Brûlé Lake.

Prior to the First World War these outfitters, with the possible exception of Brewster and Moore, were often faced with choosing one of two alternatives when a tourist party was secured. They could either find additional men and stock to help them on a temporary basis or form equally temporary partnerships with one of the other outfitters. The first choice seemed to be the more logical, but in all except a few cases the parties required more horses and equipment than one outfitter was able to acquire on short notice. For this reason temporary partnerships became the most favored means of compensating for small size.

Generally speaking, there tended to be little competitiveness in outfitting, so evident along the CPR, on the Jasper scene in its early years. This lack of competitiveness partially stemmed from the absence of outfitting concessions such as those connected with the CPR hotels — concessions which had played a part in the decisions of some outfitters to abandon the CPR line in the first place. According to its promotional material, the GTP gave equal opportunity to all. In a brochure published around 1913 entitled *The Canadian Rockies, Yellowhead Pass Route*, an entire page was devoted to recommending different guiding and outfitting companies, with Brewster Brothers (Brewster and Moore), Donald Phillips, and Otto Brothers heading the list.

Other factors accounting for the low level of competition were, perhaps, a realistic assessment of the need to help one another in order to survive and a feeling that there would eventually be enough business for all to have a share. Whatever the reasons, the resultant partnerships were sometimes quite diverse involving combinations of up to three different outfitters in the course of handling particularly large groups.

Of all the impromptu cooperative ventures at this time the ones that came the closest to resulting in a more permanent business relationship were those of Fred Stephens and John Yates. This was not surprising since these two had the most limited pack strings and could only rarely provide the necessary horseflesh to outfit a party completely on their own. Certainly by 1910 the two had crossed each other's paths on more than one occasion and quite possibly could have come to some agreement to handle a rather interesting party that was due to arrive that summer. However, an equally important consideration in their combination of forces lay in the make-up of the party itself, composed as it was of A. L. Mumm, his Swiss guide Inderbinen, and J. Norman Collie, back to his beloved Rockies after an eight year absence.

Mumm's expectations of a first ascent on Robson the year previously had, of course, been dealt a crushing blow when he and his companions met Kinney and Phillips returning from their purported conquest. Despite this setback, the British party had continued on and succeeded in carrying out an exhaustive reconnaissance of the peak without actually gaining its summit. But Mumm, a man not easily daunted, was determined to launch a further attempt on Robson and to examine the area seen from its slopes. As he had found Yates such a valuable asset in 1909, he could see no reason to look further for an outfitter and guide on his return trip in 1910.

Although Collie had always wanted to explore the area north of the Yellowhead, he could not afford the time necessary to do so until the inexorable westward push of the GTP helped to make the country more accessible. During the period since his last visit to Canada his friendship and yearly exchange of correspondence with Stephens had continued. This combined with his 1902 pledge to go out with no one but Fred determined that he too would play some part in the outfitting and guiding of the party.

The long awaited reunion between Stephens and Collie finally took place at the end of steel on July 17, 1910. Upon embarking from the train the mountaineers found their guides ready to proceed accompanied by Allan McConnochie, Yates's former partner in the Hobo Ranch, and George Swain, hired to help cut trail and manage the camp. As Robson was the main objective, the standard route up the Athabasca and Miette Rivers was followed to Yellowhead Pass at which point it was decided to retrace the trail blazed by Yates while with the Coleman party in 1908. Sticking to this trail was the easiest way to reach the Robson Glacier as once over Moose Pass it was simply a matter of following the Smoky River to its source — a route which took them across a small creek issuing from the snout of the Coleman Glacier, subsequently known as Yates Torrent.

After twenty-three days of travelling, they pitched camp on the shore of Berg Lake, but as usual the mountain itself was shrouded in cloud and snow. While waiting for it to clear several lesser peaks in the vicinity were ascended, including two that would eventually bear the names of Mumm and Phillips. But as was so often the case, the weather in the neighborhood of Robson tended to deteriorate rather than improve and, growing impatient, Mumm and Collie decided to focus attention on an exploration of the Smoky River Valley and some of its

tributaries which might hold passes over the Divide. The second side-valley examined proved to be the most intriguing as it contained a rather easy pass into British Columbia and "a splendid snow mountain" christened Mount Bess by Yates, after a daughter of Peter Gunn, the Hudson's Bay Company factor at Lac Ste. Anne.

At this point it was necessary to begin the return journey to the railhead at Wolf Creek and the question immediately arose as to which route to follow. Returning by the same path as they had come would undoubtedly be the easiest course of action, but it would also be the least interesting. Since Yates knew the area best it was left to him to suggest an alternative. He favored following the Smoky to where some Indians had told him of a pass to the Stoney (Snake Indian) River, which in turn would lead them back to the Athabasca near the former location of Jasper House. Although he had never made the passage himself he had an uncanny sense of direction.

. . . on September 2 we started down the Smoky River, intending to turn E. up the first promising looking valley, in the hopes that we should find a pass at its head over which we could take the horses. We found a very beautiful lake [Twintree Lake] in our side valley with two infinitesimal islands, on each of which was one fir tree. Yates, who is the best guide in unknown country I have ever met, by some unaccountable instinct refused to follow the valley to its head and turned up a side valley; two days later he proved to be right, for we crossed an easy pass [Snake Indian Pass] above tree-line on the old and well-worn Indian trail, descending on the other side into a beautiful valley down which a fine stream ran through the pine woods.[1]

Arriving back at the Athabasca on September 16th after a comparatively short return trip of two weeks, Mumm and Collie immediately decided to come back the following year and explore more thoroughly the new country which Yates's trail had brought to light.

John's keen guiding ability in conjunction with Fred's renowned axe work had made the pair a perfect team. In fact, their combination of forces had proved so effective that there was no question in their minds but that it should be repeated in 1911. When Mumm and Collie reappeared in July, they were once more at the ready, with Allan McConnochie again assisting them.

Striking up the Stoney River on July 24th, it took seven days of chopping downed timber to cover a mere twenty-five miles, but thereafter the going proved easier and the weather uncommonly good. On August 4th the pass discovered by Yates was regained and time allowed for Collie to commence a plane table survey. They ascended a peak on the east side of the pass for this purpose, and upon reaching its summit Mumm immediately proclaimed that it would be named Mount Hoodoo in honor of Yates's loyal bulldog. The amazing dog accompanied his master on all his travels and on this particular

Hoodoo greeting Collie.

occasion had set off with him on the climb. Even at a point near the summit where there was a steep cliff he could not bear to be left behind and had to be tied to a rope and pulled bodily up the final precipice.

From the peak the climbers saw an interesting group of mountains around Mount Bess and decided to give them more attention. Down on the Smoky again they accorded the Resthaven Icefield a detailed examination and then attempted to look into some of the valleys entering onto the river further north. However, the muskeg and burnt timber proved so overwhelming that the brief time at their disposal rapidly dwindled away. With only one week remaining they decided to spend it near Mount Bess, and on August 26th Mumm, Collie, Inderbinen and Yates succeeded in making its first ascent. The accomplishment was notable for John since with it he es-

tablished a reputation as an excellent mountaineer, an exception among trail guides. Following this success the party crossed Bess Pass, another old Indian trail, and made a brief reconnaissance of its western side before commencing the return journey to the railhead.

For the next two weeks the party maintained a leisurely pace in the best weather that Collie had experienced in the six summers spent in his Rocky Mountain travels. It was fittingly so, for when they reached the railroad at Prairie Creek it was the end of his explorations. He would never return and henceforth would have only his memories. "As one sits in one's armchair on the winter evenings and dreams of the camp life return once more, of the teepee with a roaring fire and the door snugly closed; of Fred's stories, of John's liesurely methods of playing poker, of Moritz's fears that we were lost in a strange land and that the 'grub pile' was low; all these small happenings, as they come back to one, stir the remembrances of the life in the wilds."[2]

The end of the 1911 Collie-Mumm expedition also marked the termination of Yates's and Stephens' cooperative efforts, although it was not the last time they were out on the trail together. In 1913 Yates was again engaged by Mumm while Stephens was hired by Geoffrey Howard, another Englishman, with both guides being accompanied by two packers. Howard, with no definite plans and limited time at his disposal, was invited by Mumm to accompany him on a brief exploration of the Mount Geikie (Edith Cavell) region, a proposition which found much favor with the outfitters. However, there was no formal combination of forces, and each man ran his own pack string and camp independent of the other.

For a time around 1911 it had seemed that the relationship developed between the two in their two years of work together would result in a more lasting partnership. That both ultimately decided to go their own separate way was undoubtedly attributable to their individualism and outside interests. This decision may have cost them their last chance for financial viability as within a few years both had disappeared from the Jasper scene. Small size was normal and could even be considered an advantage in the early years when tourism was on a small scale, and it would again have some advantages in the mid-twenties. In the interim, though, larger operations were the order of the day, and neither Stephens or Yates changed with the times. On the other hand, outfitters such as Phillips and the Ottos used partnerships only as a temporary means of carrying on business while they were expanding to prepare for an expected busy future.

Curly Phillips' first big break as an outfitter and guide came about as a direct result of his participation with Kinney in the attempt on Mount Robson. Kinney was a member in good standing with the Alpine Club of Canada and, as pointed out, the club was beginning to look northward by 1910. A. O. Wheeler, never one to be far from the action, was completely enthralled by the reports emanating from the Yellowhead and was determined that the club should make its own investigations "in accordance with the propaganda laid down in its constitution, viz. the encouragement of mountain craft and the opening of new regions as a national playground".[3] By 1911 he was once more working as a private surveyor, but managed to convince the government that some photo-topographical work in the region would be beneficial. In addition, the GTP, about to embark on a publicity campaign similar to the CPR's, agreed to lend financial support to an investigative expedition through the area. Wheeler's personal objective was to look into the possibility of holding one of the club's future annual camps in the vicinity of Robson. As he was unfamiliar with the country, he was glad to follow Kinney's advice for an outfitter and guide to handle this rather major undertaking.

Phillips was, of course, equally glad to receive the opportunity to conduct the prestigious party, consisting of Wheeler, Byron Harmon, the club's official photographer, and Conrad Kain, its official climbing guide. He originally felt that he would have no problem handling this group with the addition of one man to cook, but had to drastically alter his plans when some major changes took place in the party's composition as the time for departure drew near. First of all Kinney was added as an assistant, and then through the cooperation of the provincial governments of Alberta and British Columbia funds were made available to add a team capable of reporting on the area's geology, flora and fauna. Through contact with Dr. Charles D. Walcott, Secretary of the Smithsonian Institution of Washington and a long-time investigator of the Canadian Rockies, Wheeler was able to secure the desired scientists. Headed by Ned Hollister, Assistant Curator of Mammals at the United States National Museum, the group also included J. H. Riley, likewise from the National Museum, Charles Walcott Jr. and Harry Blagden, the latter two being charged with the responsibility for collecting the larger specimens of mammals required. Faced with more than a doubling in size of the party, Curly had to do some quick scrambling to find assistance.

Luckily, help was immediately available in the person of James Shand-Harvey, one of the packers who had come into the country during the construction of the railroad. Harvey had arrived in Edmonton from his native Scotland in 1905 and after a brief stint at homesteading had gone to work packing on a survey party. Most of his experience was gained during the survey of the 14th Base Line west from Lac Ste. Anne to Jasper, but he had made one brief appearance with a mountaineering party when he guided Mumm's 1909 group from Wolf Creek to their rendezvous with Yates and then accompanied them on to Robson. By 1911 he had managed to acquire a few horses of his own and with Fred Kvass, a well-known trapper, spent the spring hauling supplies from Lac Ste. Anne to Tete Jaune Cache. It

was on the completion of this venture that he encountered Phillips and accepted his proposition to cooperate with him in the outfitting of the Alpine Club-Smithsonian expedition.

Since the enlarged party would demand a substantial number of extra horses, Curly sought additional aid. Fred Stephens agreed to help and joined his horses with those of the other two outfitters when they set out from Brûlé Lake in early July. He was given the task of handling the combined pack strings while Phillips and Harvey scouted ahead, and soon his penchant for giving primary consideration to the horses' welfare got him into trouble with Wheeler.

Nearing the mouth of the Miette River, the Director found himself in a particular hurry and informed Fred that he would push on with a few of the men, choose a campsite and expect him to bring up the horses and equipment later in the day. Fred had other ideas and on seeing some good pasturage early in the afternoon he stopped, forcing Wheeler to spend the night in a makeshift shelter. Beginning the next morning "without soap or breakfast", Wheeler quickly worked himself into a temper and furiously backtracked to Fred's camp, arriving just in time to see the pack train pulling out. Accosting Fred he snapped, "Stephens, I always heard that you were a damn good man, but you're not." Unabashed, Fred retorted, "Wheeler, I always heard that you were an s.o.b., and you are."[4] The party continued on in icy silence to near the mouth of the Moose River where, after turning the horses over to Phillips, Fred, understandably, took his leave.

Phillips and Harvey pushed on, stopping the next evening at a raucous railroad construction camp known as Moose City. Here Conrad Kain, still rather new to the Canadian scene but eventually to become a prominent mountain guide and an outfitter in his own right, had a rude introduction to the ways of some of its inhabitants. Slipping out of his tent for a brief moment, he returned to find his clothes, some of the food and cook stove slickly extracted in his absence. Fortunately the losses were easily replaced and soon the party was once again underway, with each of the members involved in his own particular pursuit.

As Wheeler was experienced in topographic work, he and his assistants had little trouble in successfully carrying out their surveys, but the young American scientists proved, at least at the outset, to be not quite so adept at their collecting. Attempts to shoot game specimens provided a constant source of hilarity for Phillips and Harvey, who went to the extent of driving flocks of sheep and goat into range in order that the "experts" might obtain something suitable to stuff. Kinney, at a later date, remembered one particularly vivid example of their ineptitude:

Our climbers were having a day off from strenuous work, and had been busy here and there, when Harmon, who

ACC - Smithsonian party, 1911. Left to right — A. O. Wheeler, Curly Phillips, Harry Blagden, J. H. Riley, Charles Walcott Jr., George Kinney (seated), James Shand-Harvey and Casey Jones.

had been up Robson glacier after pictures, came rushing into camp wildly shouting "bear, bear". Out tumbled the "Big Game" hunters wildly scrambling after Harmon, the guide. Conrad and Curlie seized what weapons were handy and I trailed behind efficiently armed with two ten-inch twenty-tews. We were making a comedy of what was a serious matter for the hunters.

At last we discovered the black bear on the mountain side above us. The big game hunters knelt and began filling the mountain side with lead. Their magazines were soon emptied and Conrad and I each got behind one of the hunters and pulled the shells out of their belts and handed them the ammunition as needed during the terrific bombardment.

The bear, in the meantime, dodged here and there or else watched curiously what was going on. He was finally hit by a stray shot and scurried out of sight.[5]

Despite such setbacks, the necessary fauna, varying in size from miniscule voles to rangy bull caribou, were eventually obtained, often with the intercession of the accurate marksmanship of Phillips or Harvey.

The two guides accompanied the party as far as Berg

Lake where the steep cliffs of the Valley of a Thousand Falls on the upper Grand Fork of the Fraser (Robson) River prevented them from taking the horses further. As a result, they were forced to retrace their route and then push on up the main Fraser Valley and the Grand Fork Valley to Kinney Lake, where they were to meet the rest of the party below the offending cliffs. Effectively this meant that they completed the equivalent of another full circuit of Robson while the others leisurely awaited their arrival.

Kain, for one, could not tolerate being idle in the midst of so many unclimbed peaks. Wheeler had intimated that his assistants would get a crack at Robson, but as time went by his constant stalling made it apparent he was saving the supposed second ascent for a future Alpine Club camp. Realizing the Robson climb was not to be, Conrad vanished one afternoon and did not return that evening. The next morning he reappeared and informed a much chagrined Wheeler that he had climbed, partially in darkness, the magnificent neighboring White-horn Mountain, a peak the Director had also been hoping to save for a club ascent.

It took Phillips and Harvey five days of hard travelling, much of it through country where no pack trail existed, to attain their destination of Kinney Lake. There,

Curly Phillips' packtrain on the trail from Maligne Lake to Lake Louise, 1911.

on August 9th, Curly constructed a sizeable raft, ferried his waiting passengers and their gear across its expanse, and then brought them down some three miles to a camp he had established on the Grand Fork.

After a short delay while the survey party occupied a few more camera stations, the return trip was commenced, and Fitzhugh was regained in early September. From there it was Wheeler's intention to press the survey's work on to Maligne Lake and then to cap the season's successes by carrying right through with the pack train to Laggan, thereby completing the first trip from the new Grand Trunk Pacific to the Canadian Pacific. At the time he prophesied that this route would one day be one of the most popular scenic trips in the Canadian Rockies, and he was eventually to be proved correct for it was essentially the same as that which would be followed by the Banff-Jasper highway.

While Phillips resupplied at Fitzhugh in readiness for the proposed journey, Harvey forged on ahead to Maligne Lake with Walcott, Blagden and Harmon. En route Blagden redeemed his earlier inaccuracies by bagging a bighorn ram measuring 18½ inches around the base of the horns, the biggest ram ever taken in the lands that formed the park and eventually to go on permanent display in the Smithsonian Institution.

Phillips followed closely behind Harvey's group with his cook Casey Jones and the rest of the party except Riley and Hollister, who remained at Swift's to collect birds. It was Curly's first trip into the Maligne Lake country and to his surprise he found it easy going, due in large measure to the trail cut by the Otto brothers earlier in the year. Arriving at the lake, he had further reason to be thankful to the Ottos as his party was able to make use of the boat which they had conveniently left behind. Such good fortune allowed him and Harvey to spend their time clearing a new piece of trail from the foot of the lake to its outlet into the Maligne River.

The seventeenth of September was the proposed date of departure for the remainder of the journey to Laggan, but it proved an inauspicious choice since it marked the beginning of what was to be a five day period of rain and snow. Faced with these conditions, Wheeler, who was on a tight schedule, was forced to abandon his plans and return to Fitzhugh with the collecting party under Harvey's care. However, he believed that "Phillips could get through if anyone could" and delegated to him the responsibility of seeing Harmon, Kinney and Kain safely to the CPR line. This he was able to accomplish in twelve days but not without inflicting severe hardships on both himself and his horses in the snow-choked passes.

Immediately on reaching Laggan on September 30th, it was necessary for Curly to turn around and retrace the 120 mile route just completed in order to reach home before the passes were completely blocked for the winter.

Not wanting to make the trip alone, he was able to convince Kain to accompany him with the promise of sharing his winter trapline at the head of the Smoky River. Showing characteristic fortitude, the two travelled extremely long hours in deteriorating conditions and arrived back at Fitzhugh in the amazingly short time of thirteen days.

Before going out on the trapline, Curly completed a report for Wheeler in which he concurred in his employer's optimism about the route's future and estimated the cost of constructing a decent trail over it:

When a good trail is put in from steel to steel it will be a very popular trip. The cost of the trail will not be very great. There is about five or six miles of it that will have to be graded and "switchbacked" but very little bridging to do. Going back we had a lot of trouble on the Sun Wapta and Athabasca, but a very fair trail can be put up all these streams to the foot of Wilcox Pass for about fifty dollars per mile.[6]

Wheeler's plan to hold an Alpine Club camp at the base of Mount Robson had to wait until 1913 to come to fruition, but when it did he had no doubt as to who should be placed in charge of the outfitting. Curly had performed all that was asked of him with speed and efficiency in 1911 and had earned the right to handle the potentially lucrative 1913 venture. However, both he and Wheeler realized that, as in 1911, additional assistance would be required. The choice fell upon the Director's old friends the Otto brothers. Phillips and the Ottos were already well-acquainted and it was even their practice to share each other's facilities and equipment on occasion. For example, when outfitting two American hunters, G. D. Pratt and Phimister Proctor, in the fall of 1912, Curly noted in his diary that he stopped at the Otto's shack at Mile 111 (Cabin Creek) in order to pick up his toboggan, bear traps and folding stove.

When the time came to make arrangements for the 1913 camp, Curly had to leave his trapline in early April and go to Edmonton, where Jack Otto spent his winters. Together they decided on what remuneration they hoped to obtain from the Alpine Club and on April 4th discussed their desires with Wheeler. Apparently they were acceptable, for on that day Curly, never one to waste words, made a rather cryptic note in his diary: "John Otto and I closed a deal with A. O. Wheeler, director of the Alpine Club, to handle the Club Camp at Robson Pass in July and August. Taking the 10 p.m. train for the west tonight."[7]

The closing of a deal for outfitting was not the only hurdle which had to be overcome in laying the proper groundwork to ensure a successful camp at Robson. A major difficulty presented itself in the form of the forbidding cliffs of the upper Grand Fork Valley which had required Phillips and Harvey's extra circuit of the mountain in 1911. Descending a total of 1600 feet in the space of less than a mile, the waters flowing out of Berg Lake

Curly Phillips' flying trestle bridge.

formed a series of beautiful waterfalls, the most spectacular being Emperor Falls, which made the building of a pack trail a seeming impossibility. Yet if such a trail were not constructed, the usual route up the Moose Valley and over Moose Pass would make the task of transporting a large camp far too expensive and time-consuming to allow it to be set up between Berg and Adolphus Lakes, the most favorable location from a mountaineering standpoint. Negotiations with the GTP and the British Columbia government were carried out by Wheeler and in the spring of 1913 the latter agreed to pay the costs of having a suitable trail built, if such were possible. Curly was awarded the contract at a reported $50 per mile, and with customary zeal and inventiveness he went to work on the problem. With the assistance of Frank Doucette, his friend, trapping partner and sometime packer, he fashioned a switchback trail, involving extensive cribbing and tilling, up the steep precipices. The crowning touch to this engineering feat was a flying-trestle bridge constructed around a rock face leading up to Emperor Falls, an edifice which never failed to elicit comment from those who used it.

After finishing his trail and bridge work early in July,

it was time for Curly to join with the Otto brothers to begin the job of packing in the camp equipment. Although the attendance was to be confined to the most proficient of the club's members, it was nonetheless fairly large with seventy-three participants scheduled to appear. Since the camp was to begin on July 28th, little time was available for the outfitters to get everything to its appointed place, and the new trail immediately proved its usefulness. It was also soon appreciated by those attending the camp, who not only escaped the long pack trip over the Moose Valley route but also were allowed to view the splendors of the Valley of a Thousand Falls.

At the camp itself, which lasted until August 9th, things ran extremely smoothly. Phillips and the Ottos were kept busy carrying members back and forth to two subsidiary camps placed six miles down the Smoky and near Moose Pass, and fortunately were aided in their work by perfect weather throughout. On July 31st the ascent of Robson, the main objective of the proceedings, was made by Kain, Albert H. MacCarthy and William W. Foster, and on returning from the conquest they were greeted by Phillips with the information that it was in actuality the first ascent and not the second, as they had supposed. All in all, the decision to combine outfitting forces was shown, once again, to be the most practicable means of making a success of such a large undertaking.

In spite of the numerous temporary partnerships formed by these outfitters in the early years there were, of course, some occasions when they handled parties completely on their own. If a party was composed of only one or two patrons, it was often possible to hire temporary help and take care of them singlehandedly. This became progressively more feasible as pack strings, equipment and supplies were built up over a period of time. Fortunately, there were also some fairly dependable sources of personnel available who were willing to work on a trip by trip basis.

One of the best places to find temporary manpower adept at packing and trail work was from among the ranks of the half-breed population in the region. Born and raised in the wilderness, they knew the country to the north of Jasper as no one else, and from their earliest youth they were familiar with the ways of the Indian cayuse commonly used as pack animals, attributes not easy to find in white men.

The first to come into prominence were Tommy Groat, son of respected Edmonton resident Malcolm Groat and an early packer on the GTP, and Adolphus Moberly, who in 1908 had aided Yates in finding a route into Robson Pass for the Mumm party. Moberly was only one of a number of half-breeds of that surname who along with several other settlers of mixed blood and Lewis Swift inhabited the area enclosed within the boundaries of Jasper Forest Park, a 5,450 square mile reservation created by the federal government in 1907. Such settlement was incompatible with government plans for the park and, in December, 1909, J. W. McLaggan,

recently appointed Chief Forest Ranger and Acting Superintendent, took on the task of trying to remove them. Swift would not budge, but the half-breeds came to terms fairly easily with most of them moving northward to the Grande Cache district, one of their favorite hunting and fishing grounds. But the move did not preclude their continuing to frequent the park in their wanderings, and soon several others, in addition to Groat and Adolphus Moberly, began to come to the attention of the outfitters as possible trail hands.

Relatives of Adolphus Moberly predominated with Frank, Dave and Ed Moberly and Felix Plante being some of the more noteworthy. But it was to be Adam Joachim, a Moberly in-law, who would gain the most lasting reputation. Joachim, a descendant of both the original Iroquois canoemen brought out by the Northwest Company and the famous Hudson's Bay Company trader Colin Fraser, was born at Berland Lake in 1875 and had rather an interesting upbringing for one who eventually would make much of his livelihood working on the trail. At an early age he came to the attention of the Catholic missionary Father Albert Lacombe who provided an education for him at the St. Albert Mission School. While living at the mission he also served as an altar boy and upon completion of his schooling was sent to the Seminary in Montreal to study for the priesthood. However, a family crisis intervened and, abandoning three years of hard work, he returned home and was soon married to a daughter of Ewan Moberly. A man of his education, able to speak several Indian languages as well as English, French and Latin, was eventually bound to attract attention, landing him jobs with a number of outfitters when he was not hunting or trapping on his own.

Supplementing the half-breeds as temporary trail hands were discontented railroad construction workers and the odd down-and-out prospector wanting to make a grubstake. Life in the construction camps was somewhat less than glamorous and combined with low wages made for what one observer claimed were three equal bodies of men — those actually working on the line, those fed up and heading back to Edmonton, and those replacing them heading out. This was not a completely accurate assessment as some of the laborers stuck around long enough to take one or two pack trips, although few remained in the vicinity for any length of time. Prospectors were much the same, working as packers only long enough to set themselves up for their next venture and then disappearing back into the bush.

By employing these as well as their more permanent men, a few of the Jasper outfitters were able to make some important hunting and exploration trips on their own in the years prior to the First World War. Perhaps the most celebrated were the three expeditions of Samuel Prescott Fay between 1912 and 1914, outfitted by Brewster and Moore and guided by Fred Brewster.

Fay was the type of client an outfitter dreamed about, hiring an outfit for three to four months and returning for

Adam Joachim.

several years. A native of Boston and a Harvard graduate, he had first visited the Rockies at Lake O'Hara in 1906. At least two other visits to the Banff vicinity took place prior to 1912, but unlike his relative, Professor Charles Fay, he was more interested in hunting than climbing. It was not surprising, therefore, that when he heard of the excellent sport to be had along the new GTP line, he was attracted to the scene.

Certainly the reports were not unfounded as the wilderness north of the railroad abounded in bear, deer, moose and goat with an added attraction not plentiful in the south, caribou. But what interested Fay was solving the question as to the variety of sheep inhabiting the region north of the Athabasca River and south of the Peace River. Bighorn sheep *(Ovis Canadensis)* were known to range south of the Athabasca and Stone Sheep *(Ovis Stonei)* north of the Peace, but the species or subspecies roaming the country between was still a mystery to naturalists.

Fay appeared at Hinton in early August, 1912, and contracted Fred Brewster to handle the outfitting for his trip. Since this was to be the first hunting party handled by Brewster and Moore in their new location, Fred decided to guide it himself with one of his most trusted men, J. Beaumont Gates, assisting. On August 8th, with a seven horse pack train, the three set out, intending to get as far as possible beyond the Smoky River in the time available. Fred felt that this was the initial attempt by white men to penetrate the country west of the Smoky for purposes of big game hunting, and the trail seemed to support this assumption.

Struggling through downed timber and treacherous muskegs south of the Muddywater River, they easily bested Yates and Stephens' 1911 mark of taking seven days to cover twenty-five miles by consuming twice as much time for the same distance. The Muddywater and Jackpine Rivers, as well as Sheep Creek, were hunted unsuccessfully but not without profit, as in the process the environs of Mount Bess were examined in detail and a good view obtained of a peak some thirty miles away to the northwest which rivalled Robson in magnificence. Further examination of this mountain proved fruitless for although they were able to get within ten miles of its supposed location the weather proved so foul for the next two weeks that not a single glimpse of it was obtained.

Bad weather, a shortage of supplies and a complete lack of success in hunting also greeted the end of September, the date Fay had been expecting to arrive back in Hinton, necessitating the abandonment of both mountain and sheep hunts for 1912. Starting down the Porcupine (Kakwa) River in an endeavor to find a way home that would avoid the high, snow-covered passes, the party continued to be dogged by the weather's persistent inclemency. After striking the Smoky River, snow fell incessantly, and it was not until the end of October that Hinton was finally gained, with men and horses completely exhausted.

Unperturbed by his failure, Fay laid plans to return the next year to continue his quest, and Fred again expressed a willingness to act as guide. In the interim, though, Fay underwent a serious operation, and when the time came to resume the investigation he was in no shape to undergo its rigors. As a consequence, Fred suggested a foreshortened trip that would proceed at a more leisurely pace. Beginning from Brewster and Moore's new headquarters in Jasper, a few weeks were spent in the vicinities of Mounts Robson and Bess. Later, an additional two months were taken up in hunting sheep as far south as Laggan and caribou along the Great Divide above Fortress Lake.

But this in no way compensated for Fay's real objective, and elaborate plans were once more made with Brewster for the 1914 season. That year's expedition took on an added dimension when Fay received a commission from the Biological Survey of the U.S. Department of Agriculture to make collections of animal skins and detailed reports on the birds and mammals of the region.

Support from the Biological Survey allowed for extensions in both the range and time limit of the trip, and when Fay arrived at Jasper in June, 1914, it was with the intention of pushing right through to the Peace River.

The proposed lengthening of the expedition and the fact that Fay brought along a friend, C. R. Cross Jr. of Boston, made the need for an enlarged outfit and crew apparent. Sixteen pack horses and five saddle horses were rounded up, taxing Brewster and Moore's comparatively small pack string to its limit, and to handle them two green but willing men were utilized. They were Bob Jones, a former railroad worker who in later years would achieve a fine reputation as a park warden, and Jack Symes, an ex-North West Mounted Police constable.

Leaving Jasper on June 26th, the party was guided for the first two weeks by Jack Brewster, as Fred was tied up helping Phil Moore get started on a contract the company had to clear a trail into Medicine and Jacques Lakes. However, he was replaced as guide by his more experienced brother at the head of the Sulphur River.

The Brewster-Fay party, 1914. Left to right — Samuel Prescott Fay, C. R. "Bob" Cross, Bob Jones, Jack Symes and Fred Brewster.

The Brewster-Fay party chopping through downed timber.

Two days hence Fred and Fay again glimpsed the intriguing mountain they had seen in 1912 and decided to detour in order to study it in more detail.

The peak, when sighted, was still a long way off to the northwest, and getting close enough to obtain good views was not an easy matter. After passing through the settlement of Grande Cache at the confluence of the Sulphur and Smoky Rivers, the Smoky was crossed and the trails were found to be either old or non-existent. As Fay noted in his diary, the trails demanded great skill on the part of their guide and patience on the part of all:

We found the old trail but no one had been over it for years, — probably not since the big fire burnt it over. It has fallen in so anyone coming this way avoids it. The only people who go this way are breeds and one or two trappers. Fred and Bob Jones went ahead to chop the trees away and it was slow work. Signs of the old trail appeared now and then and how Fred followed it the way

he did was a mystery to all of us. It was a fine exhibition of a guide's seventh sense. Finally, we decided to hit across the top of the hill to find the old trail and here was our mistake, as the trail turned out to be ahead of us some ways. From here on we had lots of chopping and it was slow, tiresome work. Packs came off and sometimes three or four horses had to be repacked at once. Roachy fell under some logs and could not move until the logs were cut away. Snowball's pack went clear over his head but the ropes held him so he couldn't move. One trouble after another turned up and it was 8 p.m. before we made camp in a mess of down timber, with no feed for the horses. After a while we picked out spaces between the fallen logs, unrolled our blankets, and were soon asleep.[8]

Fighting their way up Sheep Creek, they finally caught sight of the mountain again and estimated its height at 12,000 feet. On August 3rd another excellent, but unexpected view was obtained from what was appropriately named Surprise Pass, and for the next ten days the peak was constantly in sight while the party continued northward. Fay was completely distracted by its great size and beauty and, in consultation with Brewster, decided to name it Mount Alexander in honor of the intrepid fur trader-explorer Alexander Mackenzie. Later the name would be altered to Mount Sir Alexander, at 10,700 feet the highest peak in the Rockies north of Mount Robson.

With Fay's two year old interest in the great mountain finally satisfied, his attention turned to the biological survey and the question of the sheep. Specimens similar to those sought by the Smithsonian party in 1911 were either shot or trapped and later carefully skinned and preserved in the interests of science. The fact that the collecting was accomplished in all kinds of weather and while travelling through unfamiliar country often led to uncertainty and frustration. On particularly bad days these feelings showed up in Fay's diary: "Why any sane man comes to these mountains is a mystery to me when he knows the misery he has to endure — yet we all do it again and again."[9]

The plan of the expedition had been to get to Pine Pass and then across country to the Peace River, but by the beginning of September it was obvious that the pass would be impossible to reach. As an alternative it was decided to head immediately for Hudson's Hope on the Peace and from there return to Jasper by way of Pouce Coupe, Grande Prairie and Edson. Although this would not allow for a complete study of all possible sheep ranges, Fay felt that he had already satisfactorily answered that question. From his observations he concluded that there were no sheep between the Peace River and the heads of the northern tributaries of the Smoky River, and the sheep south of his line were of the same species as found between Banff and Jasper. These conclusions were supported by the reports of Indians and half-breeds met in the course of the journey.

A change in the previously excellent weather pattern and a growing difficulty in filling out the larder immediately illustrated the wisdom of their decision to head for Hudson's Hope. Sixteen days of continuous rain and snow cut progress to a minimum, and the accommodation situation suffered a serious setback when Symes accidentally burned down the portable lean-to shelter, "the most useful article in the whole outfit." Fourteen weeks on the trail had also taken a rather devastating toll on the men's personal apparel, and by early October a day had to be taken to sew themselves back together:

Fred, whose outfit is usually in pieces, at present is sewing his hat, the crown having been slowly torn off until it is held by one corner only. Yesterday when he faced the wind his lid stood on end, making him look like some crested creature. His trousers are continually in need of repair as his supply is limited to two pair. If he had more these wouldn't be worth repairing. The ordinary person if

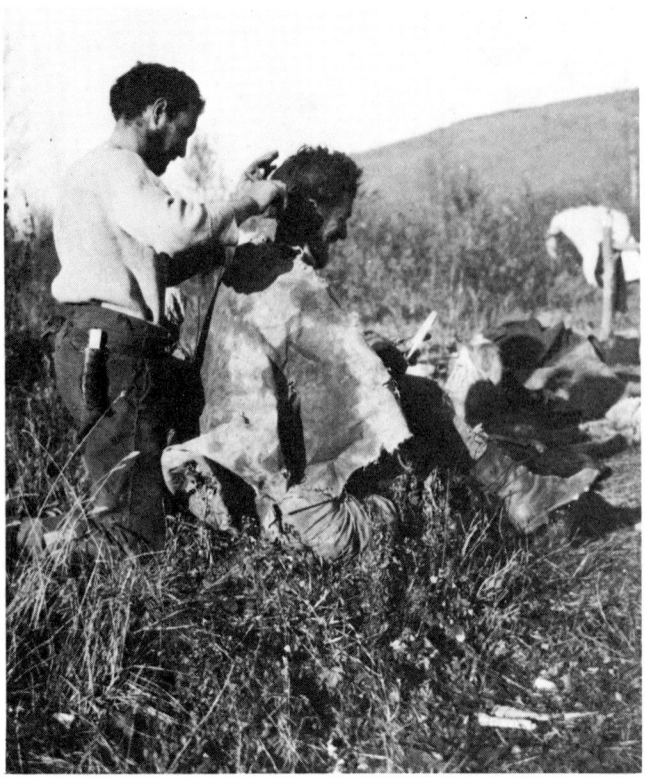

Bob Jones cutting Fred Brewster's hair in preparation for reaching civilization.

assigned to such a job would be at a loss to know which piece to sew on to which, so many are there of them. He spent the morning sewing his socks, the repairing of which was similar to a picture puzzle. However, the results were excellent.[10]

These repairs were particularly necessary at this juncture because the party soon expected to be meeting white men, a pleasure they had not experienced for almost four months. When they finally did, a startling piece of news greeted them. On October 7th they encountered a trapper named Nelson, and when questioned as to the latest news he commented that the war was still the main topic of interest. At first thinking that the United States had gone to war with Mexico, they queried him further, and finally realized that the First World War had been raging for two months.

After learning this disquieting information, the party hurried on to Hudson's Hope, reaching it on October 16th after sixteen weeks on the trail. Mission accomplished, they began the return to Jasper following the road through the farming districts of Pouce Coupe and Grande Prairie, using a wagon to carry much of the equipment. At Beaverlodge they split up, Fay and Cross continuing by road to Edson while Brewster, Jones and Symes cut across country with four pack horses and three saddle horses. Battling the first winter snows, the three finally reached Jasper on November 21st, and the longest recorded tourist pack trip in the Rockies to date, lasting some five months, was at an end.

Although probably the most important of these years, Fred Brewster's three expeditions with Fay were not the only ones handled by an outfitter on his own. In 1914 Curly Phillips outfitted an interesting party that wished to examine the same mountain which had so captivated Fay.

As intimated, Phillips was an inveterate trapper, and over a period of years he explored most of the territory between Mount Robson and Jackpine Pass. During the winter of 1913 he ran a trapline down to within a few miles of what he called "Big Mountain" and thereby became completely familiar with the entire Sir Alexander region. Elsewhere, Mary Jobe, a wealthy young New York woman who taught American history at Hunter College, had heard reports of the magnificence of the peak from those who had seen it while climbing at the 1913 Mount Robson camp. Since Phillips was the only one known to have actually visited the area, her inquiries about the possibility of reaching the mountain put her in touch with him and a trip was arranged. Travelling with Miss Jobe was Margaret Springate, a friend from Winnipeg, the two making a party sufficiently small for Curly to outfit alone. During the years from 1911 to 1914 he had constantly been building up his pack string, and the manpower situation had taken a decided turn for the better with the the appearance at Jasper of his brother-in-law Bert Wilkins in May, 1913, and both his father, Daniel, and brother, Harry, in early 1914.

The trip would be a difficult one for the ladies as it crossed country where few trails existed. In an attempt to travel as lightly and quickly as possible only four pack horses and one assistant, Wilkins, were taken along. Beginning early in August they followed a route to Robson Pass and then went northwestward in what seemed like a dreary procession of more passes, including Bess, Jackpine and Jones, until at the Big Salmon (McGregor) River further travel with horses was impossible. Among the obstacles already overcome were timber so thick and ridges so steep that at one point the men had to work twelve hours cutting out three-quarters of a mile of trail, which included twenty-four separate switchbacks. From the point where the horses were left they packed all the supplies on their own backs, an equally arduous chore since the mountain was still fairly distant. Finally they reached its foot, and Jobe, unaware of Fay and Brewster's recent naming, called it Kitchi, Cree for "great" or "mighty".

Despite the two days of bone-wearying walking to a point from where an ascent might be launched, they made two plucky but unsuccessful attempts on August 22nd and 25th. On the second try Curly and Miss Jobe attained an elevation of 7,800 feet before the difficulty of the remaining climbing and short supplies forced a retreat. After this a return to Jasper was imperative, but it was not the last time the mountain would see the two

Mary Jobe.

attempting to capture its magnificent, snow-capped summit for they would return for a renewed effort the next year. As for her outfitter's performance on the 1914 outing, Miss Jobe wrote a rather flattering assessment: "I wish to say that the main factors in our success were the splended ability, unflinching courage and determined effort of Donald Phillips."[11]

The Otto brothers, too, were relatively successful in obtaining some parties small enough to outfit on their own in the immediate pre-war years. Among those worthy of note were two composed of individuals with wide literary reputations.

One of the Ottos best customers was James Oliver Curwood, who went out with them on at least five different occasions beginning immediately before the war and continuing until the mid-twenties. Curwood had begun his career as a reporter for a Detroit newspaper, but he had later discovered a talent for writing adventure stories and went on to become America's most prolific author of this genre. Many of his works, such as *Kazan, The Wolf Dog* and *Nomads of the North,* were transformed into screenplays for motion pictures, and at one time his name on the marquee was all that was needed to ensure a sell-out house anywhere in North America.

Because he preferred to set his stories in the so-called "trackless wilderness" of Canada, his books, although in a somewhat inaccurate manner, were serving to advertise the country. This led the Canadian government to provide him with financial support to allow for further "research." Each summer for about ten years he spent three to four months in the Canadian wilds, often in the Rockies. During these visits it was his practice to take extensive sightseeing and hunting trips outfitted by Otto Brothers and usually guided by Bruce Otto, for whom he seemed to have a particular liking. In fact, in a book published in 1917 entitled *The Grizzly King,* Bruce became the main character in the story of a grizzly bear and how he survived a hunt by a crack guide and his dude. In another Curwood epic, *The Hunted Woman,* both Fred Stephens and Mrs. Jack Otto appeared as characters in a melodramatic tale set in the Yellowhead region.

A second and perhaps even more famous author to be served by Otto Brothers was Sir Arthur Conan Doyle, creator of the popular Sherlock Holmes series. Conan Doyle, his wife and children paid a visit to Jasper in the summer of 1914, just in time to have the local citizenry corral him into laying the cornerstone for the town's first church, known as "The Little White Church in the Rockies." During his stay he expressed a desire to take a short pack trip, which was provided by Closson Otto. It turned out that he was so delighted with the experience that he wrote a poem, "The Athabaska Trail," which read in part:

I shall hear the roar of rivers where the rapids foam and tear
I shall smell the virgin upland with its balsam laden air
I shall soon again be riding down the winding, woody vale
With the packer and the pack horse on the Athabaska Trail.[12]

By 1914 some of the Jasper outfitters had been able to gain a measure of security and prosperity. Their willingness to become involved in temporary partnerships had certainly played a major part in this, since they had allowed for the outfitting of parties that otherwise would have been unmanageable. Already by 1914 the gradual build-up of horses, equipment and manpower was making such combinations less necessary, but the good-will they engendered would long remain. At the outbreak of the war the future of outfitting in the area seemed particularly bright with the newly completed GTP and the soon to be completed CNR making the region much more accessible to potential tourists. It would prove so for some but not for others.

James Oliver Curwood preparing to depart from the Otto Brothers' corral, ca. 1915.
Closson Otto (front right) and Mr. and Mrs. Jack Otto (rear).

Jim Brewster and staff at Brewster Transfer Company's upper (CPR) stables, ca. 1909.

8   Artists, Hunters and the Ladies

At the same time as the outfitters of the Jasper region were co-operating in an effort to make their operations viable in the years prior to the First World War, the competition now characteristic of outfitting along the CPR continued unabated. As pointed out, this competition had already played a part in the decision of some individuals to seek greener pastures, but for those who chose to remain survival was possible given a measure of skill and efficient management. Such was also the case for a few of the new faces that appeared on the outfitting scene in the area. Though the Brewsters had a tight hold on most of the CPR concessions, there were three major conditions which allowed for the appearance of new outfitting businesses.

Certainly the Alpine Club's support of the independent outfitters was an important factor, as the annual camps and the post-camp mountaineering parties they spawned offered a considerable volume of business. Another was the ever-increasing onslaught of tourists who were annually descending on Rocky Mountains Park and wished to visit the back country. Although there were yearly fluctuations, the number of visitors increased at such a rapid rate that by 1913 the park's hotels were registering some 61,000 guests, double the amount in 1906. However, it was probably the circumstances existing within the Brewster operation which as much as anything accounted for their competitors' success.

In 1908, when Brewster Brothers added the concessions at Lake Louise and Field to the one they already held at Banff, it appeared that it was only a matter of time until the company would have a complete stranglehold on outfitting along the CPR through the Rockies and Selkirks. But there were several factors at work which tended to make this situation unlikely to occur. One of these had to do with the nature of the con-

cessions themselves. They allowed the company the sole right to solicit conveyance of any kind, be it by horse or carriage, within the confines of the railway's hotels and on station platforms. Often the carriage trade proved the more lucrative and consequently it received the most attention. This was particularly true in wet years when the convertible tally-hos used for sightseeing continued to run at full capacity while the trail business languished because of the poor weather.

In the same vein, the nature of the company's total business interests affected their trail operations. Although its historic roots were in outfitting, the expansion of its activities into other concerns, including a store, livery stable, blacksmith shop and opera house, meant that a good deal of attention had to be devoted to these matters, sometimes at outfitting's expense. The company's reputation and success as outfitters was mainly attributable to the guiding talents of Jim and Bill Brewster, but after 1905 neither could afford much time to personally lead parties on the trail.

Related to the nature of the company were some internal developments which also tended to have an adverse effect. As mentioned, the partnership which had formed Brewster Brothers in 1904 was composed of four individuals, Jim and Bill Brewster, Philip Moore and Fred Hussey. This combination seemed to work fairly effectively during its first couple of years of existence, but before too long it became increasingly apparent that the company hinged more on the colorful personality of Jim Brewster than the abilities of its other members. He was the dynamic promoter, flamboyant public relations man and maker of contacts, while Bill preferred to remain more behind the scenes and attend to the everyday details of the business. Hussey tended to identify with Jim, and for many years the two were close companions, not only on the trail in a yearly hunting trip but also in the salons of high society in the cities of the eastern United States. Moore, although a Brewster in-law after 1907, was more his own man.

Apparently these personality differences did not lead to any serious ill-feeling, but by 1906 Jim was finding the conditions of partnership too constricting for his liking and decided to pull out. In April he and Hussey sold their shares in Brewster Brothers to their partners. Jim remained in Banff until the fall of 1907 and then moved to Victoria, where he had some land interests. In the interim, his father had sold the Brewster Dairy to Frank Wellman and had also departed for the coast to open a real estate agency. Although Jim returned to Banff to spend the summer of 1908, it was not until early in 1909 that he came back to stay, this time with the intention of gaining controlling interest in the company. An agreement was reached in June, 1909 in which he acquired all shares in Brewster Brothers and then converted them into two new companies, Brewster Transfer Company and Brewster Trading Company. He retained majority control of both companies with his younger brother Fred and Fred Hussey as minority shareholders, the former holding only a nominal single share.

Moore quickly went into partnership with Fred and Jack Brewster in Brewster and Moore and headed northward. On the other hand, Bill Brewster set his sights to the south and, after settling his family in San Antonio, Texas, took part in an extended expedition to Chile. Upon returning he moved his family first to Reno, Nevada and then to Lake Tahoe, remaining there until he was approached with an interesting proposition in 1912. Glacier National Park in Montana was being developed by the Great Northern Railway, and the company's president asked newspaperman Jack Farrell, an acquaintance of Bill's, if he knew of anyone capable of handling tourist transport. Farrell claimed he knew just the man, and by the end of the year Bill was back in business with a new organization, Park Saddle Horse Company.

The unsettling period the Brewster operation went through prior to 1909 was bound to have some effect on its ability to function at peak efficiency. In fact, even after outfitting came under the aegis of Brewster Transfer Company, there continued to be ups and downs. Again this was largely a reflection of Jim Brewster's personality. When he chose to concentrate his full energies on the business it flourished, but all too often he was distracted by his involvement in local activities, from the organization of Indian Days to serving on the Board of Trade, and by his attempts to encourage tourism in the Canadian Rockies.

Being by nature a promoter, he travelled extensively appearing at expositions, sportsman shows and outdoor clubs and, through his associations with Hussey and Moore, visiting the "right" people in social and financial circles. Always the consummate showman, he often took the opportunity to play the part of the character from the "wild west" on these occasions. For instance, during a visit to England he was the guest at an earl's estate and when asked to participate in the traditional fox hunt he appeared mounted on his hunter attired in his buckskin shirt and grizzly bear chaps.

Such antics were apparently well-received, and his ability to attract new and wealthy customers for both the CPR and his own company was considerable. However, at the same time, his frequent absences from the office meant that subordinates had to look after the company's welfare, and many times the steadying hand of Bill Brewster was sorely missed. This situation was aggravated when the business took on two new aspects with the purchase of the Mount Royal Hotel from David McDougall in 1912 and the acquiring of a newspaper, *The Rocky Mountain Courier,* in 1916.

Equally unsettling to the smooth functioning of the company's outfitting branch was the manpower situation, especially after the takeover of the concessions at Lake Louise and Field. At least three guides had to be stationed at these locations for the busy summer season, and it was often necessary to have more at Banff. The guides, of course, had to be supported by a like number of cooks and numerous packers. But, with so many positions to be filled and the penchant for trailmen to drift from one outfitter to another, it was a constant battle to find really competent men at all times. Because of this the company often resorted to using only marginally efficient men and to hiring students, a practice that had occasionally been employed earlier by Wilson and Campbell. These students were often Princeton men whose fathers had prevailed on Hussey to provide them with summer jobs, and they many times left something to be desired in the performance of their duties. Wheeler described them as "babes in the woods", but he was not the only one to express his dissatisfaction. Another disgruntled patron, identifying himself only as "Disgusted," wrote on the matter to the editor of the Banff *Crag and Canyon:*

The world can stand still for no one, and yet the pace at which the old sphere has been running along the CPR line for the past year or two has been an eye-opener to one who has visited your little town and other stopping places along the road in the past. Tom Wilson, Bill Peyto and Bob Campbell were familiar to all who loved the cayuse's back and the smell of the campfire. Where are they today? Who knew so well how to throw the diamond hitch, fry a pan of bacon, make a bough bed, or tell fascinating yarns when the day's march or hunt was over? We find but a handful of the old men left, the men who have dug deep into the secrets of camp life and with their strong personalities lured us from the stock markets, the exchanges, the rush of business life in the east to forget for a time our cares by living with men who knew how to live . . . Wake up you people of Banff, wake up my old friend CPR.

Jim Brewster leading the Banff Indian Days parade, 1913.

We people to the east have known the very cream of camping in your country. You are giving us some very false coin in return for our loyalty. Bring to the fore the real, the reliable outfitter, and send back to town the youngsters who in stage "shaps" pose as wild cowboys to the innocent and unsuspecting tourist.[1]

In fairness the foregoing did not apply to Brewsters' regular men, who were as competent as any on the trail. Fortunately for the company when the new concessions were taken over they could build on a nucleus of excellent guides, stalwarts such as George Harrison, Fred Tabuteau, Bill Potts, Soapy Smith, Tex Wood and Frank Wellman, who had been with them for several years. Added to these as time went on were men drawn from a variety of sources: James I. McLeod, a former guide for Campbell who became Brewsters' head man at Lake Louise and eventually the company's general manager; Reggie Holmes, who had been associated with Elliott Barnes's outfit; Ulysse "Frog" LaCasse, a native of Ontario who started with the company as their baker in The

Birdcage but soon possessed the title of the best trail cook in the Canadian Rockies; and Stan J. "Windy" Carr, an English immigrant who worked on several prairie ranches before joining Brewster Transfer at Lake Louise in 1910. Others included Wes Latham, Art Jordan, Howard "Fat" Kane, Frank Beattie, Ben Woodworth, Jack Bevan, Ike Brooks, Ted Cook, Jack Warren, George Hankins, Ray Legace, Roy Brydon, Jack Thomas and "Lord Jim" Howard. All of these men were valuable in their own way and many would provide material for the colorful stories which would make the Brewster guides and packers legends in their own time.

One of the most notorious of the Brewster guides stationed at Field was George Hankins. He was known to all as "The Hooknosed Kid" because of a particularly obvious physical characteristic and had a brother nicknamed "Big Foot" because of an equally noticeable appendage. A native of the Columbia River country, Hankins had fought in the Boer War and on returning had gone to work for Wilson and Campbell, becoming one of their head guides. When Brewsters took over the

A group of Brewster Brothers packers known as "The Dirty Dozen," 1909. Bob Logan (1), Ted Cook (2), Bill Potts (3), Jerry Fuller (4), George Harrison (5), Jack Warren (6), Jack Giddie (7), Soapy Smith (8), Jack Bevan (9), George Hankins (10), Bert Sibbald (11) and Wattie Potts (12).

concession at Field he had remained in their employ along with his friend Jack Giddie, whose name was usually transposed to "Giddy Jack." The two had prominent reputations for living the "high life" when not on the trail, and in Hankins' case, at least, these activities sometimes carried over to times when he should have been working.

In 1909 Tex Wood was assigned to meet Hankins in Golden from where they were to take out a party bound for the Windermere region. Tex arrived at the designated meeting place only to find that his fellow employee had not yet appeared, and after a considerable wait he began to enquire around as to his whereabouts. Someone finally directed him to a house just west of town, and when he approached it he heard a terrific din coming from within. On entering he immediately realized that it was a "house of assignation" and quickly found the source of the racket. Agilely running up and down the keyboard of a piano in his boots and spurs, much to the delight of the "ladies," was "The Hooknosed Kid."

Another celebrated character who went on the trail for Brewsters was "Lord Jim" Howard, a classic case of the remittance man run amok. A younger brother of the Earl of Suffolk, the Honorable James Estcourt Howard, Viscount Andover was one of those second and third sons who were paid a substantial annual stipend as the price of their absence from the home fires. He first appeared at Banff in 1908 when he was a guest at the Brewster Bungalow, probably as a result of his brother's friendship with Jim and Bill. For several years thereafter he was regularly forced to go to work as a cook or packer because of his penchant for spending his remittance at the Banff Springs Hotel in a grand spree. After one such wild and woolly bender he was assigned to cook for a wealthy Pittsburg steel magnate. While sitting around the evening campfire a few days out on the trail the client, obviously having heard of Lord Jim's recent escapades, asked the guide, "This Lord Jim I heard about in town, is he really an Earl's brother?"

"I guess so" replied the guide.

"Do you know him?"

"Yeah, I know him."

"Extraordinary thing, imagine a real Earl's brother. I'd give a lot to meet him. Cook, do you know him?"

After what seemed like a long pause while the cook stared woefully into the glowing coals, he replied, "Yeah, too goddam well!"[2]

Several outfitters were to benefit from the developments on the Brewster outfitting scene in the years preceding the war but none more so than Jim Simpson, the man who quickly became their chief competitor. Rather interestingly, Simpson and Jim Brewster possessed a number of similar traits, among them being keen intellect and wit, a colorful personality and a streak of wildness. In addition, both had a strongly developed love for the wilderness and were especially fond of hunting. Brewster, after about 1905, had to restrict his hunting to pleasure trips a few times a year, whereas Simpson, with his smaller scale business interests, was soon able to make hunting an integral part of them.

Both men were also performers at heart and realized that showmanship could be made to work to their advantage. Any number of ploys were used to impress the tourists, a particularly notable one being Simpson's practice of studying up on his customer's interests, be they medicine or the stock market, so that he could talk intelligently with them. As he put it, this would eliminate the necessity of them having to listen to "the first eighty-seven stanzas of the cowboy's lament" while out on the trail.

Other techniques of impressing dudes were highly developed abilities to prevaricate and play practical jokes, and the adoption of distinctive attire. Brewster's sartorial trademark was his grizzly bear chaps and buckskin shirt while for Simpson it was his wide-brimmed Mounted Police stetson, drawn from a mysteriously endless supply. Brewster's interests in community activities and the encouragement of tourism were also duplicated by Simpson. He spent much of his time in the winter coaching local hockey teams and promoting the Banff Curling Club. Beginning in 1916 he also began to make frequent trips to the eastern United States and Canada to advertise the attractions of the park and his own business. The first was a honeymoon trip to New York City on the occasion of his marriage to Williamina Ross Reid. Finally, as most trailmen, both Simpson and Brewster had a well-developed fondness for whiskey and rum, or "Nelson's blood" as Simpson called it, and they went on many a tear, sometimes together.

Apart from his previously mentioned ability to obtain the outfitting contracts for the Alpine Club camps, Simpson also had increasing success in attracting important private parties. One customer who provided him with many valuable connections for the future was "the butterfly lady."

Mrs. Mary de la Beach-Nichol, daughter of former Chancellor of the Exchequer of Great Britain, had taken up lepidoptery as a hobby after her family of six children had grown up, and her collection ranked her with other such noteworthy aficionados as the Rothschilds. Being wealthy she could afford to spend a good deal of each summer traipsing about the mountains searching for new and interesting butterflies, and after her initial successful expedition to the Yoho Valley under Jim's guidance in 1904, she decided to visit the Mount Assiniboine region. The other parties must have been greatly surprised to see an old lady clad in a weather-beaten black gown and a dilapidated Panama hat with a butterfly net in one hand and an ear trumpet in the other nimbly stalking her elusive prey around the shores of Lake Magog, her guide in hot pursuit carrying the collecting box.

Jim Simpson — the big game hunter.

Despite the effect such activities must have had on his budding reputation as a "big game" guide, Jim recognized a good proposition when he saw one and agreed to accompany Mrs. Beach-Nichol again the next year. While the two previous trips had been in his own neighborhood and of short duration, this time she desired that he accompany her much farther afield and for a period of at least three months. The horses were shipped by rail to Salmon Arm, B.C., and from there he led them south around Okanagan Lake, across the Similkameen River on a barge and eventually down to Lake Chelan in the State of Washington.

While searching for specimens the pair ventured up the Ashnola River on the B.C.-Washington border and into rattlesnake country. Here Jim became quite concerned about his client's welfare since he felt that she would be unable to hear the snake's warning rattle because of her deafness. He quickly found that he need not worry as the intrepid lady was soon searching out the snakes, pinning them down with a forked stick, cutting off their heads and then skinning them out for a new collection.

On returning from their lengthy outing "the butterfly lady" was able to pronounce it an unqualified success as she had captured and identified two previously unknown varieties of moths. This led her to return for a third season in 1907 when they spent most of the summer in Jim's territory between Bow Lake and the Alexandra River searching for more as yet unidentified or un-catalogued classes of lepidoptera.

Another contact made by Jim a short time after Mrs. Beach-Nichol's final trip was equally beneficial, and interestingly it came about at his own instigation. While reading an outdoors magazine in the winter of 1909-10, his eye fell on the reproduction of a Dall sheep painting which had recently been done for the New York Zoological Society by Carl Rungius, a German-born artist then living at Greenpoint, Long Island. The quality of the work so impressed Jim that he immediately took it upon himself to write and invite the artist to visit the Canadian Rockies and apply his talents to similar work on bighorn sheep. Since Rungius had spent so much time in the field, in Wyoming, New Brunswick and the Yukon, he was at first unenthusiastic about the offer and threw the letter away. But, as luck would have it, his wife insisted that he retrieve the missive from the trash, and after several re-readings and a further exchange of correspondence with Jim, Rungius decided to accept the invitation, appearing at Banff in August, 1910.

Staying at Simpson's home, recently constructed along the river next to Bill Peyto's old cabin, Rungius quickly got to know his guide, and soon they were off on visits to Consolation Valley and Ptarmigan Lake in order that some preliminary sketch work could be done. Then in early September, with Ernie Brearley as an assistant, Jim took him up the North Fork of the Saskatchewan, over Wilcox and Nigel Passes and finally into the Brazeau basin. Here the artist spent some time sketching goats and was able to kill a small ram which, with the addition of a grizzly he bagged on Nigel Pass, provided excellent models for his canvases.

Rungius was so enthusiastic about the results of his 1910 trip that it became the first of an annual visit to the Rockies. Soon his reputation had flowered to the degree that Jim was able to convince the CPR to issue him with a yearly pass to Banff as a publicity measure. For several years Rungius and his wife continued to stay at Simpson's while in Banff, but in the winter of 1921-22 it was decided that a permanent studio was needed. Jim purchased two lots on Cave Avenue for him and immediately set to work to build the edifice according to a set of blueprints drawn up by an architect friend of Rungius'. Thereafter Jim usually supplied the outfit for

his summer pack trip while Rungius paid for the services of two men and bought the supplies. In return for the use of the outfit Jim was given a painting each year, and over the course of time their value appreciated to the extent that they were worth many times what it had cost him to forego payment for his horses and equipment.

Rungius' growing reputation soon led Simpson into relationships with such other notable wildlife artists as Archibald Thorburn, Louis Agassiz Fuertes and Henry Emerson Tuttle, and by performing services for each of them he was able to add to his collection of paintings. For Thorburn he collected bird skins which were sent to England where they were stuffed and used as models. Jim was suitably rewarded with a valuable painting of some goldfinches, the models for which had been among the specimens he gathered. Fuertes requested the skinned-out heads of big game animals which had to be sawed into parts and sent to his studio in Ithaca, New York, work which was paid for with a painting of a blue jay. Tuttle was taken out on an extended pack trip to do some sketching and so enjoyed it that he sent a painting of a goshawk as a mark of his appreciation. Ultimately these men were also partially responsible for awakening within Jim an interest in doing his own painting and in later years he became an accomplished watercolorist.

A further important offshoot of Jim's friendship with Rungius was the connections it gave him with some of America's wealthiest big game hunters. In 1903 Rungius had become a charter member of the Campfire Club of America, a social club composed of around 150 of the United States' leading outdoorsmen. Always anxious to be placed in touch with guides capable of leading them to potential world record trophies, these men were soon enquiring of the artist who it was that handled his trips. Such enquiries led to Jim guiding parties composed of those who would subsequently become some of his steadiest customers, including William N. "Billy" Beach and Joseph A. McAleenan, two of New York's foremost businessmen, and Dr. Harlow Brooks, a leading heart and lung specialist.

Outfitting and guiding big game hunters was an integral part of every outfitter's business and often his overall success or failure depended on his ability in this regard. In many seasons the income from tourists, mountaineers and fishermen was sufficient only to meet the year's expenses, and if there was to be any profit it would come from such hunting trips. Fortunately for Jim, he had a passion for big game hunting, especially for sheep which was the animal most prized by the majority of his clients.

Jim's reputation as a sheep guide and his love of the occupation were perhaps best expressed by Robert Frothingham, an eminent American sportsman who often wrote for the outdoors magazine *Field and Stream:* "Simpson is, without doubt, the best hunter and most expert stalker of Bighorn Sheep in Western Canada. To quote his own words he would rather stalk sheep than oc-

Carl Rungius with a good ram, ca. 1910.

cupy a front seat in the heavenly choir!" [3] Apart from Jim's stalking ability, his main attributes as a sheep hunting guide were unwavering patience and instinct, both of which were well-illustrated on Billy Beach's maiden attempt to procure a Canadian Rockies ram.

For several years Jim had taken his parties to different parts of the mountains in search of the elusive sheep with varying degrees of success, but it was not until around 1910 that he discovered his sheep paradise, the Brazeau River basin. This area contained an abundance of ideal sheep range, and it was here that he led Beach and his companion H. G. Morden. Soon after arriving Jim spotted some rams on a glacier late in the afternoon but decided that it would be best to leave them until the next day. Early in the morning the rams were found in the same locale and the hunt began in earnest.

Patience now came into the game, for we lay behind some rocks from eleven o'clock in the morning until five in the afternoon before they began to feed. At five-twenty

we started the stalk and here was where Jim's ability as a ram hunter stood out. The wind was quite strong and though favorable there were so many draws on the moraine it was important to avoid places that might lead down towards the sheep. Jim worked carefully and deliberately, going well above and then gradually coming down until we were within about a hundred yards. The one decided upon had a beautiful curl . . . and it took us but a short time before we were off to camp. [4]

Jim's patience in waiting six hours for the right moment and then a flawless stalk had resulted in a fine ram for Beach, and soon his instinct would provide an equally good opportunity for Morden. While sitting in camp waiting for dinner, he became uneasy and rose from his seat, mentioning that he felt there were some sheep in the vicinity. Although the others scoffed at this suggestion he nonetheless picked up his binoculars and began scanning the mountainside. Within a few minutes he was able to announce that there were eight good rams just behind

Jim Simpson after a successful hunt.

camp. A flurry of activity ensued and in no time he and Morden started off after them. None met with their approval that evening, but the next day the same bunch were trailed and an excellent trophy taken out of the thirty-eight rams they spotted.

Similar instances of instinct would stand Jim in good stead on many another hunt. In fact, in later life he claimed that he would sometimes dream there was game in a particular location and on investigating the next day would find it there.

One final interesting though much less auspicious aspect of Jim's big game hunting activity was his penchant for poaching if the opportunity arose. During the early years of the national parks' existence the regulations regarding game preservation were virtually impossible to enforce due to the absence of a well-organized and staffed warden service. Taking illegal

game was therefore a relatively safe and easy matter. Most if not all of the guides working in the Banff and Jasper areas took advantage of the situation at one time or another, although they rarely informed their clients that they were breaking the law.

Eventually, though, the creation of an effective warden service coupled with the tightening up of hunting regulations in 1909, including the licensing of guides and the registering of all hunting parties specifying their proposed route, began to bring the situation under control. Jim continued in his old habits and was finally caught in the act of taking sheep in the park. The outcome of the resulting trial was a $100 fine and the revoking of his guiding permit for the duration of the season, a rather serious threat to his income. Necessity being the mother of invention, he quickly figured out a way to circumvent the restriction. Having one of his packers sign out the register as guide, he listed himself as cook and then immediately took over the guiding of the party once safely out on the trail. Even considering the fine and this inconvenience, he was still luckier than most of those arrested for similar infractions. Just prior to his own arrest a Brewster party had been convicted on a similar charge and, in addition to fines levied on each of its members, the entire outfit, valued at some $1000, had been confiscated.

Even though poaching had its obvious dangers, on one occasion the chance Jim took was worthwhile considering the results. In fact the incident, which occurred in 1920, provided him with the sheep hunting moment of his life. While reconnoitering near the Divide at dusk on the evening of the 2nd of November, two days after the hunting season had officially closed, he spotted a single ram but was unable to get a shot. The next day he stalked the animal and found that it had joined a group of fifteen others inside the park boundary. Working from the premise that it was no worse to break two regulations than one, he decided to try to take the ram because of its obvious trophy-size curl. But when he was just about to shoot, it did a strange thing, hopping on the back of another large sheep and riding it piggy-back fashion. Adjusting his aim, Jim squeezed off a shot, unluckily just as the ram was dismounting. Feeling that the shot had gone over top of the target, he was forced to watch disconsolately while it ran off with the rest of the flock.

On the faint hope that he might get another chance, though, Jim decided to try to track the sheep in the light sprinkling of snow on the ground. Before going far he noticed that one set of tracks were blood-spattered and that they turned off from the rest. Following these to the crest of a small ridge he was amazed to see the ram standing under an outcropping of rock just below him. With no further ado he finished it off with an easy shot. When he reached his kill it became apparent that the animal had attempted to hide because his foot had been split by the original shot. It was also obvious that the ram was a real grand-daddy, and when its head was later measured at Banff it was found to have a 49 ½ inch curl, a world's record. Eventually it went on permanent display in the New York Museum of Natural History and remains to this day, according to Boone and Crockett records, the largest head ever taken. [5]

Previous to 1910, Jim had guided most parties coming his way personally, aided by Ernie Brearley and occasionally some temporary help. But the increasing business stemming from the appearance of Rungius and his friends soon meant that he had to increase his staff of guides, packers and cooks. The first assistants he chose to employ were two local lads with good blood lines for trailmen, Joe Woodworth, the son of Ben Woodworth who had done his first packing for Wilson in the 1890s, and John Wilson, Tom's eldest son who had worked with his father at the Kootenay Plains ranch since 1905. As time went on several more capable men were added to the

Simpson's record ram.

roster as conditions warranted. Included among them were Ulysse LaCasse, Jim Boyce, Howard Deegan, Tommy "Sparrow" Frayne, Max Brooks, Jack "Rosey" Powell, George "Mousie" Saddington, Verne Castella, John Musko, Percy "Beef" Woodworth, Jack Greaves, Ben Woodworth Jr. and Jack Cooley. It also became necessary as the number of parties increased for Jim to find additional pack animals, a problem which was solved by a deal worked out with Tom Wilson in 1911.

Wilson had been continuing to try convince the government to grant him leases on the Kootenay Plains ranches, without much success. In addition, the lengthy recuperation from his injuries sustained in the 1908 Christmas trip had required him to turn over responsibility for the ranches' stock to his son John. With the excellent grazing conditions present on the plains this stock had increased from the original thirty head of 1903 to one hundred and forty head by 1911. Because of his problems and attempting to capitalize on the work he had put into the ranches, Tom agreed to sell Simpson one-half interest in the stock, buildings, improvements and leases, if they should ever be obtained, for the sum of $4,000 in October, 1911. The other half-interest was temporarily turned over to his son, who in December, 1911 entered into a partnership, "Wilson and Simpson," to operate the ranches. Thus, after a strenuous spring of

Horses on the Kootenay Plains.

bronc busting in 1912, Jim had enough horseflesh to last him for many seasons.

Although Simpson handled the bulk of the parties not secured by Brewsters at this time, there were two other individuals who managed to successfully break into the outfitting business. They were William "Billy" Warren and Sidney J. Unwin, whose eventual success in establishing outfits of their own could be traced to the fortuitous acquaintance made by Warren in 1904. This acquaintance was with the plucky lady who was the Ottos' first client after they established along the GTP, Mrs. Mary Schäffer.

Mary T. Sharples was born in 1869 at Westchester, Pennsylvania of moderately wealthy Quaker parents. After receiving her early education in the local schools she went on to university to study art, and while doing so became friends with Mary Vaux, a girl of her own age with similar interests. In 1888 she accompanied Miss Vaux on her summer vacation to Glacier House where her brothers, George and William Vaux, were engaged in a pioneer effort to measure and photograph the Illecillewaet Glacier. The next summer she again appeared at Glacier House, but this time as the new bride of Dr. Charles Schäffer, a botanist connected with the Academy of Natural Science of Pennsylvania. Thereafter, until Dr. Schäffer's untimely death in 1903, the couple made an annual pilgrimage to the mountains so that he could engage in botanical work. After 1903 she collaborated with Stewardson Brown, Curator of the Herbarium at the Academy, in compiling a book from her husband's data. She was responsible for the beautiful watercolors and photographs illustrating the text. The book, *Alpine Flora of the Canadian Rocky Mountains,* was eventually published in 1907.

On her early visits to the mountains Mrs. Schäffer was not overly enamored with "roughing it." Her most distinct recollection of camping on the shores of Lake Louise in 1893 was of them having "looked out on that magnificent scene with chattering teeth and shivering bodies." However, thanks to the persistence of some of

her companions and Tom Wilson, who was given the responsibility of showing her the sights, she gradually learned to accept the rugged landscape on its own terms and to enjoy travelling in it. At a later date, she acknowledged in a letter to Tom his part in her conversion: "I owe many a lovely bit of memory to Tom Wilson who simply dragged a poor little delicate tourist to points she would not have reached had you not insisted." [6]

As her aversion changed to infatuation, she became interested in reports of the expeditions of Wilcox, Fay, Collie *et al* and along with a Quaker friend, Mollie Adams, soon wished to participate in such adventures herself. Unfortunately, she found that while it was acceptable for a lady to be a sightseer, it was not proper to take part in longer trail trips, that being the exclusive preserve of men:

We fretted for the strength of man, for the way was long and hard, and only the tried and stalwart might venture where cold and heat, starvation and privation stalked ever at the explorer's heels. In meek despair we bowed our head to the inevitable, to the cutting knowledge of the superiority of the endurance of man . . . They left us sitting on the railway track following them with hungry eyes as they plunged into the distant hills . . . [7]

So matters remained until the death of her husband when the freedom to make her own decisions brought with it the realization that she had as much right as any man to experience the dangers and hardships of the trail. In 1904, together with Mollie Adams, she convinced Wilson to set up a program of excursions which would gradually build up their ability to undergo the rigors of a trip lasting the whole summer. For the first three day jaunt into the Yoho Valley, Wilson himself acted as the guide with Harry Lang assisting as packer, but for the next trip he provided Billy Warren, a handsome young guide working for him at Field.

Born at Harlow, Essex, on January 13, 1880, Warren had benefitted from an excellent education at Saint

Mary Schäffer

Joe Barker and Billy Warren.

Mary's College. At the outbreak of the Boer War he had enrolled in the Imperial Yeomanry, and when the fighting ended he went to London to work as a clerk. Soon becoming discontented, he decided to emigrate to Canada and arrived at Banff, probably in 1903, anxious to find employment. Wilson offered him a job as a packer, and after one season he proved himself worthy of graduating to the position of guide, capable of leading local excursions while gaining experience. Such was his first trip with Mrs. Schäffer and Miss Adams as it consisted of a short visit to Moraine Lake.

Upon returning in 1905 and 1906 for further "toughening up" expeditions, the ladies were again assigned, this time by Bob Campbell, to Warren's care. The 1905 trip consisted of a week's stay in the Ptarmigan Valley, while that of 1906 was a more extensive venture, covering the area as far north as Wilcox Pass and lasting some five weeks. By that time Mrs. Schäffer had become a great admirer of Warren, for although there were those possessing more knowledge of "forest lore" and the trails, she found that "for kindness, good nature and

good judgment under unexpected stress he had no superior." [8]

When it was decided that the time had finally come to take a trip that would last an entire season, it was understood that it would be under Warren's guidance. To facilitate matters Mrs. Schäffer, now wealthy in her own right, agreed to buy all the horses, saddlery, blankets and other supplies necessary to outfit the party. She also provided sufficient funds for the hiring of another man who could act as a combination packer and cook. Warren's choice fell on Sid Unwin, a fellow Englishman who had been establishing a highly favorable reputation as a tough and dependable woodsman in the few years since his arrival.

Unwin was a young man of fairly stocky build whose lantern-jawed countenance hinted at an inner strength and endurance. He had been born in England and was the nephew of T. Fisher Unwin, one of that country's leading book publishers. Although the details of his education are sketchy, it must have been excellent since he was capable of making jokes in Latin. He also had been a volunteer for service in the Boer War, serving with an artillery battery and earning himself a decoration for bravery. Like Warren, he had returned from the war and had gone to work in London as a surveyor's clerk before being lured to Canada by the prospect of a better future. Arriving in Banff in the fall of 1904, he had immediately joined Syd Baker on a snowshoe trip to his trapline on the Saskatchewan River. The next summer he had gone to work for Simpson and Baker on the trail, and in the following winter began to run his own trapline up the Pipestone and down the Siffleur to the Saskatchewan.

The trapline proved an excellent means both to familiarize himself with the country and to toughen himself up for a life in the wilderness. The winter of 1906-07 proved to be particularly hard, and on one occasion the snow conditions were so bad on his fifty-five mile trek to the Saskatchewan that it took him ten days to snowshoe the distance. At the head of the Siffleur he found himself so tired that he fell asleep sitting in front of his campfire and only woke up when his mackinaw pants and underwear caught fire and burned into his flesh. In great pain, he made the rest of the distance to the Wilson ranch without stopping, and after perfunctorily answering Tom's queries and having a bite to eat, rolled into a bunk and slept for twenty-six hours. A week later he joined Simpson at his cabin at the mouth of the Mistaya with a piece of cloth from his underwear the size of a hand still attached to the burn. Each day thereafter as the burn slowly healed Jim cut away a small piece of the cloth with no painkiller other than a few swallows of rum available to Sid.

Such was the man who joined Warren, Mrs. Schäffer and Miss Adams at Laggan in late June, 1907. The stated objective of the expedition was to investigate the sources of the Saskatchewan and Athabasca Rivers, but in the back of the ladies' minds was the hope that they might have an opportunity to visit a lake about which Simpson had told them. Called Chaba Imne (Beaver Lake) by the Stoneys, it was supposed to lie north of Brazeau Lake, although the Indians were reticent about its exact location.

Warren began by leading his charges over their previous route to Wilcox Pass and then down the Sunwapta to its junction with the Athabasca. From there the branches of the Athabasca were followed, the west fork to Fortress Lake and then the east fork to its source at Mount Columbia. Since it was by then well into August, they turned around and headed back through Wilcox Pass where, during a heavy snowstorm, they had a chance encounter with the Coleman party headed for the foot of Robson. A few days later at Graveyard Camp, near the mouth of the Alexandra River, they met Simpson and "the butterfly lady," who were putting the finishing touches to the summer's collecting. Jim related what he knew about the mysterious lake, and before long the foursome were headed over Nigel Pass to Brazeau Lake. This they managed to reach without difficulty, but

Sid Unwin.

their luck ran out as attempts to head further north were turned back by heavy snows obliterating the trails and all but blocking the passes.

Retreating to Pinto Lake and then down the Cline River to Kootenay Plains, their fortunes improved somewhat as they met a band of Stoneys which included Sampson Beaver. Mrs. Schäffer had met Sampson the year previously and knew that he possessed as much knowledge about the surrounding country as anyone. On completion of a dinner hosted by Elliott Barnes in his rough cabin, to which Sampson was shrewdly invited, she managed to get the exact location of the lake from him. In fact, he even agreed to draw a rough map showing her how to get there. This was carefully stowed away for future reference, and the party soon continued on back to the railroad, following the route over Howse and Amiskwi Passes out to Field.

Spurred on by the new information they had so fortuitously acquired, the two ladies were determined to find their lake the following year. Arrangements were made with Warren to outfit and guide, and Unwin was again approached to act as assistant. Also recruited was Reggie Holmes, who was needed because the party was to have an extra member, Stewardson Brown, who planned to do some botanical collecting. Because of these additions, Warren put together a string of twenty-two horses for the trip, eleven new ones being purchased from Peyto's excellent stock.

Armed with Sampson's precious map, six determined riders set off from Warren's newly completed corrals near the Lake Louise Chalet on the morning of the 8th of June. This time there was little dilly-dallying along the way as the pack train headed straight across the Saskatchewan, up the North Fork and through Nigel Pass to Brazeau Lake. Here the map came into use, providing directions around the lake and then over Poboktan Pass. But soon the trail became extremely faint because of burnt timber, scree slopes and mud slides, and the guides were forced to follow some supposed old cuttings, beginning to doubt the accuracy of Sampson's sketch.

Turning up what they hoped was the right valley, it took two days of fighting snow and downed timber before they discovered a hopeful looking pass. The next day they crossed it and continued to push on for the better part of another day, expecting to see the lake at every corner. As the dispirited party halted for lunch on the 7th of July, Unwin announced that he was going to climb something and not come back until he discovered the lake.

. . . After lunch U. started out climbing to find the lake or bust, with compass, aneroid, maps, camera and field glasses, so that nothing should escape him. He left camp at about 3 p.m. and returned at 10:45, having, as he said "kept hopping all the time". He climbed about 2500 feet to the top of the ridge north of camp, dropped down 2000 feet, then up again on what seemed to be a shoulder of Mt. _____ to 8750 feet — saw the lake! Went down right to it, 5600 feet, and around and home again over the lower wooded shoulders.[9]

Later the mountain would bear the name of Mount Unwin as a fitting memorial to his efforts on that particular day and the trip as a whole. Likewise, another peak on the lake's shore would be named Mount Warren as a tribute to his part in the success.

Their hard-sought objective finally achieved, the ladies were treated to a raft tour of the lake over the succeeding few days. After this an attempt to explore its outlet to the Athabasca was frustrated by impassible timber, and it was decided they would have to retrace their steps back to Poboktan Creek and then reach the Athabasca and Miette Rivers and ultimately Tete Jaune Cache by the way of the now well-known route down the Sunwapta. When the Sunwapta was reached Brown and Holmes took their leave while the rest of the party determinedly set their sights northward. The elements were anything but propitious, moving Warren to remark after a day of constant drenchings that "in this country there are 24 kinds of weather for the 24 hours of the day — hot and cold and 22 kinds of rotten".[10]

However, they persisted and eventually reached Swift's homestead where, after being gazed upon in open-mouthed astonishment by his three children, they learned that the ladies were the first white women to appear in the vicinity. Departing from Swift's, the party next made a monotonous trip up the Miette to Tete Jaune Cache, where they again found the ladies were the first fair-skinned females to visit that rough encampment. Finally the shortening days told Warren and Unwin that it was time to be thinking about home, and after a more or less routine return trip they arrived back in Laggan on September 20th.

The 1908 trip was a tremendous feat for two ladies from such backgrounds as Mrs. Schäffer and Miss Adams, and they were accorded much praise and recognition for it. But Mrs. Schäffer realized that most of the credit was due to the two fine gentlemen who had made it possible. In later years she would state that it was "Mr. Warren's long outlook and Sid's determination" that had made the trip such a success and would describe her own contributions as "like the tail to an active horse."[11]

She would also acknowledge the men's prominent roles in the book which she began to write upon her return to Philadelphia. Relying on Tom Wilson's knowledge and his excellent library, she corresponded with him on the history of the country that her trip had encompassed. Wilson was able to provide many bits of background information mostly from his copy of the Palliser Report, the most important being that the river providing the outlet from the lake had been referred to as the Bad or Maligne River by Dr. Hector in 1859. Maligne was the name which the lake finally bore and as such it appeared in Mrs. Schäffer's book, *Old Indian Trails of the Canadian Rockies*, published in 1911.

After his two years of working for Warren, Sid Unwin secured his own outfit in 1909, probably with some assistance from Mrs. Schäffer. Even though his pack string was not large, he was able to guide some fairly important parties in the next few years. Perhaps his most loyal customer was Dr. B. W. Mitchell, a Philadelphia professor of classical and modern languages, whom he took on pleasure trips in 1910 and from 1912 to 1914. In a book which later recounted these journeys entitled *Trail Life In The Canadian Rockies*, Mitchell acknowledged his guide's abilities and deportment: "Here I desire to pay deserved and grateful tribute to that prince of guides, Sid Unwin. Unsurpassed in woodcraft and resourcefulness, unequalled in thoughtful kindness to his party, and with the charm of courteous manner that adds the touch of perfection to the little self-centered microcosm that a party in the wilderness constitutes, to him is owing through several seasons the personal safety, the perfect comfort, the entire pleasure of the expeditions."[12]

Billy Warren launching the raft on Maligne Lake, 1908.

Mrs. Schäffer was also to have recourse to Unwin's services again when she took him along as an extra guide for the surveying of Maligne Lake in 1911. Meanwhile, in 1907, Sid's sister Ethel had come out from England and had begun to help Mrs. Syd Baker set up a photo and souvenir tent to be run in conjunction with her husband's outfitting concession at Glacier House. By 1912 Sid felt that his own operation could benefit from a similar enterprise and along with Ethel and his brother Art, who had worked with Barnes and Holmes for a time, established Unwin's Curios and Souvenirs. In addition to this, he also began publishing a yearly edition of a *Guide to Banff* which listed all the points of interest in the park and advertised his ability to get tourists to them.

Bill Warren also continued to play an active role in outfitting for the next few years, running his pack train out of a headquarters established at Field. His most loyal patron continued to be Mrs. Schäffer whom he annually took to some new and interesting place, often in the company of her sister-in-law and nephew. Their relationship

grew closer each year and in June, 1915, in a romantic, almost fairy tale ending to their adventures on the trail, they married and settled down in Banff.

Not all of those who attempted to make their livelihood by establishing their own outfitting businesses in the years prior to the war were as successful as Warren and Unwin. For example, two other well-known Banff residents, Joseph Boyce and W. G. Fyfe, outfitted for a season or two before finding the going too rough. Both thereafter turned their attention mainly to the securing of government trail clearing contracts, which were becoming increasingly numerous as the parks administration began to function more effectively after the creation of the National Parks Branch in 1911.

In addition, Elliott Barnes, despite his close contact with the Alpine Club, found that after two years of trying his efforts were not meeting with the desired results. After disposing of his ranch to Wilson, he secured the position of manager of the Scott and Leeson Ranch near Morley and then, in 1910, moved on to a homestead in

Bill Peyto at "Ain't it Hell."

the Jumping Pound district. Finally, even such a hardy old-timer as Bill Peyto found that the trail no longer provided the life it once had and he too disposed of his interests.

Peyto's departure from the ranks of outfitters working out of Banff was as surprising as Wilson's had been several years earlier. With the fine reputation he had built up it seemed likely that the establishment of his own business would lead to a bright future. For a time these hopes seemed justified as his outfitting of Outram in 1902 was followed by the servicing of several other important parties in the succeeding years. Among these was Gertrude Benham, a famous English lady mountaineer, who Bill and his assistant Jim Wood escorted to Mount Assiniboine in 1904, she becoming the third person and the first woman to make its conquest. Others included Walter Wilcox in 1905 and a party composed of eight Bostonians led by J. F. Porter in 1906.

However, 1906 was the last year that Bill outfitted any major parties, the immediate reason apparently being the death of his wife in September of that year. He still advertised his services as an outfitter and guide in 1907, but it was obvious to his friends that his heart was no longer in it. About this time he admitted to Conrad Kain, who was visiting him at his mining claim on Red Earth Creek, that he would be "ten to fifteen years further from the grave" had his wife not died. By 1908 he had ceased to advertise and began to dispose of his outfit and horses, mostly to Warren.

After leaving outfitting Bill spent most of his time prospecting and working his talc claim. When not engaged in these pursuits he lived a hermit-like existence in a new home which he built on Banff Avenue, appropriately sporting a sign "Ain't It Hell" to sum up his view of life at this time. Happily, by 1910 his spirits had begun to pick up somewhat, and it was not long before he began to start guiding the odd party for Brewsters. Soon he was back to his old tricks, sparing no one including his employers.

On returning from one of his outings on the company's behalf he brought back a wolverine which he had wounded and rendered unconscious with chloroform. Arriving at the Brewster livery he dumped the ferocious animal out of the canvas sack he had been carrying it in only to find that it had succumbed during the journey. Noticing two of the Brewster brothers standing in the doorway observing him he pushed back his hat, scratched his head and with a twinkle in his eye remarked: "Oh, I know what's the matter with that polecat. It couldn't take it living here amongst all these Liberals. He was too good a Conservative to hob nob with this gang."[13]

Bill occasionally continued to go out for Brewsters until 1913 when he was able to overcome his dislike of the government enough to join the warden service. He was posted to patrol the Healy Creek-Sunshine district and later would become legendary for his exploits in this region. But that was not until the nineteen-twenties, after he returned from fighting in the devastating conflict that engulfed the world in 1914.

War Amputee Joe Woodworth tightening the diamond with one arm, ca. 1920.

9 The End of an Era

The First World War has often been described as a turning point in the history of many fields of human activity. This was certainly the case with regard to the outfitting businesses of the Banff and Jasper areas. The war marked the end of an era that had seen the outfitters and guides provide the means whereby all manner of patrons had been able to complete the exploration of those parts of the Canadian Rockies accessible from the transcontinental railroads. At the same time it coincided with developments which would result in a new type of tourist appearing in the mountains necessitating significant changes in the mode of operation of outfitters attempting to attract their patronage.

Of course, the most immediate effect of the war was the departure of many of those making their living from the trail to defend the freedom they so greatly enjoyed. As soon as word of the hostilities reached Banff a movement was afoot to form a Corps of Guides, whose combined skills would make it admirably suited to reconnaissance work. The response was excellent, but the group quickly disbanded because of the need for reinforcements in other units. Most of the participants in it did not see each other for the duration of the conflict and in the meantime several were wounded or captured in the course of performing their service.

Bill Peyto, Harry Lang and Joe Woodworth were all wounded in action, the latter losing his right arm at the shoulder. This drastic loss would seem to have marked the end of his packing activities, but after returning home and being awarded the Military Medal he set to work to rehabilitate himself. Soon he was back on the trail for Simpson, wielding an axe to good effect with his left arm and using his teeth to aid in tying the diamond hitch. Of those captured Bill Potts underwent the worst rigors in a German P.O.W. camp and for a time after his return

would occasionally scare the daylights out of his dudes when he woke up screaming from nightmares. But the individual paying the highest price for answering the call to arms was Sid Unwin.

Upon returning from a trip to the Athabasca with Professor Mitchell in the fall of 1914, Sid quickly enlisted and, because of his experience in the Boer War, was assigned to train with the 20th Artillery Battery at Lethbridge. In June, 1915 the battery was sent to England, and in January, 1916 he saw his first action in France. Meanwhile, as his brother Art had also joined up, the responsibility for handling his outfitting business had been left in the hands of his sister Ethel, who had sometimes accompanied him on the trail. With characteristic Unwin determination, she immediately applied to the government for a guide's license. The license, the first granted to a woman in the parks, allowed her to utilize the pack string and to guide small tourist parties. This was meant to be only a temporary means of maintaining the business until Sid returned from the war, but in July, 1917 word reached Banff that such was not to be. During the Battle of Vimy Ridge he was hit by shrapnel while single-handedly manning an artillery emplacement and later died of his wounds in a hospital at Leeds.

Sid's passing came as a great shock to his many friends at Banff, particularly the new Mrs. Warren. In August, 1920, she and her sister-in-law Mrs. Sharples dedicated a window in Banff's St. George's Church to Sid "as an appreciation of his fidelity as a guide and a testimony to his kindly disposition and high character."[1] Ethel Unwin, already having sold the souvenir shop in 1914, disposed of the outfitting business and went back to England in 1918. She would later return to Banff and open the Odd Craft Shop in 1922 while her brother Art

Ethel Unwin leading her first party as a guide, 1917.

established a very successful lumber and hardware business in the post-war years.

At Jasper there was an equally patriotic response among those following the trail. On arriving home from his trip with Fay in October, 1914, Fred Brewster intended to enlist immediately, but had to delay because he found that Phil Moore had already been called up for service. Moore had joined a militia unit, the 15th Light Horse of Calgary, shortly after coming to Canada and had achieved the rank of Captain before the war broke out. After reporting for duty at Winnipeg he was promoted to Brigade Major and sent overseas where he remained until transferred home in 1917. Promoted to Colonel, he was placed in charge of the garrison for Southern Alberta and was later allotted the additional task of running the Alberta conscription branch until the war's end.

Fred eventually volunteered for service in the Engineers late in the summer of 1915, after he and Jack had initiated the subsequently famous Sky Line Trail Rides to Maligne Lake and had entered a partnership in a tent camp venture, known as Jasper Park Camp, on the shore of Lac Beauvert. Because of his education and background, he was commissioned as a Major in the Second Tunnelling Division and was sent overseas in charge of a company composed mainly of miners from the Barkerville area of British Columbia. In 1917 the company was credited with the demolition of Hill 60, a strategic German observation post dominating the

French countryside. For this achievement Fred received the Military Medal and Bar.

Meanwhile, Pat Brewster had enrolled in the Royal Flying Corps and George Brewster in the Canadian Artillery, leaving the still youthful Jack Brewster to shoulder the burden of the entire Brewster and Moore operation. He performed amazingly well, fortunately being able to rely somewhat on the advice of his father who arrived in the vicinity in the fall of 1916 after his real estate interests in Vancouver had suffered a severe setback. Not only was Jack able to maintain the company's outfitting and freighting interests over the slack period to the war's end, but he also managed to buy out their partners in the tent camp, Messrs. Bone and Kenneth of the Edmonton Tent and Mattress Company.

Curly Phillips also became a member of the armed forces, but not until late in the war. Early in the war years he managed to secure a few parties to outfit, running his pack string in combination with the Ottos' out of the tent camp at Lac Beauvert for a time. Mary Jobe was taken out in the summer of 1915 for a second attempt on Mount Sir Alexander, during which Curly was able to lead her and a companion to within 100 feet of the summit, and in 1917 she accompanied him on a winter trip to the Wapiti River to supply William Rindfoos, out on yet another collecting expedition sponsored by the Smithsonian Institution. On returning from this outing Curly was called up for service in the Canadian Field Artillery, although he was granted a temporary leave early in 1918 which was spent trapping with Rindfoos. Unfortunately he never got the opportunity to go on active duty as while training at Kingston later that year he had his arm smashed when caught between some kicking horses.

When both the aforementioned and numerous other trailmen returned to their respective homes from serving their country, signs that the old order was changing were already apparent. One of these was the continuing departure of veteran outfitters and guides from the business. Unwin, of course, did not return, and by 1919 his former employer Bill Warren had decided to quit the game. Warren sought a more secure and lucrative form of livelihood and within a few years of his marriage was one of Banff's leading businessmen. In 1919 he began the Cascade Garage and Banff Motor Company with Bert Sibbald, in 1920 he acquired the old Alberta Hotel and began renovating it, and in 1921 he initiated Rocky Mountain Tours and Transport in partnership with James I. McLeod, himself a former guide.

A similar exodus occurred among those active in the Jasper area with the retirement from outfitting of both John Yates and Fred Stephens. The completion of the GTP had eliminated Yates's mail contract and by the time the CNR went through, outfitting from Lac Ste. Anne was certainly no longer feasible. It was then too late for him to try to move to Jasper and compete with the larger, well-established outfits there. Nor is it likely that he even wanted to as he had been married in 1910 and had moved off of the Hobo to a homestead of his own. There he remained with his growing family until 1920 when he moved back to the Imperial Valley in California to be near his ailing mother in her last days.

Fred Stephens' small outfit placed him in similar circumstances with relation to the bigger operations at Jasper. During the war years he began to spend much of his time back at Lacombe, where he had, at least temporarily, patched up his "double harness scrapes," and at Centralia, Washington. By the end of the war he had almost completely abandoned the trail as a livelihood and in the early twenties became a partner in a fox farm near Kalispell, Montana.

Even more significant than the departure of several individuals from outfitting as an indicator of the changing situation at the war's end was the increasing predominance of the internal combustion engine over the horse as a means of transportation.

Before the war the parks had been to a certain extent isolated from the effects of the automobile. In September, 1905, an Order-in-Council had been passed prohibiting the use of automobiles in any part of Rocky Mountains Park, a rather needless piece of legislation since there was no road connecting Banff with the outside world. But by the summer of 1909 construction on a Calgary-Banff road had progressed to the point that the occasional adventurer had attempted to make the often perilous journey to the resort. The law came down hard on such violators, and it was not until 1911 that a deputa-

tion of Calgary motorists was able to convince the Minister of the Interior to at least partially lift the restrictions. Drivers were allowed to bring their cars into town, but then the vehicles had to be parked and the keys left with the police until they were ready to return to Calgary. Some members of the Calgary Automobile Club had thumbed their noses at this regulation, and finally, in June, 1914, the Superintendent had relented, over the protests of local horse interests, allowing cars to use a limited number of streets and drives at very modest rates of speed.

Although those returning from the war might have expected some further relaxing of the rules, many were undoubtedly amazed at the state of affairs that greeted them. Not only had the government removed all restrictions by 1916, a year which saw 1,016 cars enter the east gate of the park, but it had also begun to push full-steam ahead on a motor road construction program. Concentrating on the road leading west to Castle (Eisenhower) and Lake Louise, which was eventually to link up with a road to be built over Vermilion Pass from B.C., it utilized all the money that could be scraped together from the thin wartime appropriations. At the same time the local population, which had previously been so opposed to the automobile, began to get on the bandwagon with dealerships and garages springing up virtually overnight. The extent to which things had changed was evident in the spring of 1916 when on one day a train carload of automobiles was being unloaded for delivery in town at the same time as two carloads of horses were being loaded for shipping out.

One of the first and ultimately most important purchasers of an automobile in Banff was Jim Brewster, who had initially become acquainted with its capabilities while living at the coast. Soon after acquiring his Baby Overland, he astutely perceived that the tourist business of the future would likely hinge on motorized transport. Acting on behalf of his company, which had changed its name to Brewster Transport Company in May, 1914, he proudly accepted delivery of a carload of Overland touring cars early in 1916, these being the first automobiles admitted into the park for purposes of tourist conveyance. As a consequence of this event another historic change took place when the Bow Livery, acquired in the same deal as the Mount Royal Hotel, was unceremoniously made over into a garage. Other local businessmen quickly followed Jim's lead, although on a smaller scale, and by 1919 there were sixty livery car licenses being issued annually in the park.

Because of its isolation and more limited development, Jasper did not feel the effects of the internal combustion age as quickly or fully as did Banff. But all the signs that a situation similar to Banff's would soon prevail there as well were apparent soon after the war ended. Some work was done during the war years upgrading the Maligne Canyon trail to road status and beginning construction on a road to the newly named

The conflict between automobiles and horses, ca. 1918.

Mount Edith Cavell and the mouth of the Whirlpool Valley. Then, in the summer of 1920, Jack Brewster shipped in the first car by rail, and the government began to give consideration to the idea of building a road from Edmonton using, in part, the abandoned railroad grade made available by the consolidation of the GTP and CNR lines from Edson to Moose Lake in 1916. It would be many years before this project would come to fruition, but in the meantime several other vehicles were brought in to use on the roads in the town and its vicinity. In 1921 the government began to issue its first automobile permits and chauffer's licenses in Jasper Park.

The overall effect of the automobile's widespread acceptance on outfitting and guiding is rather difficult to gauge. Understandably, its most direct influence was on the carriage trade as tally-hos and buggies soon began to disappear in favor of cars. But on examination it seems to have had some indirect influence on the trail business as well. Perhaps the major one was the change resulting from the way in which the outfitters and guides perceived the automobile and its future. The enthusiasm with which

tourists, residents and the government greeted motorized transport made it seem likely that roads would soon penetrate the most isolated mountain valleys and every tourist would scorn the horse for the car. These fears ultimately proved groundless, but at the time many trailmen decided to hedge their bets and prepare for the worst. This spurred several into developing other business interests that could be run along with or in addition to their outfitting and guiding operations.

One who in later years freely admitted that the advent of motorized tourism impelled him into making one of the most important decisions of his life was Jim Simpson. While out on one of his first trips for Wilson in 1897, he had visited Bow Lake and had been impressed with the scenery and the excellent camping area available along its north-eastern shore. Wilcox, who had visited the lake in 1895 with Peyto, had been similarly impressed and even at that early date predicted that some day it would be a favorite with tourists and that "a comfortable building, erected in a tasteful and artistic manner" would stand near its shore. Whether the two ever discussed this idea or not, it is likely that Jim had the same thought more than once in the dozens of times he camped at the spot in the next two decades. Therefore, it was only natural that when he began to contemplate the indefinite future of the horse in the post-war years, he would begin to give serious consideration to the project. A hotel or bungalow camp on the proportions of those of the CPR was out of the question financially, and so he settled on an idea for one large cabin which could be used in his outfitting business and added to or modified as future conditions warranted.

In 1920 Jim applied to the Parks Branch for a lease on five acres of land at his old camping spot but was informed that he would have to make $5000 worth of improvements before he could be granted one. This he set out to accomplish, the first job being the cutting of enough logs to build a cabin of the proportions desired. Because of the altitude the trees in the area were somewhat stunted, and he soon found that the longest feasible length of log was about ten feet. To make the building large enough he had to adapt these logs to a suitable plan, settling on an octagonal design as the most practical in the circumstances. Once the log work was completed it was necessary to have lumber, doors, windows and other hardware to complete the job, and these had to be packed over the horrendous, muskegy trail up the Bow from Laggan. Finally, by late 1922, Jim had completed sufficient work to be granted the lease, and the next summer he was able to greet his first guests, Drs. J. Monroe Thorington and William S. Ladd, two American alpinists who he was guiding on a mountaineering expedition to the Columbia Icefield.

Jim's choice of location for his lodge, christened "Num-Ti-Jah" after the Indian word for the pine marten abounding in the area, eventually proved more auspicious than even he could have foreseen. With the building of the Banff-Jasper Highway during the depression years it became one of only two places where lodging could be found between Lake Louise and Jasper. Because of the expected influx of tourists when the highway was completed, he began construction on a second lodge in 1937. This building was designed on much the same basic principles as the first but contained twenty-four rooms and it took him many years to complete it. After this facility came into use the old lodge was turned into his personal retreat, or "ram pasture," where many of his later years were spent painting, reading and reminiscing about his days on the trail.

At Jasper, the veteran outfitters also took steps to ensure that they could continue to earn a livelihood in the uncertain future. Those most closely associated with the appearance of the automobile were the Otto brothers, who like Jim Brewster in Banff realized that it was destined to play an important role in tourism. Over the years they had acquired many teams and buggies in addition to their outfitting stock and equipment. Immediately after the war the teams were put to use at a tie camp they had established at the outlet of Moab Lake in the Whirlpool Valley and on road construction, while the buggies were used to help transport guests over the rough road to the tent camp. Early in 1921 they added to these a sort of large open motor bus, which may have been a converted tally-ho, and in the succeeding few years obtained seven livery cars. Then, in 1923, they began construction of Jasper's first garage, located on main street. Known as Mountain Motors, it doubled as a headquarters for their sightseeing tours and later became the franchised dealership for General Motors products.

Fred Brewster turned much of his attention to the further development of the tent camp on returning from the war. In 1915 the GTP had agreed with Brewster and Moore and their partners to become involved in sponsoring the camp and were anxious to continue to do so after the war. Fred and Jack, now without Colonel Moore, who had left the company in 1919, were equally desirous of working closely with the railway. Together they cooperated with the GTP in building the first log kitchen and dining room in 1921 and, in 1922, erecting the first cabins on the sites formerly occupied by the ten original board floor tents. By that time Jack had also decided to quit the company and establish his own outfitting business, leaving the lease solely in his brother's hands. After helping to erect the first unit of the log building which would eventually become Jasper Park Lodge, Fred was in turn made a tempting offer for his interest by the new Canadian National Railway, which had absorbed the old GTP and CNR lines. He decided to accept and, in 1923, sold the lease to the railway. Fortunately he wisely retained the rights to the outfitting and guiding done out of the location and began to concentrate his energies on developing this concession.

Of all the Jasper outfitters the one to become involved in the most diverse interests after the war was Curly Phillips. Given his upbringing in the lake country of Ontario and his avowed love of water travel, it is not surprising that foremost among them was a boat business, which took on several aspects as time progressed. For a number of years Curly had made boats for his own use, but he soon went into boat building in a larger way. A workshop was set up in Jasper and, with the help of his father and brother, he began to turn out beautifully finished cedar and canvas canoes, specially adapted for poling and tracking, as well as larger made-to-order freight canoes, which could be fitted with inboard or outboard motors. By the mid-twenties he had compiled a fair inventory of these boats and began to use them to ferry passengers across Medicine and Maligne Lakes. As time went on these boat trips became very popular with tourists and, in 1930, he applied for and received a concession from the government allowing him the exclusive right to operate boats on Medicine, Maligne, Beaver, Mina and Mona Lakes. Also in the mid-twenties he began a project which appealed to him more than any other — the arranging and guiding of power boat trips up

Curly Phillips' power boat trip down the Peace River, ca. 1935.

the Athabasca as far as Whitecourt and down the Peace from Summit Lake to Peace River Crossing.

Curly was also for a time involved in two other innovative ventures. The first of these was an irrigated market garden worked with the assistance of his brother Harry, one of his packers Art Allan, and a local climbing guide Joseph Saladana. Begun in the summer of 1924 on Lewis Swift's property, the garden produced a variety of vegetables which were taken by truck over the old railroad grade to Jasper where they were sold to the town's residents. Although there was sufficient demand for the produce, the garden required daily attention and was subject to the vagaries of mountain weather with its frequent killing frosts. As a result, it lasted only two summers before being abandoned as unprofitable.

The second enterprise, started in the winter of 1924-25, met with much the same fate. Because of the great popularity of stories about the adventurous life of trappers travelling by dog team in the far north at this time, Curly surmised that there were undoubtedly many people who would like to have the experience for themselves. With his great skill as a trapper and love for dog sledding, he felt that there was no one more qualified to provide such a service than himself. Evolving from this was the idea for a "dude trapline" which, as his advertising material pointed out, would give people a true picture of what trapping was all about:

Most everyone is familiar with the term as applied in the

West to the city man, or "dude", and from which is derived the terms "dude ranch" and "dude wrangler". To these I am going to add an entirely new one in my "dude trapline". It's a new idea which grew partly out of the many inquiries I have had in the last few years from city people who wanted to take a trip by dog-team, and to have the experience of winter travel in the great Northland, and partly I must confess to a genuine love of the life that has such an appeal to me. And incidentally help others to do the same, and show them the real thing. Not the lurid faked up romance, but as it really is when placed on a commercial basis, and means of making a living.[2]

For the preceding few winters he had been running a trapline from north of Hinton to the Old Man River and then north-easterly across the Hay, Berland and Little Smoky Rivers. Here he chose to inaugurate his scheme, and at first the response proved excellent. However, as time went on, clients became harder to come by, and after three years, because of lack of interest, it too had to be discontinued.

Apart from its influence on many outfitters' decisions to diversify their interests, the automobile brought about another interesting change which affected them. This was in the type of tourist entering the parks after they became accessible by road. The day of the at least moderately wealthy tourist-explorer, who wished to visit unexplored lakes, valleys and mountains and could afford to hire men and outfit for several months, was over. In his place came a tourist, likely from a middle class background, who in most cases would desire to see the maximum amount of country in the minimum time and at the least expense possible. Many of this new breed, if they wished to go out on the trail at all, demanded that their outings be inexpensive and only of a few days duration. Trips of this nature, many outfitters soon found, were just not a paying proposition. This was well-attested to by Phillips' complaint to a prospective customer in 1925, when he was feeling a bit glum about the future:

... The average tourist business never pays in July and August unless you can book big parties for long trips. If you are going to give first class service you have to keep good reliable men on the payroll all the time and if you cannot keep them busy you are bound to lose. So I have decided to leave my horses out on the range this summer. Last season I lost $1500 in July and August, so this season I am taking no chances. It would cost me around $200 to get an outfit in and fitted up for your party and to take them back to the range afterwards. And all I would take in on a week's trip for the horses use would only be $210, which is too small a margin to make it worthwhile ... The day of the packtrain is pretty well over, as the tourist of today wants speed and the only way to get it is where there is good roads and motor cars ... We have wonderful country here and I have spent 17 years building up an outfit and a business only to find when I got to the top that there was nothing there and no possible future to the business.[3]

Because of problems of this nature it was not until after the mid-twenties that many outfitters were back to their pre-war levels of business, even though by 1920 visitor statistics had recovered from their wartime doldrums.

Despite the fact that outfitting and guiding had some drawbacks as an avocation in the immediate post-war years, there were, nonetheless, numerous new operations which came into existence. While a few of these were composed of new people, most involved men who had worked for one of the old outfitters and had decided that it was time to strike out on their own. These included Jim Boyce, Pat Brewster, Tex Wood, George Harrison, Soapy Smith and Bill Potts along the Canadian Pacific line, and Jack Brewster, Bert Wilkins and Jack Hargreaves along the Canadian National line. Of course, the consideration motivating most of these individuals' decisions was a monetary one, since the $60 to $70 a month they made working for one of the other outfitters did not seem like much compared with the returns evidently to be had from running their own pack string. In the early twenties a typical price for outfitting a party of two would vary anywhere from $25 to $40 per day depending on the length of the trip and the number of men and horses required.

With a few exceptions, the new concerns which appeared had a definite advantage over the older outfitters, that being their size. As Phillips' complaint pointed out, during the early twenties the major outfitters sometimes lost money because they had to keep large numbers of men on the payroll whether they were on the trail or not, a problem avoided by most of the new people. They usually had only enough horses to handle one or two parties at a time and did much of the guiding themselves, cutting the hired staff to a minimum. Because of this they were often quite able to make a profit handling the types of trip that many tourists were interested in. It was sadly ironic that men such as Stephens and Yates had departed the scene before this situation occurred, as these conditions would have accommodated their desires quite admirably.

The very predictable result of the abundant new outfitting and guiding ventures making their appearance were complaints that too many trail businesses were being allowed to establish in the parks. It seemed to the older outfitters that their guides were taking advantage of them, accompanying the cream of the parties for a year or two and then, after getting well-acquainted, making arrangements to outfit them on their own. Such practices would eventually prove ruinous to all, and in an effort to correct these and other abuses eleven of the leading Banff area outfitting concerns held a meeting in May, 1922. This parley resulted in the formation of the Rocky Mountain Outfitters Association whose objective was "to have one official body who will be empowered to negotiate with the dominion and provincial governments in all matters pertaining to the outfitting business throughout the Rocky Mountains, such as the interprovincial recognition of guides' licenses, betterment of trails in the park, game and fishing regulations etc."[4]

Although the original meeting was composed solely of Banff area interests, the Association's Secretary, Louis S. Crosby of Brewster Transport, was instructed to communicate with the major outfitters in other areas of the Rockies, including Jasper, Windermere and Waterton, to invite their cooperation. Some response was received and the organization continued to function for a couple of years, although its name was amended to the Rocky Mountain Guides Association. After its demise later in the twenties, it was not until 1944 that a new group, the Alberta Licensed Outfitters, was formed to look after the interests of trailmen.

The departure of many veteran outfitters and guides from the business, the appearance of motorized transport and roads, the large number of new outfitters entering on the scene and the creation of a trailman's organization were signs that the old age of trail life was over. But the major manifestation of this fact was in a new type of trip which became popular in the twenties, the conducted trail ride. This was essentially composed of a large group of tourists travelling a specified number of days over a predetermined route and usually, but not always, stopping at pre-arranged camping spots. To a great degree the out-fitters' involvement in these rides was an attempt to meet and make a profit from the post-war tourists' desires.

The earliest and probably least structured of the conducted trail rides were the "Off The Beaten Track" trips arranged and accompanied by Caroline B. Hinman. Hinman was born in Cincinnati but lived most of her life in Summit, New Jersey, where she served from 1915-21 as the Secretary of the Board of Education. Finding that she had an all-consuming passion for travel, she went on a conducted tour of Europe and was so taken with the idea that she arranged a tour of her own to the continent in 1914. Before this, however, she had visited the Canadian Rockies during the Alpine Club camps at Cathedral Mountain and Mount Robson in 1913 and had been impressed with what she saw. A second visit to the mountains was made in 1915, when she accompanied Mary Jobe and some other friends to Mount Sir Alexander under the guidance of Phillips.

In 1916 Miss Hinman took a party to the mountains

Caroline Hinman.

in Glacier Park, Montana, but it was not until 1917 that she arrived with her first group to be conducted through the Canadian Rockies. Composed mainly of well-educated teen-age girls from wealthy families in the United States, as all the Hinman tours were, the party of ten was outfitted by Jim Simpson for a three week trip to Assiniboine, Sawback Lake and the Ptarmigan Valley. Impressed with Jim's services, she came back to Banff in 1919 and was again outfitted by him, this time for a trip north of the Saskatchewan as far as Nigel Pass.

The guides and packers working on these trips found the experience to be a little out of the ordinary. Not only were they required to camp some distance away from the girls but also often felt that they were coming under the close scrutiny of the chaperones in order to head off any hanky-panky. On one occasion a packer had a few of the girls out for a boat ride on a mountain lake when he noticed the glint of the sun catching glass on a nearby ridge. Using his binoculars he was amazed to see someone ensconced on a lofty perch observing his every move with the benefit of a similar optical aid.

The first two Hinman trips in the Rockies proved so successful that they inaugurated several decades of similar outings. For the years 1920-22 Curly Phillips was the annual recipient of her business with excursions covering the entire area within Jasper Park and the environs of Mount Robson. Then, in 1923, the tours began the first of sixteen summers under the guidance of Jim Boyce. He had been successively cook and guide on the first two trips outfitted by Simpson, and Miss Hinman had been so taken with him that after he started in business for himself she would rarely go out with anyone else. It was during her years on the trail with Boyce that she was tabbed with the nickname "Timberline Kate" because of her penchant for choosing a campsite with a good view near timberline or on a high pass. The "Off The Beaten Track" tours in the Rockies eventually expanded to include up to three different groups each summer and, in addition to travel by pack train, began to include boat trips in the thirties and automobile trips in the forties.

At the opposite end of the spectrum from the Hinman tours were the Banff to Mount Assiniboine Walking and Riding Tours which were highly structured in their route and itinerary. A. O. Wheeler had for many years given the idea of permanent camps in the more remote regions of the mountains serious consideration and by 1920 was able to convince his friend J. B. Harkin, Commissioner of Dominion Parks, that such camps were desirable. To get his plan underway he acquired a lease on some land at the Middle Springs near Banff and also sublet the Alpine Club's property at Lake Magog near Mount Assiniboine. He then approached Ralph Rink, a Swedish trailman who had worked for Brewsters at Lake Louise in 1912 and had done some guiding in the Kootenay country, with an offer to become both the Alpine Club's official outfitter and a partner in a horse transport business for

R O C K Y :: M O U N T A I N S :: O F :: C A N A D A

Banff to Mt Assiniboine
---*The Matterhorn of the Canadian Rockies*---
via Spray Lakes Route.

A PUBLIC WALKING OR RIDING TOUR FOR 1921   GOOD TROUT FISHING
STARTING FROM BANFF TWICE A WEEK DURING JULY, AUGUST AND SEPTEMBER

The Tour is for the benefit of the general public—specially designed for Tourists, Mountaineers, Artists, Scientists, Botanists, Fishermen and Lovers of Nature.

The Tour lies amidst magnificent mountain scenery. By it the most spectacular beauty spots of the Canadian Rockies may be visited at a moderate cost.

Now is Your Opportunity!   *Do Not Miss It!*

MAGNIFICENT SCENERY   EXCELLENT FISHING
COMFORTABLE CAMPS   NO BAGGAGE NECESSARY
GOOD FOOD AND CAMP BEDS PROVIDED

From the main route, special trips may be arranged to Kananaskis Lakes, Kananaskis Pass, Palliser Pass and Whiteman Pass. To the Royal Group of Mountains, the British Military Group, the French Military Group. To Mt. Whiteman and Mt. Redskin. To Marvel Lake, Lake Gloria, Sunburst Lake and Cerulean Lake. Return trip via Valley of the Rocks, Golden Valley, Citadel Pass, Healy Creek and Bow River can be arranged.

The Alpine Pack Train

will operate in conjunction with the Tour and will carry all baggage desired and take charge of special trips.

Camp charges at the rate of $5.00 per day.
Saddle ponies, $3.00 per day.
Baggages charges, $1.00 per lot of 40 lbs. between camps.   Special trips by arrangement.

For full particulars apply to A. O. WHEELER, Director Banff-Assiniboine Walking Tour, BANFF, ALBERTA, Canada.
Information concerning The Canadian Rockies and matters connected with them willingly supplied on application—no charge. Write to above address.

BANFF MIDDLE SPRINGS CAMP---*OPEN TO ALL UP TO CAPACITY*

In conjunction with the Banff-Assiniboine Walking and Riding Tour, a comfortable Camp will be in operation at the Banff Middle Springs, on a magnificent site, from whence a glorious view sweeps the wide panorama of the Bow Valley and its encircling mountain peaks. Open to the public, up to capacity, whether going on the Walking and Riding Tour or not.

Rates per day, $4.00.   Saddle ponies for those who wish to ride.
Accommodation limited—make your application early.
FOR GOOD FISHING take the Walking and Riding Tour to SPRAY LAKES.
(Write for full details).

STOVEL COMPANY LIMITED, WINNIPEG

A Wheeler party at Sunshine camp, 1920. A. O. Wheeler (second from left) with Rink's packtrain in the background.

the camps. Rink accepted and joined Wheeler in Ralph Rink and Company. The outfit was run under the name of the Alpine Pack Train.

As the idea for the walking and riding tour was to make a circuit — from Banff up the Spray Valley and Bryant Creek to Assiniboine and then returning via Sunshine and Healy Creek — Wheeler quickly decided that it would be necessary to have other camps en route. Government permission was also granted for these, and they were located at the former Eau Claire lumber camp seven miles up the Spray River from Banff, at Goat Pass near Lower Spray Lake, at Trail Centre near Spray Falls above Upper Spray Lake, and at Sunshine on the open meadows near the head of Sunshine Creek. The distance between the camps varied from seven to sixteen miles, the latter being judged the maximum for a hiker or rider unused to the rigors of mountain travel.

After entering his agreement with Wheeler in the spring of 1920, Rink's first task was to build the cabins and corrals at the two permanent sites of Middle Springs and Assiniboine. Meanwhile, Wheeler turned his attention to the promotion of the tours in the press: "If you are worn and tired from the daily grind of life's battle and routine existence; if you need revitalizing and a real rest; if you are nervous, neurotic or dyspeptic; come and try it for a week or two. The cure is certain and for the remainder of your life the pages of your memory's scrapbook will be replete with scenes and experiences that will occur again and again with the thrill of joy."[5]

The round trip price for the tour, which was to take five days, was listed at $35, or $50 if a horse was desired. Horses could also be hired by the day at $3 each and baggage could be carried by pack horse at the rate of $1 per 40 pound lot or $3.60 for the whole trip. Provisions were also made for a longer stay at Assiniboine if the patron desired.

In these circumstances the tour was inaugurated in July, 1920, and for two years it proved quite popular. However, by 1922 it began experiencing problems. One of these stemmed from Wheeler's allowing the idea to circulate that it was being run under the auspices of the Alpine Club. The fact that some members of the club voiced their concern and that Wheeler had to defend his actions to the club's executive on several occasions was undoubtedly damaging. Another difficulty developed because of the complaints of several outfitters that the incorporation of Rink's pack train with the tour constituted unfair competition. They were afraid that the tour would act as a cover for outfitting longer trail trips, a practice not allowed by the terms of Wheeler's agreement with the government. As Wheeler and Rink were contemplating something exactly of this nature, the resultant government instructions prohibiting horse trips beyond one day's journey from the tour was another serious blow.

Because of these developments and competition from other conducted trail rides, attendance dwindled to just thirty-nine participants in 1924, and by 1926 the tour had ceased entirely. Ralph Rink and Company disposed of its pack string and some equipment by auction in May, 1928, the partnership was dissolved, and Rink went into business for himself. Wheeler sold his leases and improvements on the camps at Middle Springs and Assiniboine to Pat Brewster in 1930.

A third conducted trail ride was initiated by Jack Brewster in 1924. Jack had always been the junior partner of Brewster and Moore, and despite the fact that he had kept the company afloat during the difficult war years, had never received the recognition he deserved. Therefore it was not surprising when he split with his brother Fred, bought up much of the Otto brothers' pack string and equipment, and struck out on his own in 1922. Although he was already establishing a reputation as one of the area's foremost big game hunting guides, he recognized that he needed something to attract customers to his new business during the summer months as well. He found what he was looking for in a scheme known as "The Glacier Trail," an annual pack train trip from Jasper to Lake Louise and return.

The first year's trial run of the concept proved to be somewhat of a fiasco simply because of lack of experience and the fact that Jack tried to hurry too much. Thereafter he allowed the pack train to proceed at a more leisurely pace, leaving Jasper at the beginning of July and arriving at Lake Louise three weeks later, and then start-ing out on the return journey with a new party on August 1st. Along the route there were twelve camps established, the major one at Mount Castleguard where a three day layover allowed the group to explore the fringes of the Columbia Icefield. By 1927 "The Glacier Trail" was proving extremely popular and continued to attract a good patronage until the beginning of the Depression.

Even though the Hinman, Wheeler and Brewster tours were important factors in the history of post-war outfitting, they paled in significance compared with the ultimate in the annual group trips in the mountains, the Trail Riders of the Canadian Rockies. The Trail Riders had their origin in a trip taken by a party of fourteen fishermen in 1923 under the guidance of Walter Nixon, a pioneer outfitter and guide of the Windermere district. Nixon, a native of Ontario, had come west and begun ranching in the upper Columbia Valley around 1905. He had also occasionally served as game warden in the Kootenay River and Leanchoil districts, but most of his

Jack Brewster with a "Glacier Trail" party on the Saskatchewan Glacier, ca. 1924.

Walter Nixon leading the Gibbon party over Wolverine Pass, 1923.

spare time had been spent guiding. This developed to the point where he had established an outfitting and guiding business at Invermere and had begun to take out several important parties, as the 1923 one was. It included H. B. Clow, president of Rand McNally mapmakers, Reginald Townsend, editor of *Country Life in America* magazine, R. H. Palenske, a noted Chicago artist, John Murray Gibbon, General Publicity Agent for the CPR, and Byron Harmon, now a well-established Banff photographer.

The party set out from Lake Windermere and fished the Kootenay River until convinced by Clow to visit what he considered to be the most beautiful country in the mountains, the Wolverine Plateau near Tumbling Glacier. While camped at this spot a blizzard necessitated a layover of several days, and as the group sat around the teepee campfire passing the time, the subject of discussion fell on trail riding. One of those present, likely Gibbon, suggested the idea of an Order in which buttons of various grades would be awarded to those riding fifty, one hundred, five hundred, one thousand and two thousand five hundred miles of mountain trails. Being kindred spirits, all agreed, and Gibbon was allotted the position of Secretary-Treasurer, in charge of promoting the idea.

Because of its obvious benefits to the CPR, which *de facto* became its sponsor, Gibbon threw the whole weight of his influential position behind the scheme and was able to elicit a tremendous response. Within a year the membership holding the various badges stood at well over two hundred people, many of them very distinguished and important individuals. Among these were honorary president Charles D. Walcott and council members J. B. Harkin, W. T. Hornaday, Sir James Outram, Carl Rungius, Mary Vaux Walcott and Mary Schäffer Warren. The outfitting interests were likewise

well represented with Jim and Bill Brewster, Jim Simpson, Bill Potts and George Harrison serving on the council and most of the others holding the 2,500 mile badge.

The organization quickly formulated a constitution whose stated aims included the improvement of old trails and the building of new ones, the study and conservation of bird and animal life, the preservation of the National Parks of Canada for the use of the public, and the publication and distribution of maps of existing and proposed trails. However, the main objective was to be the encouragement of travel by horseback through the Canadian Rockies, an objective to be achieved by means of an annual trail ride. Originally the idea was to have a three day ride on an interesting trail, which officials would go over beforehand to select the appropriate campsites, and then finish with an annual pow-wow and general meeting in a huge tent called the Sun Dance Lodge. This would be erected at a suitable location, preferably in proximity to one of the CPR bungalow camps or hotels. The outfitting and guiding would be placed in the hands of the Rocky Mountain Guides Association on the understanding that they would give the best rates possible. This turned out to be approximately $10 a day per person.

After the first year's ride in the Yoho Valley, the response proved so overwhelming that it was necessary to have both three and five day rides and to break the groups into "squadrons," which would start at different points and rendezvous at the site of the pow-wow. In addition, Fred Brewster organized a Jasper group in 1925. The first enrollees signing up at Jasper Park Lodge were Lewis Swift and the visiting Field Marshall Earl Haig and Countess Haig. But even the squadron idea did not prove capable of handling all comers, and it was soon necessary to have more extended trips lasting from eight to twenty-five days in addition to the three and five day "official" rides. Phil Moore, under whose direction the rides fell in the mid-twenties, also secured the government's permission in 1927 to build cabins at points suitable to allow the Trail Riders to start circle rides, much in the mode of Wheeler's tours.

These trail rides were unquestionably valuable business-wise for the various outfitters in the Rocky Mountain Guides Association. Those benefiting most directly were Bill Potts, Walter Nixon, Pat Brewster, Soapy Smith and Fred Brewster, who not only took out the official rides but also made their outfits available to those wishing private rides afterwards. These patrons were not inconsiderable in number, since by 1929 the Trail Riders could count some 1,500 members with over a hundred of them holding the 2,500 mile badge. In fact, during that year the officials of the Trail Riders claimed, with some justification, that it was largely due to their organization that the outfitters and guides, who only a few years previously were being driven out of business by the motor car, were once again working at capacity.

Although the creation of the Trail Riders played a major role in the revitalization of outfitting and guiding, it also marked the end of the pioneer era in that business at Banff and Jasper. No one was more aware of this than

the organization's executive, who decided to pay tribute to the work of those who had opened up the country and had thereby made their present enjoyable travels possible. In planning the first annual ride, to be held in the Yoho Valley on July 17, 1924, they decided that it would be appropriate to invite Tom Wilson as their special guest. Furthermore, his historic contribution was to be recognized by the unveiling of a bronze plaque mounted on a large boulder at the mouth of the valley bearing the inscription:

Tom Wilson
Trail Blazer of
the Canadian Rockies
Lake Louise 1882
Emerald Lake 1882

Tom agreed to attend and on reaching the camp was greeted with speeches of welcome from Colonel Moore and Mrs. Walcott. Called upon to respond, he seemed to be quite uncharacteristically at a loss for words. Undoubtedly his mind was far away, comparing the horde of riders preparing for the morrow's ride up the Yoho with his own initial prospecting trip up the valley in 1884. Yes, the old days of the trail were gone forever.

Jim Simpson, 1965.

Epilogue

Although the end of the pioneer era in outfitting and guiding at Banff and Jasper saw significant changes in the business, it did not mark the end of the careers of all the early trailmen of these areas. Along with several newcomers, some of the old guard continued to earn the bulk of their livelihood from trail-related activities in the succeeding decades.

Jim Simpson maintained his reputation as the foremost outfitter in the Banff area, drawing from a wealth of clientele built up over many years. Mountaineers and hunters in particular sought him out, impressed either from their own experience under his guidance or hearing of his prowess from others. After the completion of the original Num-Ti-Jah Lodge in 1922, he gradually began to shift the focus of his operations away from Banff to Bow Lake. In the twenties he used the lodge as a base camp for the hunting and climbing expeditions he took out from Banff, but during the thirties it became his main headquarters. After the second lodge was sufficiently completed to accommodate guests, saddle horses were provided for those desiring day or short overnight trips. However, the pack outfit was also kept in trim to allow for the handling of longer trail trips taken out from the lodge. Jim continued to guide parties on his own, particularly hunting parties, until age crept up on him, and after the Second World War he began to turn complete responsibility for the business over to his son, Jim Simpson Jr. Even at that, though, he often accompanied parties out as cook until he was well into his seventies.

Pat Brewster, along with Simpson, rated as one of the principal outfitters operating out of Banff by the late twenties. After having worked for Brewster Brothers and Brewster Transport in the south and Brewster and Moore in the north, Pat finally achieved a modicum of independence in 1925. Returning from the war he had gone back to work for his brother Jim, handling the company's interests at Glacier for the five years previous to the closing of Glacier House by the CPR. At that time he approached Jim with the proposal that he be leased Brewster Transport's entire outfitting department since it was becoming rather burdensome to the company. Jim agreed, and after christening his acquisition Brewster's Mountain Pack Trains, Pat immediately set about rebuilding the trail business which had been allowed to languish for several years.

Because the CPR concession accompanied the lease, Pat was provided with an increasing supply of customers as the twenties progressed and had to build up his pack string to huge proportions. The record year proved to be 1928, when he had 488 head of horses working out of Banff, Lake Louise, and Field. Soon after, however, business plummeted with the onset of the Depression and the operations were drastically reduced. By the mid-thirties Pat had to be content with the business he could garner from such customers as the Alpine Club, the Trail Riders and a few loyal hunters. Later he began a series of permanent camps at Hillsdale, Egypt Lake and Sunburst Lake which complemented and served as bases for his outfitting endeavors for a number of years.

Jim Boyce was another of the successful outfitters who began working out of Banff in the twenties. Boyce was a native of Pembrooke, Ontario who had come to Banff to join his father Joe in 1911 and had begun working on the trail for Simpson in 1916. Soon he had a reputation for producing the lightest and tastiest bannock ever to emerge from a campfire reflector and gained a great following among his employer's customers. In 1921 he and Max Brooks, a fellow employee of Simpson's, decided to go it on their own and after purchasing some stock from Soapy Smith and the Stoneys joined together in a partnership known as Boyce and Brooks. This was dissolved in 1924, by which time Jim had begun to outfit and guide the first of his numerous Caroline Hinman tours. As time went on the Hinman trips grew in popularity until they reached the point that he had to provide as many as fifty-five horses for each outing. He also had to be prepared to go tremendously far afield, on one occasion trailing his pack string far to the north of Mount Robson. During the thirties, as was the case for most outfitters, his business suffered a setback, and he became involved in ventures such as managing Skoki Ski Lodge, running a dog team, and working on highway construction. But his first love continued to be the trail, and he kept his hand in at it until selling off the last of his horses in 1952.

Not all of those who engaged in outfitting and guiding along the CPR through the mountains chose Banff as their headquarters. Both to west and east along the line, former Brewster men, including Tex Wood, George Harrison, Bill Potts and Soapy Smith, successfully carried on their businesses.

Tex Wood had left Brewsters in 1915 to join the warden service, being posted to Peyto's district while Bill served overseas. One of the duties he was instructed to perform in his job was rendering assistance to the distinguished geologist of the Smithsonian Institution Dr. Charles Walcott, who was investigating the Cambrian geology of the Canadian Rockies. In 1919 Tex decided to leave the wardens and after acquiring his own outfit began to regularly escort Walcott and his wife, the former Mary Vaux, on their summer expedition from Lake Louise. This work was supplemented by contracts from both the Smithsonian Institution and the American Museum of Natural History which required him to make geological and faunal collections on his own and by a large clientele of New York lawyers he took on annual hunting trips. Except for a brief period during 1923-24, which was spent working in the movies in Hollywood, he kept his horses at Banff or up the Spray Valley, but he ran his outfit primarily out of Lake Louise. Finally, in 1938, he found the country becoming too crowded and left for the Windermere district to open a dude ranch for young boys from wealthy families.

George Harrison, undoubtedly Brewsters' most loyal and valuable guide also chose the war years as the time to sever his connection with the company. He had spent the years from 1910 to 1915 as head guide at Lake Louise and then had been transferred to Glacier when the company acquired the CPR concession at Glacier House from Syd Baker. Because the area appealed to him, George decided that it would be his choice of locale for a business of his own, and in 1918, after sixteen years with Brewsters, felt that the time was ripe. His reputation as a hunting guide gained through long years of experience immediately brought many parties he had handled for his former employer back his way. Fortunately, after the closing of Glacier House, he was able to obtain the lease to the old CPR section house at Glacier, which he used as a headquarters until his retirement in 1945.

Bill Potts began his first attempts at outfitting in conjunction with two other returned war veterans, his brother Wattie and Stan Carr, and with the assistance of his brother-in-law Frank Wellman. Wellman had purchased the Morley Trading Company store and moved his family to Morley prior to the war, after having operated the Park Dairy at Banff from 1907 to 1913. Later he had disposed of the store and had acquired the old Dave McDougall ranch near Morley, from where he had outfitted and guided the occasional party. In the spring of 1918 he entered an agreement with Simpson and Tom Wilson, to whom John Wilson's share in the Kootenay Plains stock had reverted, to purchase 140 head of horses. Once these were rounded up and moved to his ranch, Wellman donated a large number of them and his entire supply of outfitting equipment to Bill and his partners so that they could get the Potts Outfitting Company underway.

Wattie remained only one year with the company while Carr stayed slightly longer, departing for a three and a half year stint in California in 1921 and then returning to work on the trail in the Yellowhead region. Bill was left to run the operation himself, and he continued to maintain Morley as his headquarters, although he often leased livery facilities at Banff as well. Despite the support his business received from the Trail Riders, he decided to leave outfitting and guiding in the thirties in order to join the warden service and eventually became the Chief Warden of Banff National Park.

Soapy Smith, like Harrison, was one of Brewsters' most loyal employees, serving respectively as harness maker, cook, packer and guide from 1905 to 1922. During this period he had continued to spend the winter months at his Jumping Pound ranch after coming in from his summer's work in the mountains. However, in 1922 he was able to buy a piece of the Wellman property from Mrs. Wellman, Frank having died in the flu epidemic of 1919, and he began a new ranch known as the Rafter 6. For a short time he abandoned the trail to concentrate on the raising of horses, but soon began to take parties out on his own. His most notable trip was in 1924 when he outfitted and guided the American writer Lewis R. Freeman and Byron Harmon on a trip to attempt the first complete photographic coverage of the Columbia Icefield. Assisted by Ulysee LaCasse and Bob Baptie, he successfully led the party on the second recorded crossing of the Saskatchewan Glacier by pack train, a feat given wide coverage in Freeman's subsequent article in *National Geographic Magazine* and his book *On The Roof Of The Rockies*. Thereafter, Soapy remained active in outfitting and guiding, particularly with the Trail Riders, until two years before his death in 1948.

Along the Canadian National line much the same situation occurred as did on the Canadian Pacific. Some of the old time outfitters continued to live at least partially from the trail, and they were joined by a few newcomers. The major outfitters in the area after 1925 included Curly Phillips, Fred Brewster, Jack Brewster, Hargreaves Brothers, Jack Hargreaves, Alex Wylie and Stan Clark.

Curly Phillips was married in 1923, and although he continued to outfit, he would seldom go out on the trail himself. Many of his earlier customers, including the Alpine Club and Miss Hinman, remained loyal to him, but they were taken care of by one of his most trustworthy guides, usually Adam Joachim or Dave Moberly, while he devoted his attention to the boat trips. These and his winter trapline kept him occupied until the mid-thirties when, in line with his progressive thinking, he began formulating a new scheme.

This was an idea for using airplanes to get hunters to previously inaccessible areas, and in 1937, he proved it was possible by flying two American hunters from Finlay Forks across the Lloyd George Range to Tuchodi Lake. Intending to devote more attention to such enterprises, he sold his pack string to Bert Wilkins upon returning from this trip. However, he never got the opportunity to pursue his plans, because in March of the following year, despite three decades of experience at winter travel in the mountains, he fell victim to an avalanche while scouting out the possibilities for a ski cabin near Elysium Pass.

Fred Brewster's activities in the early twenties continued to be centred around the developments at Jasper Park Lodge, which he used as the headquarters for his outfitting. As the clientele arriving at the Lodge gradually increased, his Sky Line Trail Rides to Maligne Lake became very popular. In 1928 he decided to expand his services and, with the railroad's assistance, was able to lease a parcel of land on the shore of Medicine Lake to use in conjunction with his trail business. At this site the Medicine Lake Chalet was constructed, and it became the first location in a system of camps and chalets known as Fred Brewster's Rocky Mountain Camps. As time went on these included Maligne Lake Chalet and Tonquin Valley Camp, used for riding, hiking, boating and fishing, camps in the Little and Big Shovel Passes and Tekarra Basin, used in connection with the Sky Line Trail Rides, and the Black Cat Ranch on Solomon Creek outside the park's eastern boundary, used for big game hunting parties. Fred was also one of the early enthusiasts of skiing in the area, becoming an original member and president of the Jasper Park Ski Club in 1936, and later he began to use some of the camps and chalets for winter ski camps. After Phillips' death he obtained the boat concession at Maligne and Medicine Lakes, and continued to run it along with his outfitting business until his retirement in 1962.

Jack Brewster, although he maintained Jasper as his home, tended to go much further afield in pursuing his business interests. His main reputation was as one of Western Canada's foremost big game hunting guides,

and his search for productive new territory kept him constantly on the move. Eventually the Cassiar country of British Columbia began to receive much of his attention in this regard. Beginning in the late thirties, upon the completion of the Banff-Jasper Highway, he constructed the Columbia Icefield Chalet for Brewster Transport and was soon offering a saddle horse service in the summer and pack trips into the Brazeau country for hunting parties in the fall. Because of his skill in log work, he was asked to assist in the construction of the Alaska Highway during the Second World War, holding the position of superintendent of camp and hospital construction for three years at Whitehorse. Shortly after the war he returned to Banff and built the Brewster Motel on the site of his father's original lease, and ran it until his death in 1951.

Jack Hargreaves was, perhaps, the most successful of the new outfitters and guides who established at Jasper, his appearance there being related to earlier developments at Mount Robson in an enterprise known as Hargreaves Brothers. Jack and his three brothers, Frank, George and Roy, had spent much of their youth travelling around the country with their rather footloose father. George and Roy had been the first to leave home, and in 1905, they had been involved in cutting a trail from Golden to Tete Jaune Cache.

Jack had first come to Jasper at age eighteen to play hockey in the winter of 1913-14. The next summer he had begun to work for Otto Brothers and, in the winter of 1917, had accompanied Phillips and Miss Jobe on their trip to the Wapiti. After that he had enlisted and gone overseas until the war's end when he returned and proceeded to Mount Robson. There he and his brother Frank decided to file on homesteads with an eye towards involvement in the tourist business. They erected several log buildings as well as a small store and before long were joined first by their brother George and later by Roy. Together the four began to outfit and guide parties, using about seventy head of horses and concentrating mainly on the Berg Lake area.

Although they carried on business under the name of Hargreaves Brothers, each one maintained his own separate part of the pack string and share of the equipment. This arrangement continued until 1924, when Jack found he wasn't seeing eye to eye with his brothers and decided to pull out. He moved on to Jasper, purchased some horses and equipment from Ralph James of Pocahontas, and began to take out hunting parties in 1927. Thereafter, both he and Hargreaves Brothers ran separately for many years, Jack himself having up to eighty-five horses on the trail at one time.

Alex Wylie, although he had not worked for any of the established outfitters, was well-acquainted with packing in the mountains by the time he began his own outfit in 1918. After coming out from his native Scotland in 1887 at age five, he had spent his youth in Edmonton and had begun freighting for the Hudson's Bay Company to

Athabaska Landing in 1898. In 1905 he had left for the mountains, intending to take a holiday but ending up working for N. H. Jock and Jack Gregg, pioneer ranchers at Prairie Creek. Jock had obtained a contract with the GTP and, in 1906, Alex had helped him freight supplies to the McLeod River and then pack them on to Prairie Creek. The next year he packed for the railway, making a round trip from Swift's through to Tete Jaune Cache and back every eight days with a twenty-three horse pack train assisted by two other packers. After that he had worked with survey parties on the GTP until 1910, when he had hired on as a packer for a government survey of the Coal Branch area.

During the war years Alex had raised horses on his family's ranch at Nisku, south of Edmonton, and after its completion he returned to the mountains with the intention of settling down. Bringing about twenty head of horses with him, he set about looking over the country for a suitable location and, after considerable investigation, decided on Jasper. Although he was never a large outfitter, in the years prior to his retirement in 1939, he achieved some success with day trip tourists and sometimes combined his horses with another outfitter's string to take larger parties on longer treks. For a number of years he also had the job of delivering Jasper's water supply from an outlet of Cabin Lake using two large water tanks drawn by teams.

Stan Clark had one of the most interesting backgrounds of those becoming involved in the trail business in the early twenties. After graduating from college, where he had been captain of his football team, he had entered the employ of the Canadian Forestry Service. Soon he had become Superintendent of Rocky Mountain Forest Reserve and had done most of the pioneer work in establishing the Athabasca Forest Reserve north of Jasper. At the outbreak of the war in 1914 he had immediately enlisted and because of his training was placed in charge of British forestry operations in France. After returning from overseas he had acquired a large parcel of land across the Athabasca from Entrance and began setting up a large horse and cattle ranch. In 1922 he was approached by Major Townsend Whelen, the leading ballistics expert of the United States Army, with a request to accompany him on a sheep hunt in the country west of the Smoky River. Although he wasn't planning on getting into the outfitting and guiding line, the success of this trip convinced him to do so. Whelen wrote up the account of their hunt in a three part series entitled "In Virgin Game Mountains of the North" which appeared in *Outdoor Life* in 1923 and 1924. Because of Whelen's reputation, Clark was soon inundated with requests for his services in a similar capacity and continued to be a successful big game outfitter and guide for several years.

Regardless of how and when they got into outfitting and guiding, where they established themselves or how long they stayed with it, all these individuals had something in common. The blood of the trail ran strong in their veins, and as long as they lived they were never able to get the memory of those challenging and exciting days out of their minds. Then, like the explorers of old, they were driven to seek just beyond the next ridge, they were allowed to live in closest contact with nature in some of the most magnificent surroundings which God had put on earth, and they were able to share a camaraderie with their fellow travellers that was the lot of few men. These trailmen reminisced freely about their experiences and way of life, but perhaps the one to best articulate their feelings for "the good old days" was Tom Wilson, who had begun the whole story.

Tom had become discontented with the mountains by the end of the First World War, largely because of his continued failure to obtain title to the Kootenay Plains ranches. Resigning his position of justice of the peace and magistrate which he had held for several years, he moved to Vancouver in 1920. Soon finding that city did not agree with him, he went on to Enderby, British Columbia, where he intended to retire permanently. But the old lure proved too strong. After his visit to attend the initiation of the Trail Riders in 1924, he realized how much he longed for the mountains and trails of his younger days, and in January, 1927, returned to Banff. From then until the time of his death in 1933 he provided "local color" for the CPR at the Banff Springs Hotel, his main function being to entertain guests and newspaper reporters with stories drawn from his vast repertoire of trail lore. One of these stories concerned his days spent packing for the railway and ended with a poem he liked to call "Memories of Golden Days."

Good old days on the trail and evenings around the campfire,
And when the coffee pot upset just as it was beginning to boil,
And the sugar and salt got wet,
And sometimes the beans went sour and the bacon musty,
And the wind blew sparks in your eyes and ashes on your blankets,
And the butt of the biggest bough hit the small of your back,
And the mosquitoes almost crowded you out of the tent,
And you heard the horse bell getting fainter and fainter,
And you knew damn well they would be five miles away in the morning,
But just the same, O Lord, how I wish I could live them all over again.

To Major Fred Brewster - Old time Memories.
from his Friend Tom Wilson
Sept 6th 1929

Notes

Chapter 1

1. Archives of the Canadian Rockies, Copy of Wilson scrapbook, Newsclipping, n.n., n.d. Much of the information about Wilson's early life is obtainable only from newsclippings written by journalists after interviews with him in the late twenties, when he was a sort of story-teller for the CPR at the Banff Springs Hotel. These interviews commonly included a goodly sprinkling of 'tall tales' and thus some of Tom's claims must be viewed with a degree of scepticism.
2. Thomas E. Wilson, *Trail Blazer of the Canadian Rockies* (Calgary: Glenbow-Alberta Institute, 1972), p. 19.
3. Wilson scrapbook, Letter from Tom Wilson to J. B. Harkin, 1924.
4. *Ibid.*, Ina Burns, "Mountain Miracle", *Calgary Herald*, n.d.
5. In his book Fleming refers to the packer in charge as George Wilson but Tom's later recollections about accompanying the party make it seem likely it was him.
6. Sandford Fleming, *England and Canada, A Summer Tour Between Old and New Westminster* (London: Sampson Low, Marston, Searle and Rivington, 1884), p. 243.
7. *Ibid.*, pp. 248-49.
8. *Ibid.*, p. 258.
9. Wilson scrapbook, J. E. Middleton, "Eastern Tenderfoot Meets Tom Wilson," *Toronto Mail and Empire*, September 8, 1930.
10. *Ibid.*
11. Sandford Fleming, "Memories of the Mountains," *Canadian Alpine Journal*, I, (1907), p. 32.
12. Walter D. Wilcox, *The Rockies of Canada*, (New York: The Knickerbocker Press, 1916), pp. 115-16.
13. Glenbow-Alberta Institute Archives, Wilson Papers, Barrett to Wilson, November 1, 1924.
14. Walter D. Wilcox, "Early Days in the Canadian Rockies," *American Alpine Journal*, IV, (1941), p. 177.

Chapter II

1. Wilson Papers, Wilcox to Wilson, January 18, 1930.
2. Archives of the Canadian Rockies, Taped interview with James Simpson, March 9, 1969.
3. *Ibid.*
4. Wilcox, "Early Days . . .," p. 181.
5. Wilcox, *The Rockies of Canada*, p. 120.
6. Jimmy Simpson, Sr., "Peyto . . . of Peyto Lake," *Canadian Golden West*, VI, (Winter, 1971), p. 31.
7. Ralph Edwards, *The Trail to the Charmed Land*, (Saskatoon: H. R. Larson Publishing Company, 1949), p. 12.
8. Walter D. Wilcox, *Camping in the Canadian Rockies*, (New York: G. P. Putnam's Sons, 1897), pp. 170-74.
9. *Ibid.*, p. 214.

10. *Ibid.*, p. 209.
11. *Appalachia*, I, (June, 1876), p. 1.
12. Philip S. Abbot, "The First Ascent of Mount Hector, Canadian Rockies," *Appalachia*, VIII, (January, 1896), p. 2.
13. *Ibid.*, p. 3.
14. Princeton University Archives, Thompson-Little Collection, P. S. Abbot to C. E. Fay, October 17, 1895. (Copies available in Archives of the Canadian Rockies.)
15. Stanley Washburn, *Trails, Trappers and Tenderfeet In The New Empire of Western Canada*, (New York: Henry Holt and Company, 1912), p. 6.
16. Princeton University Archives, J. Monroe Thorington Collection, James Simpson to J. Monroe Thorington, November 18, 1968. (Copies available in Archives of the Canadian Rockies.)
17. Washburn, p. 175.
18. Martin Nordegg, "Pioneering in Canada, 1906-1924," (memoirs of Martin Nordegg, n.d.), p. 36.
19. Thompson-Little Collection (Supplement), Wilcox to Thorington, December 5, 1944.

Chapter III

1. Charles E. Fay, "The Casualty on Mount Lefroy," *Appalachia*, VIII, (November, 1896), p. 150.
2. Thompson-Little Collection, Abbot to Wilson, June 28, 1896.
3. *Ibid.*, p. 228.
4. Wilcox, "Early Days . . .," p. 188.
5. H. E. M. Stutfield and J. N. Collie, *Climbs and Explorations in the Canadian Rockies*. (London: Longmans, Green and Co., 1903), pp. 26-27.
6. *Ibid.*, pp. 41-42.
7. Archives of the Canadian Rockies, Tom Wilson, "A short history of the early work in developing the resorts and tourist trade in the Canadian Pacific Rockies," p. 2. Wilson wrote this manuscript in the late twenties to point out all the work he had done for the CPR for which he had never received credit or reimbursement.
8. Wilson scrapbook, Wilson to Harkin, November 30, 1922 and n. d., 1924.
9. Edwards, *The Trail to the Charmed Land*, pp. 35-36.
10. Charles E. Fay, "Old Times in the Canadian Alps," *Canadian Alpine Journal*, XII, (1922), p. 101. The time reference is an allusion to the hour and day of Abbot's fall in 1896.
11. R. F. Curtis, "The Making of Abbot Pass," *Appalachia*, IX, (1899-1901) p. 36.
12. Thompson-Little Collection, Fay to Thompson, August 17, 1898.
13. Charles L. Noyes, "Mount Balfour and the Waputehk Snowfield," *Appalachia*, IX. (1899-1901), p. 31.
14. Stutfield and Collie, p. 84.

15. J. Norman Collie, "Climbing in the Canadian Rockies," *The Alpine Journal*, XIX, (1898-99), p. 454.
16. *Ibid.*, pp. 457-58.
17. Stutfield and Collie, p. 135.
18. *Ibid.*, p. 97.
19. Archives of the Canadian Rockies, Excerpts from a diary by J. Norman Collie, 1900.
20. Thompson-Little Collection (Supplement), F. Stephens to Wilcox, December 31, 1902.
21. J. Monroe Thorington Collection, J. Simpson to Thorington, October 26, 1968.
22. Glenbow-Alberta Institute Archives, Memoirs of Charles Lumley, p. 38.

Chapter IV
1. *Calgary Daily Herald*, December 3, 1901.
2. Thorington Collection, Simpson to Thorington, December 4, 1968 and November 18, 1968.
3. Scott Polar Institute, Diary of Edward Whymper, July 27, 1901. (Copy available in Archives of the Canadian Rockies).
4. *Ibid.*, August 8, 1901.
5. Wilson Papers, Whymper to Wilson, August 9, 1901.
6. A. O. Wheeler, "Some Memories of Edward Whymper," *Canadian Alpine Journal*, XXVIII, (1941), p. 84.
7. Wilson Papers, Contract between T. E. Wilson, Field B. C., Liveryman and the CPR, 1902.
8. Memoirs of Charles Lumley, p. 3.
9. Archives of the Canadian Rockies, Taped interview with Jack Fuller, February 6, 1969.
10. Archives of the Canadian Rockies, Unpublished manuscript "Mountain Men" by N. "Tex" Vernon-Wood.
11. Thorington Collection, Simpson to Thorington, December 23, 1968 and July 30, 1969.
12. Thompson-Little Collection, Collie to Thompson, March 10 and 13, 1902.
13. Stutfield and Collie, pp. 296-97.
14. Thorington Collection, Simpson to Thorington, October 26, 1968.

Chapter V
1. Wilson Papers, Whymper to Wilson, May 29, 1905.
2. Stutfield and Collie, p. 247.
3. B. W. Mitchell, *Trail Life in the Canadian Rockies*, (New York: The MacMillan Co., 1924), p. 196.
4. Thorington Collection, Simpson to Thorington, July 30, 1969.
5. *Ibid.*
6. Wilson Papers, Fay to Wilson, April 4, 1898.
7. *Ibid.*, Oliver to Wilson, April 7, 1908.
8. Newsclipping, "Canada's Mountain Beauty Spot," n.n. March, 1906.
9. Wilson Papers, Wheeler to Mrs. Wilson, September 27, 1933.
10. *Ibid.*, Wheeler to Wilson, June 8, 1906.
11. Yoho Camp Circular, *Canadian Alpine Journal*, I, (1907), pp. 169-70.
12. A. O. Wheeler, "The Origin and Founding of the Alpine Club of Canada," *Canadian Alpine Journal*, XXVII, (1938), p. 94.
13. Frank Yeigh, "Canada's First Alpine Club Camp," *Canadian Alpine Journal*, I, (1907), p. 55.
14. Alpine Club of Canada Archives, Minutes of the Annual Meeting of the Alpine Club of Canada held at the Yoho Camp, July 11, 1906.
15. *Ibid.*, Minutes of the Annual Meeting of the Alpine Club of Canada, 1909, President's Address.
16. Report of 1910 Camp, *Canadian Alpine Journal*, III, (1911), pp. 189, 195.

Chapter VI
1. Washburn, p. 135.
2. A. P. Coleman, *The Canadian Rockies, New And Old Trails*, (London: T. Fisher Unwin, 1911), p. 347.
3. George B. Kinney and Donald Phillips, "To The Top Of Mount Robson," *Canadian Alpine Journal*, II, (1910), p. 40.
4. J. Monroe Thorington (ed.), *Where Clouds Can Go*, (New York City: The American Alpine Club, 1935), p. 320.
5. Canada, Department of the Interior, *Annual Report*, 1915, Part V, p. 65.

6. J. E. C. Eaton, "An Expedition To The Freshfield Group," *Canadian Alpine Journal*, III, (1911), p. 2.
7. Archives of the Canadian Rockies, Untitled manuscript concerning a trip to Maligne Lake in 1911 by Mary T. S. Schäffer, p. 27.
8. Jasper-Yellowhead Historical Society, "Reminiscing" by Fred Brewster.
9. Canada, Department of the Interior, *Annual Report*, 1915, Part V, p. 65.

Chapter VII
1. J. Norman Collie, "On The Canadian Rocky Mountains North Of The Yellow Head Pass," *The Alpine Journal*, XXVI, (1912), p. 11.
2. *Ibid.*, p. 17.
3. A. O. Wheeler, "The Alpine Club of Canada's Expedition To Jasper Park, Yellow Head Pass And Mount Robson Region, 1911," *Canadian Alpine Journal*, IV, (1912), p. 91.
4. Thorington Collection, Simpson to Thorington, November 18, 1968.
5. *Ibid.*, Kinney to Thorington, September 7, 1934.
6. Donald Phillips, "Fitzhugh to Laggan," *Canadian Alpine Journal*, IV, (1912), p. 91.
7. Thorington Collection, Unpublished manuscript, "Tracks Across My Trail, The Trapping Diaries of Donald (Curly) Phillips," ed. by J. Monroe Thorington, entry of April 4, 1911.
8. Archives of the Canadian Rockies, Fred Brewster Collection, Unpublished manuscript, "Diary of a Trip from Jasper to Hudson's Hope, Peace River" by S. Prescott Fay, entry of July 25, 1914.
9. *Ibid.*, entry of August 13, 1914.
10. *Ibid.*, entry of October 2, 1914.
11. Mary L. Jobe, "The Expedition To 'Mt. Kitchi'," *Canadian Alpine Journal*, VI, (1914-15), p. 200.
12. Arthur Conan Doyle, "The Athabaska Trail," quoted from Caroline Hinman advertising pamphlet, 1925.

Chapter VIII
1. *Crag and Canyon*, August 14, 1909.
2. Archives of the Canadian Rockies, Taped interview with Tex Vernon-Wood and Stan Carr, August 18, 1970.
3. Robert Frothingham, "Bighorns on the Brazeau," *Field and Stream*, March, 1917, p. 385.
4. William N. Beach, "Land of Heart's Desire," *Field and Stream*, August, 1920, p. 376.
5. Simpson's ram was the world's record until 1952 when a new system of determining record sheep heads, taking into account such points as symmetry and massiveness as well as length of curl, was instituted by Boone and Crockett. At that time a head taken by Martin Bovey of Minneapolis in 1924 while hunting with the pioneer outfitter and guide Bert Riggall of Waterton Lakes jumped from fourth to first place.
6. Archives of the Canadian Rockies, Letter from Mary S. Warren to Wilson, n.d.
7. Mary T. S. Schäffer, *Old Indian Trails of the Canadian Rockies*, (New York: The Kinckerbocker Press, 1911), pp. 4-5.
8. Mrs. Charles Schaffer, "The Valley of the Saskatchewan with Horse and Camera," *Bulletin of the Geographical Society of Philadelphia*, Vol. V., No. 2, (April, 1907), pp. 37-38.
9. Archives of the Canadian Rockies, Mary Schaffer Warren Collection, Diary of Mollie Adams, entry of July 7, 1908.
10. *Ibid.*, entry of July 28, 1908.
11. Archives of the Canadian Rockies, Letter from Mary S. Warren to Raymond Zillmer, February 28, 1928.
12. Mitchell, p. 78.
13. Archives of the Canadian Rockies, Mabel Brinkley Collection, "Bill Peyto," unpublished manuscript.

Chapter IX
1. *Crag and Canyon*, August 7, 1920.
2. Thorington Collection, advertising leaflet, "Introducing Donald 'Curly' Phillips 'Dude Trapline'", 1924-25.
3. *Ibid.*, Phillips to Dr. P. G. Woodward, May 17, 1925.
4. *Crag and Canyon*, May 6, 1922.
5. Newsclipping, n.n., May 15, 1920.

154

Photo Credits

Index

PRINTED IN CANADA

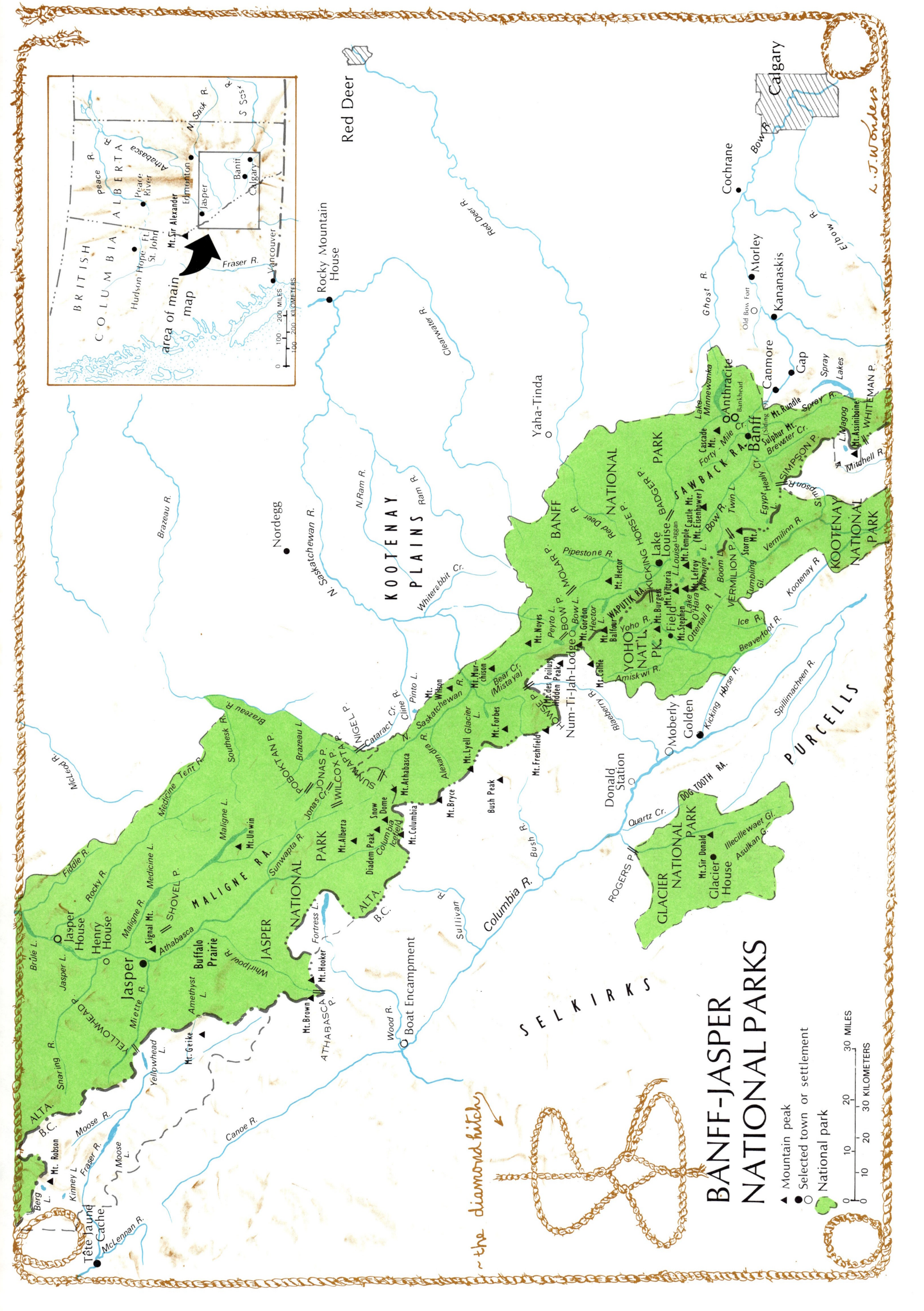